DALRY ROAD

MOTIVE POWER DEPOT,

EDINBURGH

Still at work for British Railways as No. 57559, former Caledonian Railway No. 821 McIntosh 0-6-0 of the '812' Class works a Leith North to Princes Street passenger service between Craigleith and Murrayfield. *David Anderson*

0-4-4T No. 15149 (formerly CR No. 106) of the '104' Class, built for use on the Balerno Branch and seen here at the coaling stage at Dalry Road shed. *CRA Archives*

DALRY ROAD MOTIVE POWER DEPOT, EDINBURGH

A HISTORY, 1848–1965

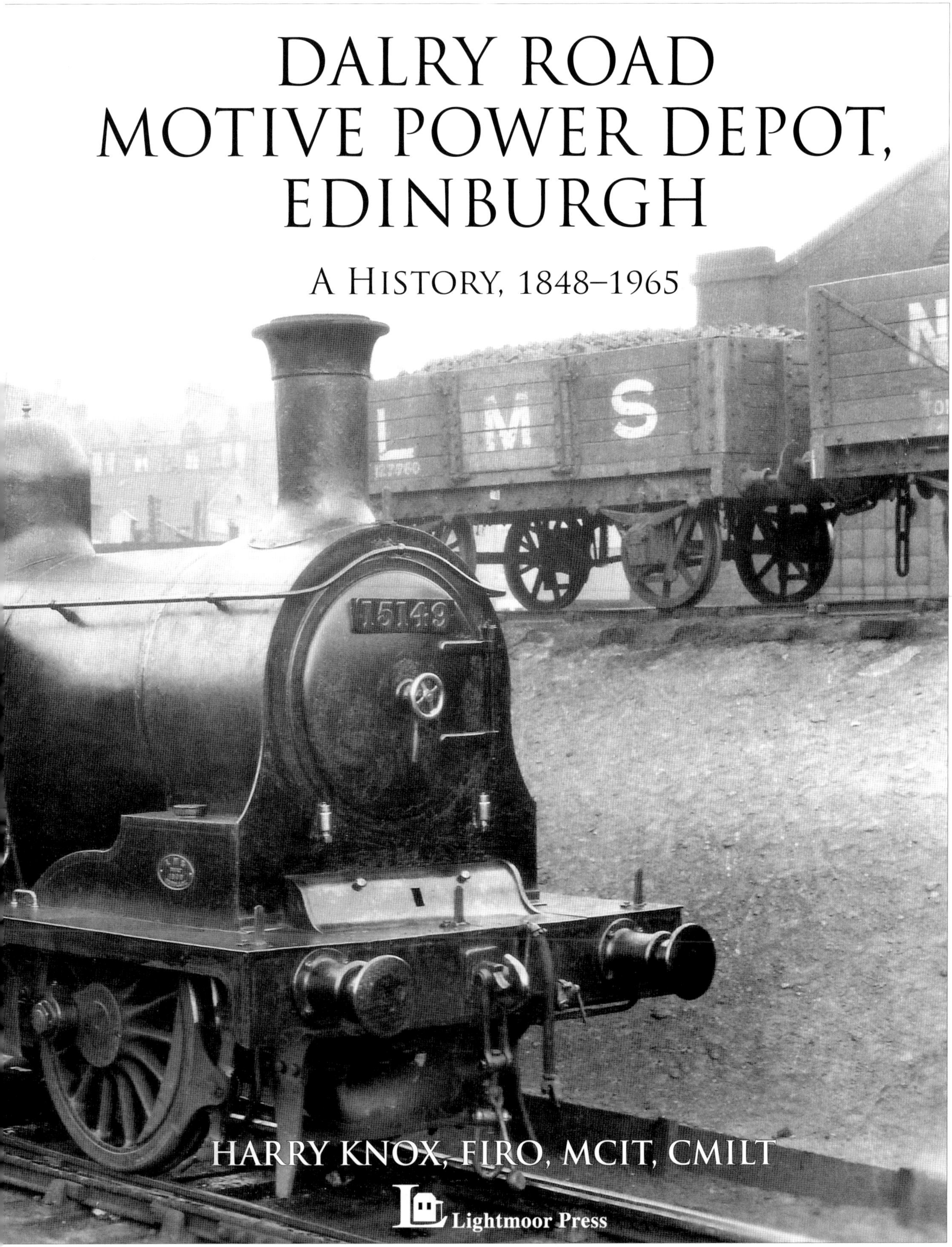

HARRY KNOX, FIRO, MCIT, CMILT

Lightmoor Press

This book is dedicated, with love, to my dear wife, Heather, my travelling companion for the past thirty years, with thanks for her unfailing encouragement and support. And so our journey together continues!

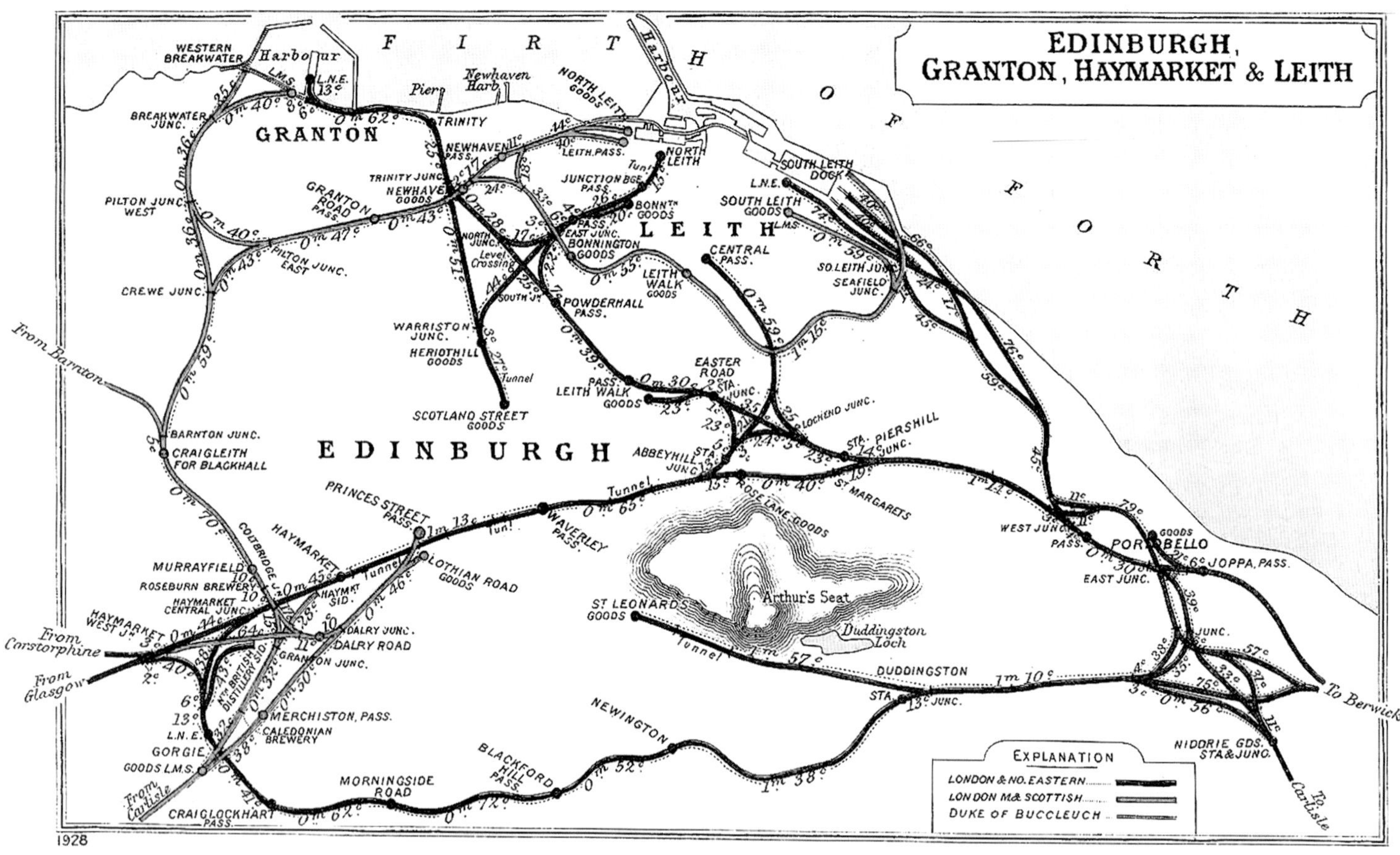

Railway Clearing House map of the railways in, and around Edinburgh. *Author's collection*

Published by LIGHTMOOR PRESS in conjunction with the CALEDONIAN RAILWAY ASSOCIATION

Designed by Nigel Nicholson.

British Library Cataloguing-in-Publication Data. A catalogue record for this book is available from the British Library.
ISBN 9781 911038 41 2

LIGHTMOOR PRESS
Unit 144B, Lydney Trading Estate, Harbour Road, Lydney, Gloucestershire GL15 4EJ
www.lightmoor.co.uk
Lightmoor Press is an imprint of Black Dwarf Lightmoor Publications Ltd.

Printed in Poland; www.lfbookservices.co.uk

Contents

Ex-LM&SR 'Royal Scot' Class 4-6-0 No. 46107 ***Argyll and Sutherland Highlander*** **of Polmadie shed, Glasgow takes coal at Dalry Road coaling stage.** *D. Simpson/David Spaven*

INTRODUCTION

Having completed some five works, including a history of both of Edinburgh's two North British Railway motive power depots – Haymarket (formerly Edinburgh & Glasgow Railway Company 1843) and St. Margarets (North British Railway 1844) – and with time now hanging heavily on my hands, I have yet again succumbed to suggestions made by well meaning colleagues to turn my attention to that other railway company which was to serve Edinburgh, and complete the trilogy of Edinburgh locomotive shed histories. The company was the Caledonian Railway Company, never to be quite as large as the North British Railway, but it was much, much grander in every way and their engine house in Edinburgh was, of course, Dalry Road.

Now, at this juncture I must admit to having spent my youth in a village, my home village, which sat astride a route of the former Caledonian Railway. This was the village of West Calder, lying on the 1869 'short cut' deviation from Midcalder Junction to Cleland, authorised under the Caledonian Railway Cleland & Mid Calder Railway and Branches Act of 1869. I must also mention here the fact that the Caledonian Railway was always, in every publication, to refer to Mid Calder as Midcalder, as they did with West Calder (Westcalder) – but these were two of the three 'Calders', being the villages of East, Mid and West Calder, so this nomenclature is incorrect.

It still being wartime, on the rare occasions I was taken 'into town', usually by my Grandmother, it was always using the former Caledonian Railway (by that time the LM&SR) from West Calder to Edinburgh Princes Street, with the 'ten' train. This was the 08.13 from Glasgow Central (09.05 from Holytown), due at West Calder at 10.03, and was sometimes even seen to be headed by a wartime, black (very) LM&SR Stanier streamlined Pacific, always yet another memorable event on what was already an exciting occasion. These rare wartime treats, as such journeys really were, are remembered with great affection. So it was ex-Caledonian and LM&SR engines with which I was to be brought up initially, and I was well familiar with Dalry Road MPD, or 64C as it was classified by BR, as seen in the passing. Enjoyable days indeed, but oh, how I wish I could have seen, and experienced, the Pullman expresses over this line.

I commenced my own railway career at the former Caledonian railway station, Shotts Central, lying on the same deviation line as mentioned above, where I was appointed as junior clerk in October 1956. It was whilst working at Shotts that I came to know several Hamilton footplatemen who worked in on a daily basis with the Motherwell District trip working, M23. They tolerated my presence on the footplate and in time became my mentors in the management of steam locomotives. To them, my thanks for a 'master class' in handling ex-Caledonian Railway and LM&SR locomotives which was to prove invaluable in my future career. The station master, one John Dyer, formerly station master at Law Junction, was a dyed-in-the-wool Caledonian man and I was to blot my copybook, as it were, by in early 1957 applying to be transferred to Haymarket MPD as an engine cleaner. He suggested that, as Haymarket was the NBR, I had made a mistake and really meant Dalry Road shed, but I was adamant, and he never spoke another word to me from that day on, right up to the day I finally left Shotts.

Later promotions, post-footplate days, saw me appointed as a relief station master in the Glasgow South District, when I was aged 21 years, covering the former Caledonian territory right down to Beattock, and I became well acquainted with many of the stations in this old Caledonian district. The very first station I ever served at as station master was Maxwell Park on the Cathcart Circle, but I was to be interim SM at many other ex-Caledonian railway stations on the main line, as well as covering the operating posts in Glasgow Central station, Motherwell Yardmaster's office and that at Mossend Yard. Earlier, whilst still a clerk in the Motive Power Department at Haymarket, I was seconded for the best part of the summer of 1961 to Dalry Road MPD and so gained a valuable insight to the men and work at that depot.

So it is to this same small Caledonian Railway Locomotive Depot at Dalry Road that I now turn, in an attempt to chart the history of same. In one respect this is not an easy task, since, unlike the sheds at St. Margarets (64A) and Haymarket (64B), there were no Charlie Meachers, Willie Hennigans or Norman McKillops to record shed life over the years at Dalry Road (64C), and thus much useful and valuable information has now gone, along with the denizens of that particular shed, to that great railway Valhalla. As stated, I had the pleasure, for a short two months in the summer of 1961, of having been loaned from Haymarket as a clerical officer to assist in the shed office at Dalry Road and made the acquaintance of some of the men there. Given the paucity of relevant information in 2017 regarding Dalry Road MPD, it is intended that this work also looks at the developments in the areas and lines that the depot served with motive power.

Since this has largely been a journey into the unknown for me, I am indebted to good friends who were able to supply invaluable information and (hopefully) keep me on the straight and narrow. In particular, I must thank Dr Campbell Cornwell and David Hamilton, both founts of knowledge, who have exposed and helped put right my sad lack of knowledge of early Caledonian Railway locomotives. Sincere thanks also to Stuart Sellar, David Anderson, David Spaven, John Furneval, Rae Montgomery; also Donald Peddie, Archivist of the Caledonian Railway Association Photographic Library, and with a special thanks to Hamish Stevenson, for allowing access to the respective collections of historic photographs and for permission to use the images so kindly loaned. Thanks also to my friend Ian Musgrave and my one-time colleague Harry Archibald for their kind and most useful photographic contributions, and to Robert Dey for the supply of relevant signalling diagrams. My most sincere thanks also must go to Jim MacIntosh, Douglas Yuill, Jim Summers and other fellow members of the Caledonian Railway Association, and also to Donald Cattanach of the NBR Study Group, for all assistance rendered during my researches. I must also acknowledge the valuable help provided by Christine Simm of the

SRPS regarding Rugby Specials, and, last but certainly not least, the gift of early photographs of Granton Gas Works, given me by my old and much missed dear friend, the late Wallace Lockhart, who had been Personnel Manager there for many years. As always, I must acknowledge my admiration of the skills and professionalism of both publisher Neil Parkhouse and designer Nigel Nicholson of Black Dwarf Lightmoor Press, in their ability to transform a manuscript of mere words into a format pleasing to the general reader at large, and to the Caledonian Railway Association for their continued support of my work. I am grateful to Stuart Sellar, Jim Summers, Dr Campbell Cornwell and Jim MacIntosh for proof checking images/captions and the actual manuscript, and to David Hamilton for proof reading some relevant chapters and putting me right regarding Caledonian Railway locomotives.

A special thank you to Chris Hawkins of Irwell Press for kind permission to include information from the chapter from my first book, *Steam Days at Haymarket*, dealing with footplate work at Dalry Road.

As in my previous works, time in this book is quoted using the 24-hour clock and Imperial measurements apply, and any errors which might be spotted are down to me, and me alone.

Harry Knox FIRO, MCIT, CMILT.
Linlithgow, 2018

Stanier 'Black Five' No. 44701 heads a stopping passenger service from Kingsknowe, past the new Slateford Junction signal box in April 1960. The original Slateford Junction box is on the left-hand side. The new box was later to become an S&T Dept training centre. *Stuart Sellar*

Glossary

Pre-Grouping companies and other railway abbreviations.

BR	British Railways (later British Rail)
D/E	Diesel Electric (Traction)
DMPS	District Motive Power Superintendent
DMU	Diesel Multiple Unit
E&BR	Edinburgh & Bathgate Railway
ECML	East Coast Main Line
ECS	Empty Coaching Stock
E.E.	English Electric Company (diesel locomotive builders)
EGR	Edinburgh & Glasgow Railway (later NBR)
EL&GR	Edinburgh, Leith & Granton Railway
EL&NR	Edinburgh, Leith & Newhaven Railway (became EL&GR)
EMU	Electric Multiple Unit
EP&DR	Edinburgh, Perth & Dundee Railway (later Edinburgh & Northern Railway, then North British Railway)
G&SWR	Glasgow & South-Western Railway
GJR	Grand Junction Railway
GNoSR	Great North of Scotland Railway
GPK&AR	Glasgow, Paisley, Kilmarnock & Ayr Railway (later G&SWR)
LE	Light Engine
L&MR	Liverpool & Manchester Railway
L&NWR	London & North Western Railway
L&YR	Lancashire & Yorkshire Railway
MR	Midland Railway
MS&LR	Manchester, Sheffield & Lincolnshire Railway
NBR	North British Railway
R&CR	Rutherglen & Coatbridge Railway
RCH	Railway Clearing House
SNER	Scottish North-Eastern Railway
SCR	Scottish Central Railway
TOC	Train Operating Company
W&CR	Wishaw & Coltness Railway Company
WCML	West Coast Main Line
WM&CR	Wilsontown, Morningside & Coltness Railway

1 The Caledonian Railway Comes to Town

In 1836, the Directors of the Grand Junction Railway, later to be part of the great London & North Western Railway (L&NWR), having connected the 83 miles between Birmingham and Newtown Junction (later Earlestown Junction) at Warrington in Lancashire, turned their attentions to the possibility of promoting a direct line which would connect London to Scotland, with Glasgow being the goal. Joseph Locke, by that time already a noted railway civil engineer, was asked to survey a possible route, or routes, for such a line north from the border city of Carlisle. Locke considered two alternatives using the natural valleys scoured out by rivers: the first was a line of route following the River Annan (Annandale), and the second the River Nith (Nithsdale), lying further to the west. The Annandale route did, however, present the most severe and difficult physical barrier, formed by a saddle between the Lowther and Moffat hills lying immediately to the north of the small village of Beattock. Thus Locke, faced by this virtual barrier of hills of no little consequence, and being of the opinion that two separate cross-border routes would not, and could not, be viable, opted for his second choice, this being the easier Nithsdale route, although it was the longer option at 417 miles. In doing so, he had not lost sight of the value of connecting Edinburgh to the chosen route but considered that the Edinburgh traffic could run over the soon to be constructed Edinburgh & Glasgow Railway (E&GR) from Glasgow.

In 1837, Locke was asked to reconsider his initial report and he therefore resurveyed the Annandale route, but for the first time took into consideration just how this route could actually be connected with Edinburgh. He reported that the Annandale route was indeed viable, but involving long and heavy gradients on the way, using a natural corridor lying between the Moffat Hills and the Lowther Hills in order to clear the summit (Beattock Summit), lying at 1,016 feet above sea level in the Lowther Hills. There was a possible connecting line to Edinburgh leaving this route between Symington and Thankerton, then running via Biggar on a line running on the southern side of the Pentland Hills to access Edinburgh (see Chapter 12). In doing so, Locke displayed his great professionalism and understanding of practical railway operation, by commenting not on the problem posed to the progeny locomotives by steepness of the gradients, but by the greater inherent dangers posed in the descent of same, and lack of suitable braking force. In 1840 an alternative line of route to Edinburgh was surveyed by a Mr D. McCallum, this route leaving the main line slightly further to the north of Symington in the Clyde Valley, near the village of Carstairs (at what was to become Carstairs Junction), running parallel to the north side of the Pentland Hills, and accessing Edinburgh via a slightly easier and more direct route from the west.

This Annandale route was to be approved by a Parliamentary Commission in 1841 and opened the door to the formation of a new railway company to promote the railway and build it. In early 1844 a group of a mere nine interested people assembled in London and were to form the backbone of this new Caledonian Railway Company, appointing Joseph Locke and John Errington as engineers of the line. The support of local landowners was also to be sought. Locke had, meanwhile, been asked to resurvey McCallum's route from Carstairs to Edinburgh and duly recommended this to the Directors as the best option, suggesting that the railway should terminate on a chosen site on Lothian Road, immediately to the south of the Union Canal's terminating point in the city, at Port Hopetoun, in the west side of central Edinburgh. This route, 27½ miles in length, required that agreement be reached with seven local (Midlothian) landowners, two of whom were openly hostile to the proposed railway, although by the time that the Caledonian Railway had obtained their authorising Act of Parliament on 31st July 1845, suitable financial terms had secured the approval of the whole seven. The first Board of Directors, including the two engineers of the line, consisted of seventeen other members under the chairmanship of John James Hope Johnston MP, of Annandale. The development and the growth of the Caledonian Railway to become what was without doubt the premier Scottish railway company, self-promoted as '*The True Line, True to Time*', has been well documented elsewhere and is a fascinating story in its own right, but this book is interested only in the Caledonian in and around the capital, the home ground of Dalry Road locomotives, drivers and firemen, and that is where the story must now go.

The 27½ miles from Carstairs Junction to the terminus in Lothian Road (101.6 miles from Carlisle) was not to be the easiest line of route. Running to the north of the Pentland Hills, the line climbed steadily away from Carstairs (Dolphinton Junction) and crossed the difficult Carnwath Moss; it ran on an average rising gradient of 1 in 217 for the nine intervening miles to Cobbinshaw Summit, lying around 950 feet above sea level and crossing more natural wetlands and mosses on the way, after which the line then fell away on an average falling gradient of about 1 in 149 for the remaining 15.5 miles to Slateford Junction on the outskirts of Edinburgh, not an easy road by any stretch of imagination. The remaining few miles into the terminus were, to all intents, level. Intermediate stations were to be provided at Carnwath (1¾ miles from Carstairs Junction), Auchengray (6 miles), Cobbinshaw (9 miles), West Calder & Torphin (12½ miles) (later renamed Harburn), Midcalder & Kirknewton (17¼ miles) (very quickly renamed Midcalder and eventually renamed Kirknewton once more in 1982), Slateford (24½ miles) (renamed King's Knowes in January 1853 and later still Kingsknowe), the new Slateford (January 1853) (25¼ miles), Merchiston (1882) (26¼ miles) (see Chapter 3) and Lothian Road (27½ miles). A further intermediate station was provided to the north of the village of Currie (later renamed Curriehill) (22 miles) (see Chapter 3). Within that distance a total of twenty-four telegraph block posts (signal boxes) controlled train running on the main line – initially by the Time Interval System of Working, but later the more secure Absolute Block Working facilitated by the Electric Telegraph – and access to the various sidings and branches connected thereto. This line of railway crossed the County March

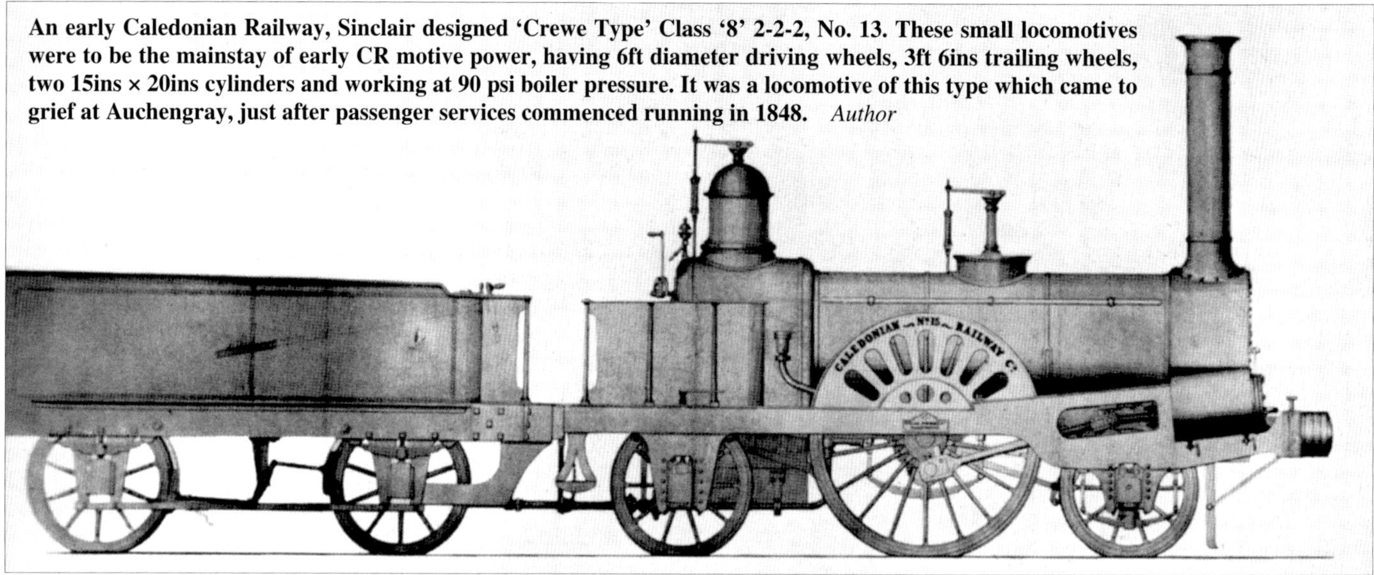

An early Caledonian Railway, Sinclair designed 'Crewe Type' Class '8' 2-2-2, No. 13. These small locomotives were to be the mainstay of early CR motive power, having 6ft diameter driving wheels, 3ft 6ins trailing wheels, two 15ins × 20ins cylinders and working at 90 psi boiler pressure. It was a locomotive of this type which came to grief at Auchengray, just after passenger services commenced running in 1848. *Author*

between Lanarkshire and Edinburghshire (later Midlothian) at Cobbinshaw and ran wholly within that latter county through to Edinburgh. In doing so, it ran almost parallel to the south side of the Edinburghshire (Midlothian)/Linlithgowshire (West Lothian) County March, which was marked by a stream, the Breich Water, and then the River Almond into which the former stream flowed. West Lothian, and that particular portion of south-west Midlothian crossed by the new line, were both to be unusual in terms of geology from the other adjacent counties in the Central Belt of Scotland. All the adjoining counties were underpinned by rich seams of coal,

McIntosh Class '104' No. 106 in CR livery pauses after taking water at Edinburgh Princes Street station whilst employed on Leith North Branch passenger workings in January 1913. This engine was finally scrapped in May 1936.
A.G. Ellis/Hamish Stevenson collection

but by a geological oddity of the Carboniferous Era (359 to 299 million years ago) the two counties of West Lothian and South Midlothian were to sit astride a vast field of oil-bearing shales, a field around three miles wide and stretching for 25 miles north-eastwards from Cobbinshaw to pass under the River Forth at South Queensferry; in all, a shale oil field measuring some 75 square miles in area. This geological feature and the additional rich, thick seams of limestone also present were to have a significant bearing on the future development of the Caledonian Railway, as shall be seen. The presence of oil shale, however, was not to mean that West Lothian did not have any rich coal seams; these and other rich mineral workings, such as ironstone, fireclay and in particular a seam of rare canneloid coal (see Chapter 2), were located along the western edge of the county, workings to which both the NBR and, at a later date, the Caledonian Railway were to serve, with the transportation of coal and other mineral traffic being shared (see Chapters 2 and 8).

The Caledonian Railway had also entered into an agreement with Edinburgh Town Council to lay in a water main alongside the railway, fed from Cobbinshaw Loch, to provide an additional water supply for the city, and, of course, from which the Caledonian Railway was to enjoy a free supply of water for its own needs until the Union Canal (and its feeder, Cobbinshaw Reservoir) was purchased by the NBR in 1849.

The Caledonian Railway had, as is said in Scotland, *a guid conceit o' itsel* – and quite illegally, in an act of opportunistic plagiarism, it misappropriated nothing less than the Ancient Royal Coat of Arms of Scotland as its own Coat of Arms, plus the Motto of the Order of the Thistle, which was to later adorn many of the locomotives of the company. Remembered by very few, if any, now, the Caledonian Railway Company was to become noted for the splendour of its beautiful ultramarine, blue locomotives, if not necessarily for the quality of its early rolling stock

The Caledonian Railway was to be beset by rivals on all sides, and in Edinburgh the initial rival concern was of, course, the Edinburgh-based Edinburgh & Glasgow Railway Company (E&GR). Whilst this latter concern (part of the bigger North British Railway after 1865), was eventually to stride through the centre of the city in no uncertain manner in 1846, the Caledonian followed in an almost apologetic manner two years later, reaching Edinburgh

Lothian Road to the left of station. The left-hand entrance is that of the Caledonian Hotel whilst that on the right is the pedestrian entrance to the station. Vehicular entrance was from Rutland Street on the right. Quite a nostalgic image with the (old) trams still on the streets and the sheer bulk and grandeur of the Caledonian Hotel is seen to advantage. The actual passenger station lay at street level below and behind the hotel. The pedestrian entrance on the frontage is now part of the Pompadour Restaurant, and the hotel is the Waldorf Astoria Caledonian Hotel. There was also a pedestrian entrance from Lothian Road to station located in the lower part of the station to left-hand rear. *Author's collection*

from Carstairs Junction on 15th February 1848. The new railway terminated in a wooden building some 180 feet in length and 54 feet wide, located on the south-western side of Lothian Road, at that time almost on the western outskirts of the city. Described as a glorified wooden shack, this station was to be the Caledonian Railway's major passenger base in Edinburgh for the next twenty-two years. Main line Anglo-Scottish services commenced running in March 1848, with passenger train services from Edinburgh to Glasgow via Carstairs following on the 1st April 1848 (see Chapter 7). Although the main line had been constructed as a double line, there was but a single platform within this 'shack'; it was served initially by a single line of railway from the vicinity of the Gardiner's Crescent overbridge, which split into three sidings, forming the platform line and another two storage sidings, all under cover. On the north side of the station another single approach line (the second of the double main lines), split into three or four goods sidings, all equipped with wagon turntables of varying dimensions. Thus, from the outset, the efficient operation of the new Caledonian Railway passenger and goods facilities in Edinburgh was to be hamstrung by the limitations imposed by these two single access and exit lines. With the opening of this Edinburgh terminus it appears that the company was in no hurry to commence express passenger running, preferring, as they explained, *'to allow the line to consolidate'*.

However, the explanation given as to why there was a delay in commencing train running also indicates that both of the engineering functionaries of the Caledonian Railway, as well as the BoT Inspecting Officer, Captain Simmons, had some serious doubts as to the condition of the trackbed of their new railway, especially where it crossed boggy terrain. This was perhaps not without cause, because in the same month as passenger services commenced, March 1848, there was indeed a serious derailment, with fatalities, of an Anglo-Scottish express train at Auchengray, caused in part by unstable track (see Chapter 15). That this delay was sound policy goes without saying, for the later excellent condition of the Caledonian Railway metals was to be specially commented upon by G.P. Neele, Superintendent of the Line for the L&NWR. In his *Reminiscences* he wrote:

> *'Certainly, the road bed of the Caledonian Line was always well and firmly maintained, and although our permanent way Engineer, Mr. Worthington, did not like comparisons, the solidity and stability of the line north of Carlisle was most marked; hard cinder slag, broken into small sections, being the leading feature of the ballast.'*

Despite some grandiose plans to replace this original wooden shed in Edinburgh (which was to be closed in any case in 1870) with a larger, Italianate stone structure, more appropriate for Scotland's capital city, this aspiration was not to be. The company, at that time beset by financial problems, sought yet another Act of Parliament

The station master (right), station inspectors and platform staff at the 'new' Princes Street station (circa 1910) are gathered together at the ticket barriers for Platforms 6 and 7 for the photographer. Note the interesting train departure boards overhead. *CRA Archives*

by which it could legally restrict the overgenerous dividends already promised to shareholders. Thus a second attempt at the provision of a worthy Caledonian Railway terminus in Edinburgh was to result in yet another wooden structure, not dissimilar to the one it was replacing and once more lying just as inconveniently placed as its predecessor, on Lothian Road. This replacement was, perhaps fortuitously, destroyed by fire on 16th June 1890, just before completion.

A third attempt was then made to provide Edinburgh with an appropriate Caledonian Railway station. This fine neo-Baroque, stone building was designed by the noted architectural practice of Peddie & Kinnear (Edinburgh) and was to cost £120,000 (a mere one tenth of the cost incurred by the NBR in rebuilding Waverley station). This new Caledonian station conveniently lay at street level and, sometime later, as the city boundaries expanded outwards, directly in the heart of Edinburgh's fashionable West End. The dimensions of this new station were 850 feet in length and 190 feet in width, providing some 18,000 square yards of area covered by a bayed roof. In the construction of this new Caledonian Railway station the company proved itself to be no more sympathetic to existing Edinburgh historic infrastructure than the NBR had been in earlier days,[1] and it spent considerable sums of money demolishing many existing buildings in the northern part of Lothian Road and the south side of Rutland Square, including St. George's Free Church, The Royal Riding Academy and the Scottish Naval & Military Academy.

The final station, still a long, low building, was opened in 1894, having been perspicaciously constructed to allow, at a somewhat later time, the construction of a hotel over it and lying along the eastern side and north frontage. This was to be the large, palatial, and very popular Caledonian Hotel, which was built in the manner of all grand railway hotels and constructed in distinctive red sandstone above the station; it opened its doors in 1903. Over the forthcoming years the hotel hosted many celebrities, including many of Hollywood's most famous film stars; amongst these, in the early 1950s, was that most famous singing cowboy, Roy Rodgers, *plus* his equally famous horse Trigger, both photographed descending the main staircase in the hotel in a publicity shot for the *Scotsman* newspaper. In Caledonian Railway days, the hotel boasted 250 rooms and 70 bathrooms. The Caledonian Hotel, when constructed, was not to be to everyone's taste, and indeed it was to be described by the Cockburn Association as an architectural excrescence and an eyesore which had utterly ruined the fine views along Princes Street from the Mound.

The new Princes Street station, ever popular and successful, was extended between 1899 and 1903, moving even closer to Princes Street. It was now ideally located in the centre of what was by this

1 See *Edinburgh St. Margaret's: A History*, by H. Knox, Lightmoor Press, 2015.

CR No. 89, a Class '66' 4-4-0 and one of Drummond's last designs for the CR (1891), the members of this class of locomotive were to do some sterling work between Edinburgh Princes Street and Carlisle with trailing loads of 'equal to fifteen'. *CRA Archives*

time Edinburgh's affluent West End, and known to both the local populace and users alike as the 'Caley' station. Large, light and airy, with seven curved platforms providing adequate standage for all the traffic running at the time and to come, the station was nevertheless regarded by the company as suffering from the problems posed by its inherent restrictive terminal configuration and plans were set in motion to convert it to a through station, company eyes still being concentrated on access to Leith (see Chapter 3). By the early 1900s, train services from Edinburgh to Lanark, Carstairs and the south, Ayr, Moffat, Peebles, Oban, Stirling, Perth and Dundee were departing from Princes Street station on a daily basis.

The last British Rail station master at Princes Street was Roderick (Roddie) McKenzie, who later was to become station master at Edinburgh Waverley, before the grade of station master was dispensed with in the early 1960s.

The 'Caley' station (Edinburgh Princes Street) closed in 1965 and was largely demolished in 1968, albeit with the exception of the hotel, and although sadly long gone, is still fondly remembered by the regular users, one of whom was the author. The main entrance to the former station (still extant) is now part of the frontage of the Pompadour Restaurant within the hotel proper. The magnificent five-star Caledonian Hotel, now an integral part of Princes Street and the West End, still stands today, but re-branded by the Hilton Hotel chain as the Waldorf Astoria Caledonian (Edinburgh) Hotel, albeit still referred to, and also known far and wide, as the 'Caley Hotel' by city residents and many others. Recently, £14 million has been earmarked for a complete refurbishment, and this sum, on top of the £51.7 million paid by the current owners, the Caledonian Operating Company, to the Hilton Group for the building, signifies a vast investment indeed.

An unidentified 'Princess Coronation' Pacific heads a stopping passenger train in Princes Street station on the 15th June 1955. The train is most likely the 11.37 departure for Glasgow Central via Shotts. Ex-LM&SR Stanier Pacifics appeared regularly on this service and also on the following Glasgow train, the 13.30 departure. The train is formed of a very clean rake of coaches in BR carmine and cream (also known as blood and custard) livery. *Stuart Sellar*

With passengers waving from the windows and relatives watching on the platform, 'Black Five' No. 45155 and Class 'B1' No. 61245 head the 10.30 (SO) to Heads of Ayr out of Edinburgh Princes Street in July 1964. *Stuart Sellar*

2 INDUSTRIAL GROWTH AROUND EDINBURGH (WESTERN APPROACHES)

Before Caledonian metals had even reached Edinburgh, the company, with ambitions to break into the lucrative shipping traffic at Granton and Leith, had in 1846 sought Parliamentary approval for a new line of railway from Slateford to Granton but this was not granted. In 1847 the Caledonian made a second attempt for another new line, termed the 'Edinburgh Union Line'; this time authorisation was granted under the Caledonian Railway Edinburgh Stations and Branches Act, 1847, for construction of a new branch line from Slateford to Haymarket (for additional information, see Chapter 3), but one recalcitrant landowner, John Laing, refused his permission and thus frustrated the scheme and completion was to be much delayed.

No sooner had the Caledonian Railway reached Edinburgh than it was also to cast an envious eye on the passenger traffic being carried by the E&GR between the capital and the second city of the British Empire, Glasgow. At that time the E&GR – with a line of route so nearly perfect, to all intents level except for the final mile, and 46½ miles in length (from its Haymarket Terminus) – was engaged in a ruinous war for passengers with not one, but two competing canals, in what should have been a no contest. The canals were respectively the Union Canal (Edinburgh to Falkirk) and the Forth & Clyde Canal (Grangemouth via Falkirk to Glasgow and the River Clyde). The competition had led to the E&GR charging the nonsensical fare of 6d (2½ pence) per Third Class single journey between the two cities, as did the canals, in order to compete. The Caledonian Railway, themselves enmeshed in a financial mess of immense proportions, partly due to poor management, sat on the side-lines watching this situation until, with the E&GR on the verge of bankruptcy, the Caledonian made its move and in November 1849 proposed amalgamation with the E&GR. The latter company, despite its problems, lacked nothing in the way of business astuteness and made demands which the Caledonian Board took on face value as a final position, rather than as a starting point in negotiations; in December of that same year, the Caledonian Railway, with amalgamation now a non-starter, decided to enter into full competition for the Edinburgh and Glasgow inter-city rail traffic, despite the fact that the then through rail link between Edinburgh (Lothian Road) and Glasgow (Buchanan Street station) via Carstairs Junction was a wholly uncompetitive 58¾ miles, compared with the 46½ miles enjoyed by the E&GR. It was to prove another no contest, with both companies now entrenched in the ruinous 6d per single journey fare; the Caledonian and the E&GR were soon both in much deeper financial trouble.

But it was not only the inter-city passenger traffic passing on E&GR (and later NBR) metals, but the sheer quantity of mineral freight traffic being handled by that latter company that stimulated Caledonian Railway interest. Given the industrial interests springing up in the east of Scotland, the then-new Scottish shale oil industry very much to the fore in both West and Midlothian, and the coal, ironstone, fireclay and limestone mining also being undertaken in the area crossed by the Caledonian Railway on its way into Edinburgh, there was a great demand for efficient and effective means of bulk transportation. Unfortunately for the Caledonian, the largest developing industry in the area, the Scottish shale oil industry, was centred upon the vast oil-bearing shale fields covering some 75 square miles lying mainly under West Lothian. This vast field outcropped at Cobbinshaw, deep in Caledonian territory, but thereafter was to run in a north-eastward direction across the county to pass under the River Forth at Dalmeny; thus after clearing the summit at Cobbinshaw the Caledonian Railway's Carstairs to Edinburgh line was to run parallel to the southern edge of the shale fields without actually passing over same. However, this line of route did lie on the very rich Burdiehouse limestone seam, a seam varying in thickness from 35 to 40 feet and lying parallel with and immediately below the shale seams of the Upper Oil Shales Group. Between Cobbinshaw and Harburn, this limestone seam was to be both mined and quarried immediately west of Torphin level crossing, where long sidings were laid in and opened in 1912, giving access to the limestone pits and lime kilns lying adjacent to the south side of the railway; access to these was controlled from a small signal box, Harburn Lime Works (all closed in 1963). The workings of this same seam of limestone close by the village of East Calder also prompted the Caledonian Railway to construct the later Camps Branch (see Chapter 3). This limestone was also to be worked at Westfield Pit, located on the west side of Newpark station, opened and rail-served after the coming of the Mid Calder to Cleland Railway in 1869 (see Chapters 4 and 11).

Likewise, the largest and very productive West Lothian coal fields lay on the western edge of the county, centred on Fauldhouse, Whitburn, Bathgate, Armadale and Bo'ness, all these locations being served by the North British Railway and earlier constituent companies. High on the Monklands moorlands, there were rich reserves of quality splint coal and ironstone, both of which were already in high demand by the iron masters who had set up their major iron and steel works in and around Motherwell and Coatbridge, both locations deep in Caledonian territory. The Caledonian Railway Company was to cast envious glances at the mineral largesse lying on its major rival's doorstep, and the means by which it was to gain access is discussed at Chapter 6.

East of Edinburgh it was the same story with high quality coal being produced in ever increasing tonnages from the rich East Lothian coalfields and being conveyed by the NBR to Leith and Granton for shipping. It was upon access to the rich and very productive Lothian coal measures on the south side of the capital that Caledonian attention was centred, when consideration was being given to Locke's initial proposal that the Edinburgh Branch from the West Coast Main Line should be extended to Edinburgh via Penicuik, a rural town lying on the River South Esk and a centre of the paper-making industry, but also sitting astride this coalfield. The docks at Leith were not only used for exporting, in the main, coal, but also received inwards traffic in no small quantities, including esparto grass (used in the paper making industry generally

Stanier '5MT' No. 44881 of Perth shed sets out for home with an express passenger train from Edinburgh Princes Street in April 1962. Edinburgh Castle overlooks the scene. *Stuart Sellar*

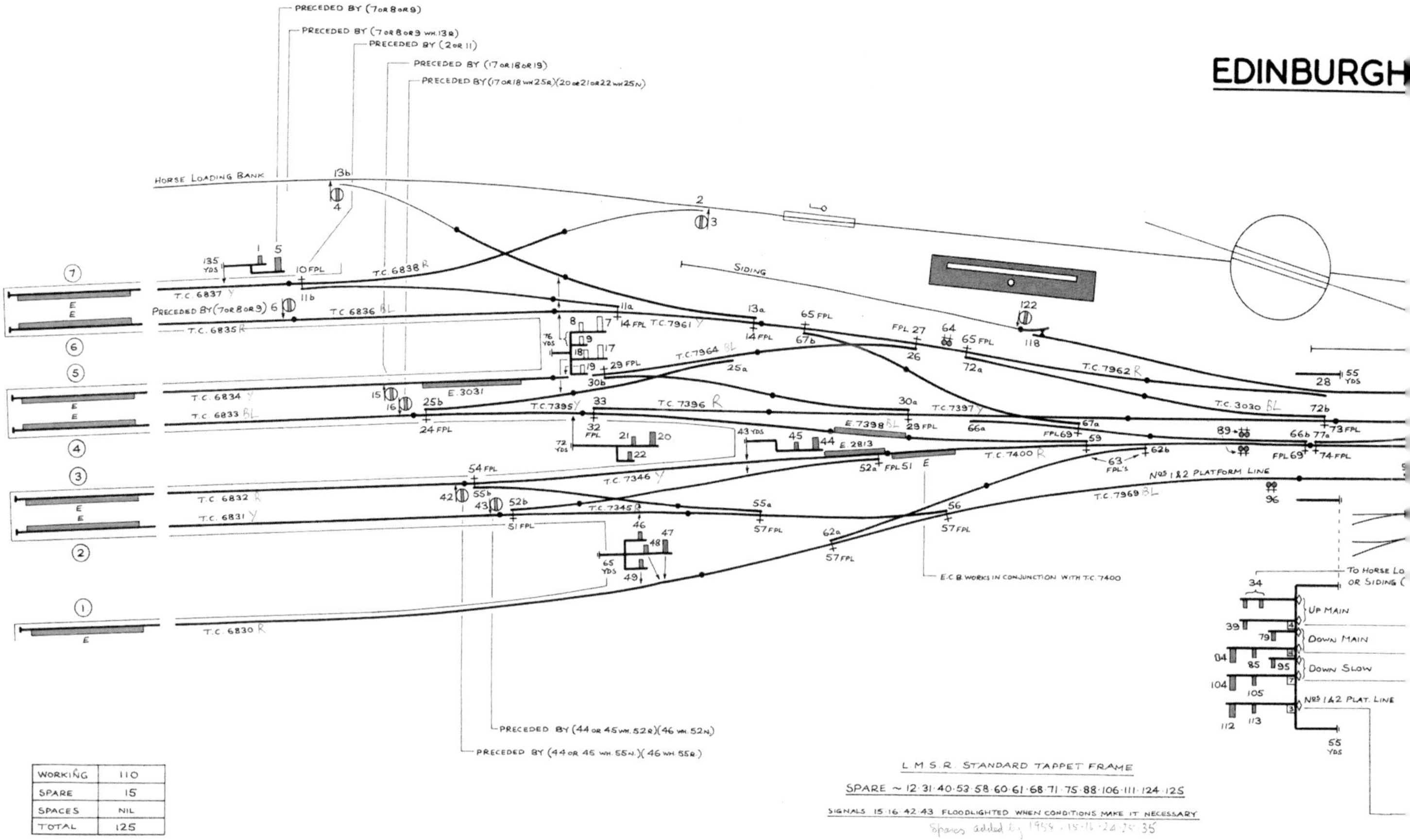

EDINBURGH

PRECEDED BY (7 OR 8 OR 9)
PRECEDED BY (7 OR 8 OR 9 WH. 13a)
PRECEDED BY (2 OR 11)
PRECEDED BY (17 OR 18 OR 19)
PRECEDED BY (17 OR 18 WH 25a)(20 OR 21 OR 22 WH 25N)

HORSE LOADING BANK

SIDING

NOS 1 & 2 PLATFORM LINE

UP MAIN
DOWN MAIN
DOWN SLOW
NOS 1 & 2 PLAT. LINE

TO HORSE LO[ADING BANK] OR SIDING

E.C.B. WORKS IN CONJUNCTION WITH T.C. 7400

PRECEDED BY (44 OR 45 WH. 52a)(46 WH. 52N)
PRECEDED BY (44 OR 45 WH. 55N)(46 WH. 55a)

WORKING	110
SPARE	15
SPACES	NIL
TOTAL	125

L.M.S.R. STANDARD TAPPET FRAME

SPARE ~ 12·31·40·53·58·60·61·68·71·75·88·106·111·124·125

SIGNALS 15·16·42·43 FLOODLIGHTED WHEN CONDITIONS MAKE IT NECESSARY

Spares added by 1958 · 15·16·24·25·35

In the closing days of Edinburgh Princes Street station, 'Black Five' No. 45483 awaits departure from Platform 4 with a local passenger service to Glasgow Central via Shotts. The fireman is keeping a good lookout for the guard's signal. *J.L. Stevenson/Hamish Stevenson*

Edinburgh Princes Street signalling plan, as drawn by BR in 1957 and amended 1958. *R. Dey collection*

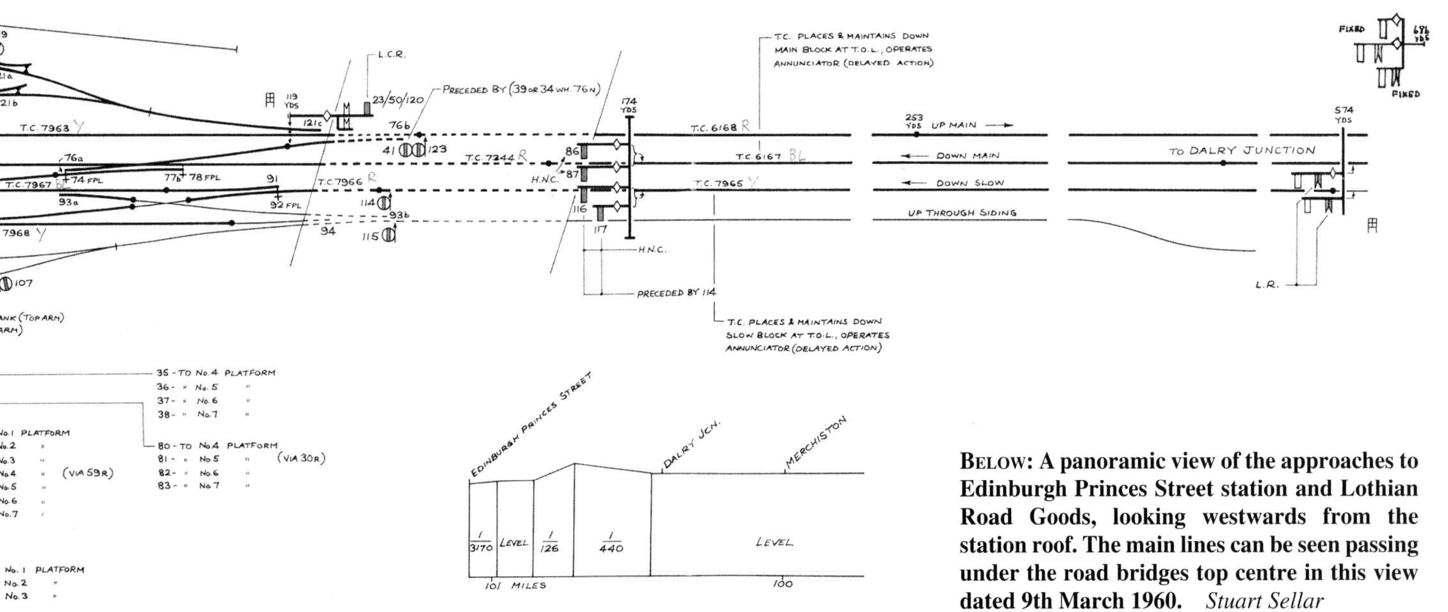

BELOW: A panoramic view of the approaches to Edinburgh Princes Street station and Lothian Road Goods, looking westwards from the station roof. The main lines can be seen passing under the road bridges top centre in this view dated 9th March 1960. *Stuart Sellar*

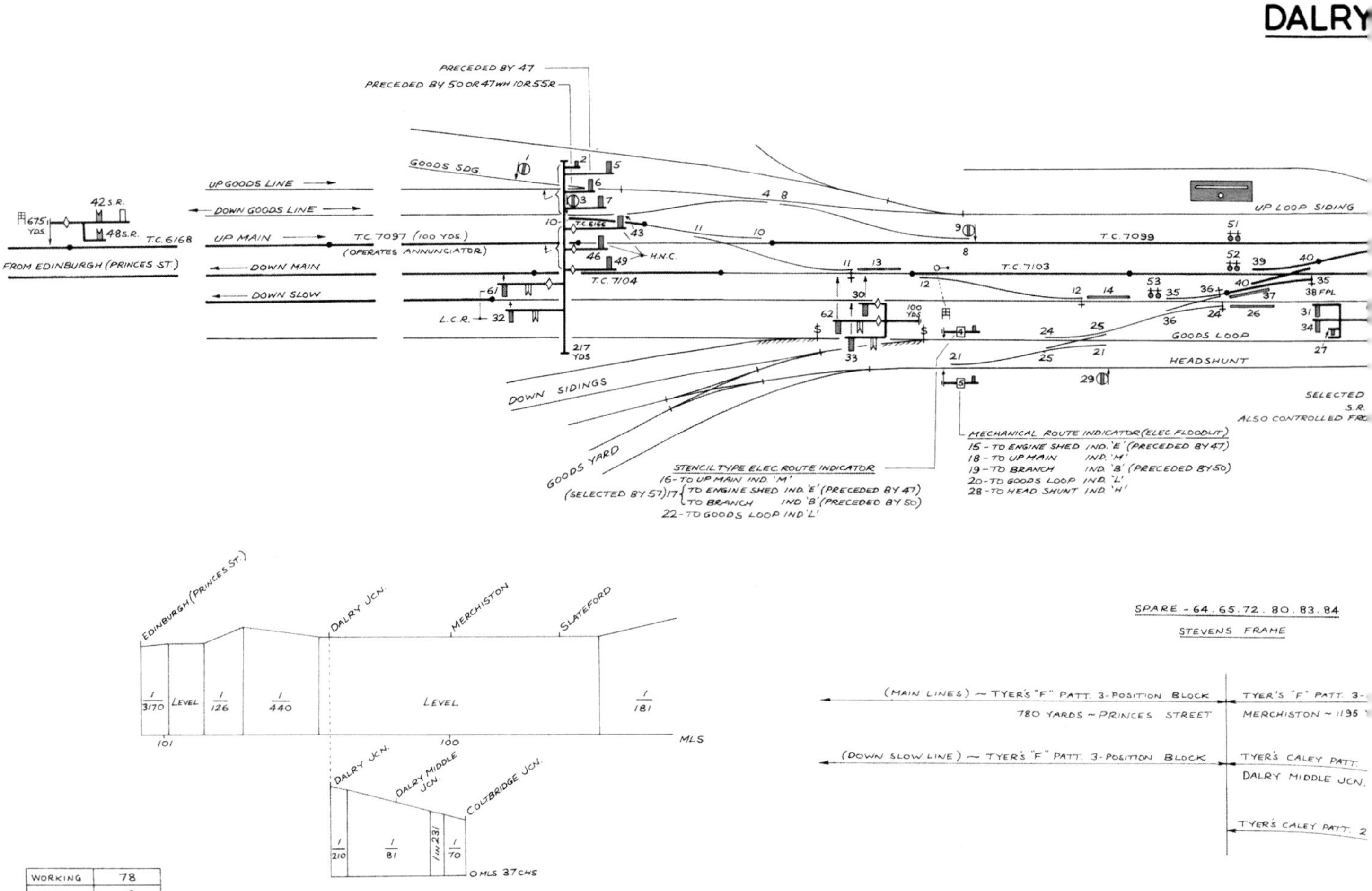

DALRY

PRECEDED BY 47
PRECEDED BY 50 OR 47WH 10R55R
GOODS SDG.
UP GOODS LINE
DOWN GOODS LINE
UP MAIN
DOWN MAIN
DOWN SLOW
FROM EDINBURGH (PRINCES ST.)
675 YDS.
42 S.R.
48 S.R.
T.C. 6168
T.C. 7097 (100 YDS.)
(OPERATES ANNUNCIATOR)
T.C. 6166
H.N.C.
T.C. 7104
L.C.R.
217 YDS
T.C. 7099
T.C. 7103
UP LOOP SIDING
GOODS LOOP
HEADSHUNT
38 FPL
100 YDS
DOWN SIDINGS
GOODS YARD
SELECTED
S.R.
ALSO CONTROLLED FRO

STENCIL TYPE ELEC. ROUTE INDICATOR
16 - TO UP MAIN IND. 'M'
(SELECTED BY 57) 17 { TO ENGINE SHED IND. 'E' (PRECEDED BY 47)
TO BRANCH IND. 'B' (PRECEDED BY 50)
22 - TO GOODS LOOP IND. 'L'

MECHANICAL ROUTE INDICATOR (ELEC. FLOODLIT)
15 - TO ENGINE SHED IND. 'E' (PRECEDED BY 47)
18 - TO UP MAIN IND. 'M'
19 - TO BRANCH IND. 'B' (PRECEDED BY 50)
20 - TO GOODS LOOP IND. 'L'
28 - TO HEAD SHUNT IND. 'H'

EDINBURGH (PRINCES ST.)
DALRY JCN.
MERCHISTON
SLATEFORD
1/3170
LEVEL
1/126
1/440
LEVEL
1/181
101
100
MLS
DALRY JCN.
DALRY MIDDLE JCN.
COLTBRIDGE JCN.
1/210
1/81
1 IN 231
1/70
0 MLS 37 CHS

SPARE - 64. 65. 72. 80. 83. 84
STEVENS FRAME

(MAIN LINES) ~ TYER'S "F" PATT. 3-POSITION BLOCK
780 YARDS ~ PRINCES STREET
TYER'S "F" PATT. 3-
MERCHISTON ~ 1195
(DOWN SLOW LINE) ~ TYER'S "F" PATT. 3-POSITION BLOCK
TYER'S CALEY PATT.
DALRY MIDDLE JCN.
TYER'S CALEY PATT. 2

WORKING	78
SPARE	6
SPACES	–
TOTAL	84

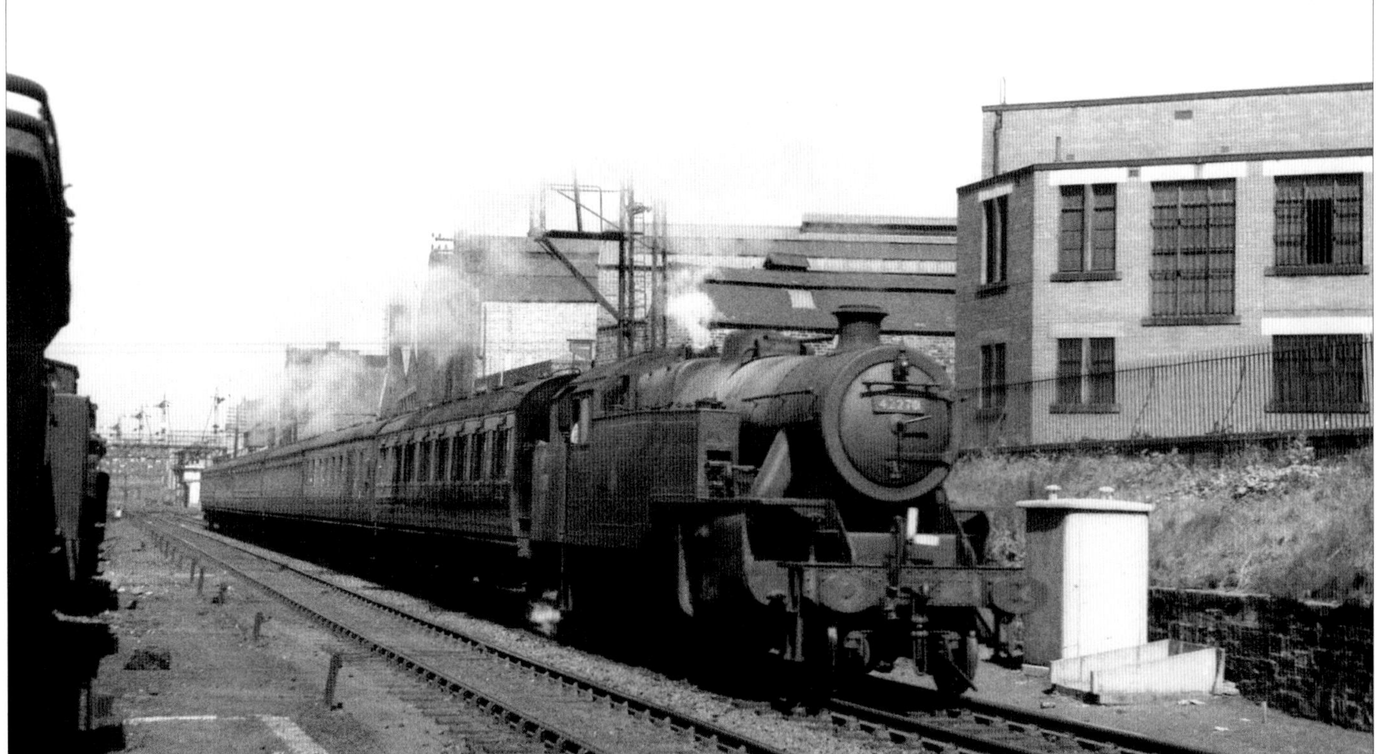

Fairburn 2-6-4T No. 42270 passes Dalry Road shed whilst working an Edinburgh to Glasgow stopping passenger service. Dalry Junction signal box can be seen to rear. *J.L. Stevenson/Hamish Stevenson*

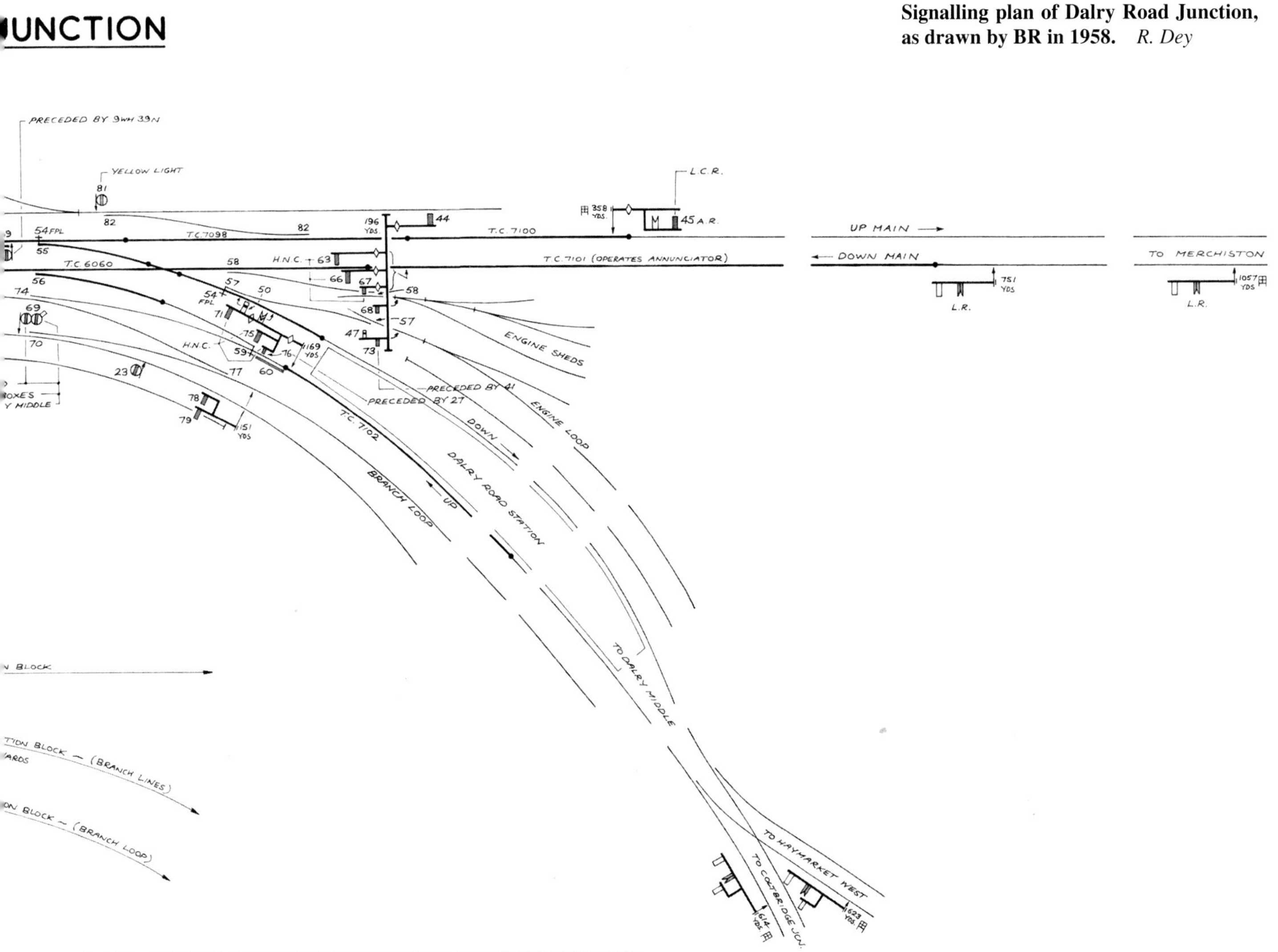

Signalling plan of Dalry Road Junction, as drawn by BR in 1958. *R. Dey*

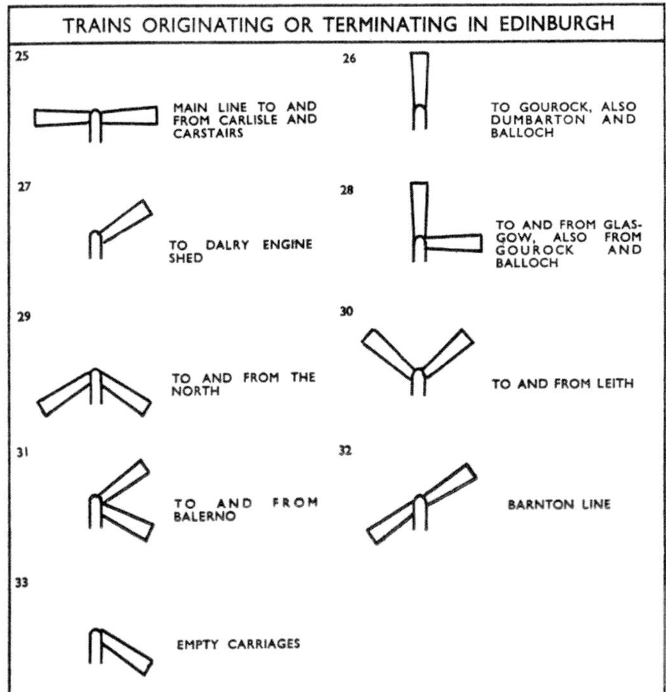

The Caledonian Railway 'Bow Tie' route indicators as applying to trains to and from Edinburgh. *Author's collection*

but with the Caledonian Railway having a particular interest in the paper mills lying on the Balerno Branch); in LM&SR days the ex-Caledonian rail network was to gain the benefit in transporting all the foregoing imported commodities to destination via Leith Docks, including, in particular, the later Norwegian iron ore traffic, of which, more later.

Within the city of Edinburgh itself, sitting on vast reserves of very high quality, fresh water, brewing was to be a major industry in the city, with some thirty-five brew houses and maltings being recorded as being in production over the years, and in this respect the Caledonian Railway, in choosing McCallum's recommended route into the city, was quickly to have a ready-made foothold with one of the developing major brewing concerns, that of William McEwan & Co., centred in the Fountainbridge area of the city and lying immediately adjacent to the Caledonian main line in the ward of Dalry. McEwan's Brewery, almost as old as the Caledonian Railway in Edinburgh itself, went into production in 1856 as the Fountain Brewery, which was very quickly rail-connected thereafter and was soon establishing itself as one of Edinburgh's major brewing concerns with significant export business within the UK and also to the wider British Empire. This brewery (closed 2004) was later to become part of the famous Scottish & Newcastle Brewing Group, now part of the Heineken & Carlsberg Group.

The Caledonian Railway was also to serve other brewing concerns

A misty morning at Dalry Road, where the ashpits are unusually quiet. Fairburn 2-6-4T No. 42270 stands, simmering gently before moving off shed to its next turn of duty. Dalry Road station canopy can be seen mid left behind coaling stage line, the signals for the western approaches to Dalry Junction are on the right. *David Anderson*

in and around Edinburgh. Indeed, it was the constant presence of wood smoke haze over the city from not only domestic fires, but also from these breweries and maltings, which was to lead to Edinburgh becoming known as 'Auld Reekie' (Old Smoky).

Also within the city boundaries the quarrying of a high quality, honey-coloured sandstone was conducted at some fifteen quarries including probably the largest, deepest (110m) and most famous, Craigleith Quarry. Quarrying started here in 1615 and continued until the quarry was finally closed in 1942. Widely used in the construction of Edinburgh's New Town, the hard sandstone was in high demand as a building material by the capital's architects. Indeed, the famous Nelson's Column in London was constructed of Craigleith sandstone. On closure the quarry was allowed to fill with water and became a source of cooling water for the nearby Granton Gas Works. Later it was infilled with inert waste and is now the site of a giant Sainsbury's supermarket. The Edinburgh, Granton and Leith Branch skirted the quarry immediately to the north of Craigleith station and sidings were laid in by the Caledonian Railway to gain the stone traffic coming from same.

To the south of the then new main line, Edinburgh's own river, the Water of Leith, flowing south-eastwards from its source high in the Pentland Hills, was to power an extraordinary number of mills of all types – paper, grains, spices and tobacco (snuff) – and leather tanning, all offering rich pickings for the transportation of both raw materials and finished products, plus a very productive quarrying activity around the river; all this lay deep in Caledonian Railway territory.

Elsewhere, lying closer to their industrial home in the west, there were other traffic opportunities, and the Caledonian Railway, soon to be serving the immense iron and steel industries of the Lower Clyde Valley and around Coatbridge, was not to be slow in tapping into these valuable mineral reserves. Coal was said to be the Caledonian's 'bread and butter' and the coal train workings around Hamilton and Motherwell were of eye-watering proportions. The similar extension of lines of railway in and around Edinburgh was to commence very soon after the Caledonian gained a toe-hold in the city. Whilst the NBR held sway with the largest tonnages of West Lothian coal being carried by that company, the Caledonian Railway was also later to enjoy a significant share of this coal, from the Benhar pits, lying up on the Benhar and Polkemmet moors, and also the United Collieries' Loganlea/Woodmuir/Foulshiels pits located close by West Calder.

The development of the Scottish shale oil industry, referred to above, largely came about after Sir James Young's patent of 1850 expired in 1864, when Scotland was thereafter to see a boom in the sheer number of oil companies (in excess of 120 new oil works in total) springing up in and around the two counties and elsewhere. Most were in fact to be nothing more than crude oil producers, with the crude oil being conveyed to the larger works which had refining capability and capacity, whilst others were smaller refining plants produced paraffin oil only. By the turn of the 20th century, through bankruptcies, amalgamations, fires and closures, only twelve major oil companies were to be left in production, and these, soon to be only nine, amalgamated in 1919 to form Scottish Oils Ltd. But the important factor for the railway companies was that there was still a requirement for crude oil to be transported to central refineries, the main one, and soon to be the only one, being Pumpherston oil works and refinery near Uphall. The refined end products also demanded transportation, and all this was reflected in the complicated Caledonian trip train diagrams which were developed to serve the needs of that expanding industry and which resulted in the Camps Branch becoming the main arterial link for the exchange of shale oil traffic between the Caledonian and North British Railway companies. Fortuitously for the Caledonian Railway, the rich oil-

ABOVE: A pedestrian's view of Dalry Middle Junction signal box from the street below, with BR Standard 2-6-2T No. 80060 heading a train for Stirling which will take the Wester Dalry Branch at this junction. *D. Simpson/David Spaven*

RIGHT: Camps Junction signal box and level crossing in late BR days. *Harry Archibald*

bearing seams of shale (fifteen in all, of which only seven were ever to be worked) also outcropped on Cobbinshaw Moor, adjacent to and south of their West Coast Main Line of Railway. Here both shale mining and oil production were quickly to spring up, with the construction of an oil works with retorting facilities high up on the bleak moorland at Tarbrax. Coal was also to be mined on these high moors, some of which fuelled the retorts at Tarbrax Oil Works whilst the remainder was taken by rail to Pumpherston refinery. The Tarbrax crude shale oil and coal traffic, the Westwood crude oil traffic, and the Coltness limestone workings at Harburn, Newpark and Camps were to keep two Carstairs trip engines and two Dalry Road trip engines in full time employment until the demise of the industries in the early 1960s.

An early speculator in the developing Scottish oil industry was to be a noted Caledonian Railway Locomotive Superintendent, Benjamin Connor (see also Chapter 6), when in 1866 he invested heavily in the then new Glasgow Oil Company (Broxburn) Ltd. Albyn Oil Works at Broxburn, had been founded by Robert Bell, a leading light in the new industry of the time, but the venture failed not just once but twice, and the oil company was, very soon, to be wound up. Connor lost heavily, as did his friend and fellow Locomotive Superintendent of the North British Railway, William Hurst, who was another early investor.

It was not just industrial growth in the Lothians which was to provide valuable traffic for the railway, however, as both West and Mid Lothian, lying west of Edinburgh, consisted of rich agricultural land where arable, livestock and dairy farming were all being undertaken, with the latter providing a regular flow of milk traffic to rail (see Chapters 3 and 10). Milk was being forwarded daily, by both special milk trains and normal service passenger trains, and the author remembers well the daily procession of tractors and trailers, conveying the milk in conical steel 'churns', each containing 18 gallons of milk, to West Calder station for onward transmission to Edinburgh. The owner of each churn was identified by a small brass plate with his name etched and affixed thereto. This traffic lasted until the late 1950s, but thereafter, with the spread of road milk tankers collecting milk in bulk from each of the individual farms, the use of churns was superseded and the milk traffic was largely gone from the railway scene by 1960. Never popular with the station staff at West Calder, and with no road access to the Up-side platform (for Edinburgh), these heavy churns had to be manhandled across the running lines between the platforms. In total, Edinburgh Princes Street station and Lothian Road Goods station handled between 8,000 and 10,000 gallons of milk daily if the Edinburgh & Dumfriesshire Dairy bulk milk traffic from Dumfries is included.

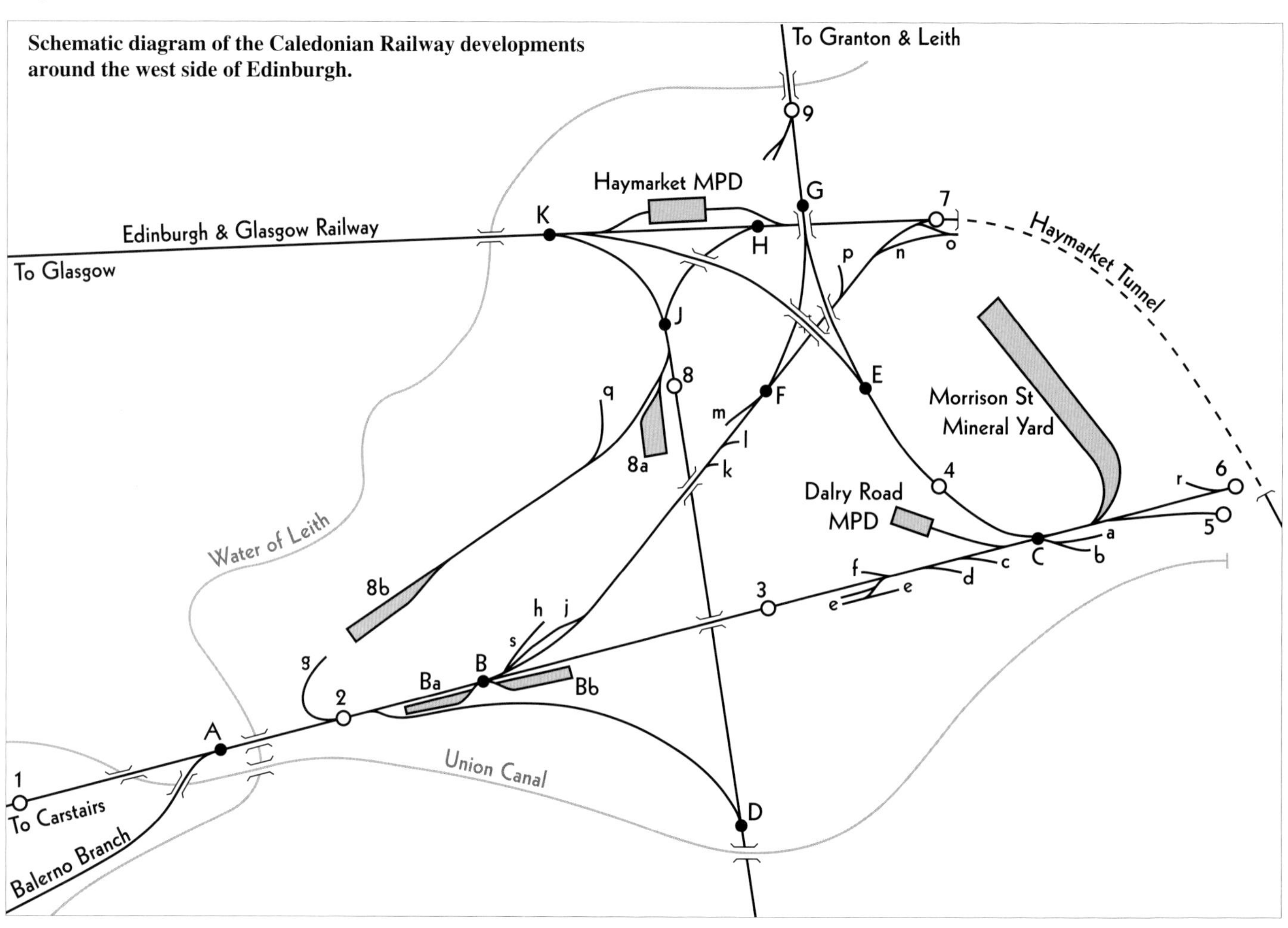

Schematic diagram of the Caledonian Railway developments around the west side of Edinburgh.

Key to map

1. Kinsknowe station
2. Slateford station
3. Merchiston station
4. Dalry Road station
5. Lothian Road Goods
6. Edinburgh Princes Street station
7. Haymarket station
8. Gorgie East station
8a. Gorgie East Yard
8b. Gorgie Cattle Market sidings
9. Murrayfield station

A. Balerno Junction
B. Slateford Junction
Ba. Slateford Carriage sidings
Bb. Slateford Yard
C. Dalry Junction
D. Craiglockhart Junction
E. Dalry Middle Junction
F. Granton Junction
G. Coltbridge Junction
H. Haymarket Central Junction
J. Gorgie Junction
K. Haymarket West Junction

a. McEwan's Fountain Brewery
b. West End Engine Works and Robertsons
c. Dalry Manure Siding
d. Old Cattle Bank
e. Harrison Park and Edinburgh & Dumfriesshire Dairy Co.
f. Angle Park Stone Sidings
g. Gorgie Markets
h. McEwans Maltings and McKenzie & Moncur Iron Works
j. Blacks

k. Lorimer & Clark's Caledonian Brewery
l. Tynecastle Sidings
m. Corporation Stone Sidings
n. Duff Street Sidings
o. Caledonian Distillery
p. James Hunter & Beattie
q. Gorgie Mills (Cox's Glue Works)
r. Dewar Place electricity generating station
s. Slateford Laundry

3 Caledonian Railway Developments in the Edinburgh District

Given the industrial developments outline in Chapter 2, it is unsurprising that the Caledonian Railway sought to gain a share in both the various mineral extraction projects taking place in and around their Edinburgh territory, and the sheer quantities of coal being conveyed to Leith and Granton docks.

As described at Chapter 1, the Caledonian Railway was to enter the Edinburgh city boundaries in a somewhat understated manner, its new main line running on a falling gradient to the city limits at Kingsknowe (originally called Slateford) where it crossed the Union Canal. Running parallel to, and immediately north of the canal, it crossed the Water of Leith by a handsome stone viaduct on the approach to the second Slateford station (opened January 1853) with the Union Canal crossing the same Water by a handsome, Telford designed, stone aqueduct lying parallel to the south. At Slateford, with plenty of open space lying adjacent, the Caledonian was to construct a large marshalling yard, in 1896 consisting of six dead-ended sidings, but by 1908 there were ten dead-ended sidings and by 1933 the yard consisted of eleven dead-ended sidings all lying on an east/west axis with buffer ends at the eastern end. Passenger coaching stock was initially stabled and serviced in the carriage sidings provided adjacent to the northern side of Princes Street station but when more commodious facilities became essential in the early part of the 20th century the west sidings at Slateford were pressed into use as a carriage stabling, cleaning and servicing facility. In 1928 the LM&SR decided to centralise all carriage cleaning, servicing and stabling at Slateford, and this remained the position until October 1958, when construction work on the new Craiglockhart curve, opened in 1959, required closure of the carriage sidings.

In chronological order, the proliferation of Caledonian Railway sponsored railway schemes in and around Edinburgh, included the following.

1853, Slateford to Haymarket Branch

As stated in Chapter 2, the Caledonian Railway had early aspirations to access not only Leith and Granton to obtain a share of the lucrative shipping traffic being undertaken there, but also to access Waverley Bridge station itself. Finally, in 1847, the company was authorised to construct, amongst other things, a branch line from Slateford to Haymarket, termed 'The Edinburgh Union Line'.

The actual Bill presented to Parliament in 1846 sought powers as follows:

- *To construct a new Branch Railway from the Caledonian Railway, near where it crosses a stream called the Moat Burn, which runs between the farms of Gorgie Mains and Gorgie Farm, in the Parish of St. Cuthbert's, through said Parish to the Parish of Cramond to, or near to, Granton Pier, in the last-mentioned Parish.*
- *A Branch Railway from the Branch Railway, above described, near Tyne Castle toll bar in the Parish of St. Cuthbert, to the Edinburgh and Glasgow Railway at or near Haymarket Station in Edinburgh, of the aforementioned Railway.*
- *A Branch Railway from the Caledonian Railway, near Dalry House in the Parish of St. Cuthbert's, to the Branch Railway first described, at or near the point where the same proposes to cross over the Edinburgh and Glasgow Railway, and:*
- *A Branch Railway from the Edinburgh and Glasgow Railway at a point about 440 yards to the westwards of the Signal-house, near the Engine-house at the said Haymarket Station, to the Branch Railway first described, at or near the point where the same is proposed to cross over the Turnpike road, leading from Edinburgh to Glasgow, all in the Parish of St. Cuthbert's.*

The Bill received Royal Assent on 22nd July 1847 for both the extension of their Edinburgh (Lothian Road) station and the construction of the branch as described. However, the Caledonian Railway Directors were under the impression that all was now plain sailing and that the path to obtaining the most economical way of reaching Leith – via the E&GR and NBR joint Waverley Bridge station and the EL&GR lying at right angles to same and rail connected to this joint station and on to Leith via the Scotland Street Tunnel – was now within their grasp. *But*, the Act merely gave the Caledonian the right to construct a physical connection between the two companies' lines at Haymarket. It did not confer upon the Caledonian any rights to run trains to Haymarket and through to Waverley Bridge station without consent in writing from the NBR, the EL&GR *and* the E&GR – since the latter's station formed part of the Joint NBR/E&GR Waverley Bridge station and with the EL&GR owned Canal Street station adjacent to Waverley Bridge. In January 1851 the E&GR Directors apparently agreed to the creation of a Junction from the Caledonian Haymarket Branch to the E&GR main line at Haymarket.[1] A rather ambiguous note in the Minutes of the E&GR dated November/December 1853 states that:

> *'CALEDONIAN RAILWAY and NBR reported now to be under joint management, and the E&GR sought to bring CR traffic into Edinburgh Waverley Bridge Station.'*

The subsequent history of this branch and its construction, is mired in controversy with much left unexplained even to the present day. There is a difference of opinion amongst railway historians as to exactly when this branch was constructed, with the Cobb's *The Railways of Great Britain, a Historical Atlas* opting for 1851. The truth of the matter is that a recalcitrant landowner, John Laing, caused delay to the best laid plans of the Caledonian Railway Company and it was not until early 1853 that a start could be

1 E&GR Minutes, BR/EGR/1/13.

A view of Granton Junction and the former CR Slateford to Haymarket branch, now ground frame controlled with a single line connection in the Haymarket direction. The line to Coltbridge Junction leads off left. An unidentified BR Standard 2-6-4T heads a Stirling bound passenger train on the Wester Dalry Branch. *Stuart Sellar*

made on the actual construction. It appears, from what transpired next, that both the line and the physical connection with E&GR metals at Haymarket were completed very quickly by late 1853, since on 22nd October of that same year the Caledonian Railway advised the Board of Trade (BoT) that the line was ready for opening. By 1855, however, nothing more had happened regarding the BoT inspection, and on the 17th March 1855 the Caledonian once again wrote to the Board of Trade regarding inspection of the new works. An inspection was carried out by Colonel W. Yoland on 23rd March 1855, but he refused permission to open the line of route until the signalling arrangements controlling the junction at Haymarket East had been properly finalised. Further BoT inspections were carried out on 23rd April and 19th May 1855, but yet again, and quite incredibly, the signals at Haymarket East Junction, controlling access to the Slateford Branch, had still not been provided, and once more the opening of the line was rejected.

On 15th June 1855 the Caledonian Railway Company formally advised the BoT that they now wished to postpone the opening of this branch line and would be in touch at a later date. It appears from correspondence between the Caledonian Railway and the NBR later that same year that the E&GR had, in light of the Caledonian's decision to defer indefinitely the opening of the branch, removed the connecting junction at Haymarket station without any reference to the Caledonian.[2] However, following the quite justified complaint from the latter,[3] re-emphasising that this connection was made under Parliamentary Powers (The Edinburgh Station and Branches Act 1847), the E&GR had the junction points re-instated at their own cost, but not until early February 1859. The pressure to do so came partly from the Edinburgh, Perth & Dundee Railway (EP&DR) in order that their traffic from Leith to the south could be transferred to the Caledonian Railway at Haymarket (should that company choose to take it on!).

It is well known that the E&GR and the Caledonian Railway enjoyed a relatively close working relationship in the early days and contained within E&GR Director's Minutes is clear evidence that the E&GR were prepared to help the Caledonian to access Leith and Granton. They were also supportive of the EP&DR attempts to have their traffic conveyed to Haymarket, where the transfer to the Caledonian Railway metals could be easily effected, but the EP&DR declined to accept the rates for the proposed Caledonian & Leith traffic, as quoted by the E&GR, and final agreement was not reached until December 1858.

The North British Railway Company, standing alone and seeing the way the wind was blowing with the E&GR, had as far back as 1853 sought a permanent interdict, prohibiting the Caledonian Railway any right of access to their metals and station. The E&GR and the Caledonian appealed the interdict. The appeal was heard on 16th December 1853 at the First Division of the Court of Session in Edinburgh and *The Scotsman* reported the proceedings on the 17th as follows:

Waverley Bridge Station.

The Application for interdict by the North British Railway Company against the Caledonian and the Edinburgh & Glasgow Railway Companies was taken up on Wednesday by the First Division. Interim interdict had been granted on the 11th November last, by Lord Deas (who meanwhile) took the case to the First Division,

2 E&GR Board Minutes of 30th October 1855.

3 E&GR Minutes, BR/EGR/1/17: letter of 15th November 1855 from the Caledonian Railway, discussed by Directors refers.

prohibiting the Caledonian Company taking possession at, or use of the Joint Station at Waverley Bridge as their station; or from acting upon the Agreement of Amalgamation between them and the Edinburgh & Glasgow Railway Company, so far as regarded the use and occupancy of said joint station.

The case having been fully debated, The Lord President, in giving judgement said that the questions raised between the Parties were undoubtedly very important for both of them but involved matters the settlement of which might be attended with some difficulty. But the question they had to decide was simply whether or not they ought to continue the interdict. Now he could not shut his eyes to the contract that had been entered into between two of these companies,[4] which was in fact a contract to make the station the joint one for the use of both these parties. His Lordship referred to reports submitted to the half yearly meetings of the amalgamated companies in September last, in which one of the objects of amalgamation was plainly stated to be to make one station at either terminus accommodating the joint traffic. Although the parties denied they were acting on that agreement in this matter, it was evident he said that the objective they had in view in availing themselves, as they alleged, of the power the statutes gave without any agreement at all. He could not therefore, view the matter otherwise than an attempt on the part of these two companies, to carry into effect, this agreement, and he certainly thought that the NBR were entitled to be protected against the intrusion of this third party, into their station. There might be nice questions raised as to the extent to which the NBR and the E&GR were entitled to introduce traffic of another company, which had a terminus of its own in Edinburgh, but he could not think that the introduction of the traffic of another company, which had a terminus of its own in Edinburgh, almost at the threshold of the station and plainly for the occupying the station, was in accordance with the fair interpretation of the clauses of the Act of Parliament. The case of the Scottish Central, joining the Edinburgh and Glasgow line at Polmont and Castlecary might be in perfect accordance with these clauses, for the Scottish Central had no communication of its own in that direction, but the proceeding now disclosed appeared to him to be an attempt to transfer to the Caledonian Company, a right to enter that station in conjunction with the Edinburgh & Glasgow Company, which he conceived, might be attended with great inconvenience, and positive injury to the NBR, a measure which, if it had been proposed at the time, was one that would not probably have been gone into. Looking to all these matters, he thought that the interdict ought to be continued.

Lord Ivory concurred. If all three parties had consented, there might have been no objection to the Caledonian using this station, and superseding their own, but without the consent of the two contracting parties, no third person could be introduced.

Lord Robertson was of the same opinion, looking upon the arrangement as an attempt to trip up the heels of the NBR which was a rival line.

Lord Rutherford had no hesitation in concurring with their Lordships. He did not mean to say that there might not arise cases of considerable difficulty in regard to this station, but he considered that they all should pass the note and continue the interdict, that these questions might deliberately considered. There could be no doubt that this terminus being the joint property of the NBR and the E&GR Companies, each company was only entitled to use it for traffic which was fairly and honestly brought upon their lines, whether local traffic or through traffic communicated to them from other lines and passing over a portion of their lines from distant quarters. Thus, the E&GR use this station for all its northern traffic, and the NBR uses it for traffic from the east and north of England, and if a question should arise about the junction at Greenhill, he should hesitate very much before he interdicted the traffic from that junction, for there was so much of the E&GR line used, and fairly used, that it was not a question as to the use of the line. But when they found that the Caledonian Railway, having its own station in Edinburgh, besides entering this station under an arrangement to which the rights of traffic brought from that rival company, was only brought in, as his Lordship had remarked, at the threshold of the station, he would hesitate about saying that this was a case within the meaning of the Act of Parliament in providing for the traffic of one line being received upon another.

The Court accordingly passed the note, and continued this interdict prohibiting the use of this joint station by the Caledonian Railway.

And so, the Caledonian Railway lost the battle to secure passage through Edinburgh to access Leith and the docks thereof. However, the Caledonian, with an interest in the traffic passing to and from the EP&DR, were still seeking an arrangement whereby EP&DR traffic bound for the Caledonian Railway should be worked over the E&GR, by that company's locomotives, to be handed over to the Caledonian Railway at Haymarket.

As discussed above, there things remained in abeyance until June 1859, when the whole question was considered by the General Committee of the Caledonian Railway and remitted by them to Board Level. However, the matter was largely, and most effectively, to be taken out of Caledonian hands later that same year, when William Cawkwell, General Manager of the L&NWR, advised both the Caledonian Railway Board and the BoT in London in a letter dated 10th October 1859, that a Royal Train, conveying HM Queen Victoria, travelling from Edinburgh to Bangor, was planned to run over West Coast Main Line metals in the October of that same year. He stated that this train *would* require to run over the rail connections at Haymarket (East) to this erstwhile branch, in running via the NBR and E&GR from the Queen's station at Meadowbank, near Holyrood House, to Slateford, Carstairs and Carlisle, on the occasion of the Royal Visit. That prompted some action at last, with the BoT (unwilling to incur Her Majesty's displeasure) quickly agreeing to a temporary opening of both the junction and the branch line, and the Queen passed over this branch, in safety, a mere four days later, on the 15th October 1859, and did so again on the 17th September 1860. However, BoT approval was given with conditions, in that the branch was not to be considered suitable for the travelling public at large. Despite this clarification, and given everything that transpired during this period, the running of these Royal workings does beg the question 'just how was this conducted?'

Given the NBR's stance that Caledonian engines would never run on their metals, one wonders did Her Majesty suffer the indignity in having not two, but three engine changes in this very short distance? That is, the NBR working the train from St. Margaret's to Waverley Bridge station, where the E&GR took over and worked to Haymarket East Junction, where a Caledonian engine was waiting to work the train forward? If this were the case, then HM would quite definitely not have been amused. The answer is,

4 The NBR and the E&GR.

of course, a resounding NO and common sense prevailed. In fact, and thanks to G.P. Neele's attention to detail, it is recorded in his *Reminiscences* that:

'The Queen and Prince Consort left Edinburgh St. Margaret's Station at 09.00. The Royal Train by which Her Majesty travelled, was under the special direction of Mr. Cawkwell, General Manager of the L&NWR, and the Marquis of Chandos, the Chairman of the same Company was also present, and passing through Waverley Bridge station, entered on the Caledonian system at Haymarket Junction at 09.10, thence travelling via Mid Calder, Carnwath and Thankerton, it made its first stop at Abington at 10.15 for water. Carlisle was reached at 11.45 and the North-Western engines were attached.'

The second journey mentioned was made on the 17th September when the Queen, accompanied by the Prince Consort and a large household entourage, were travelling from Edinburgh St. Margaret's station to Gosport. Once again it is recorded that leaving Edinburgh at 19.00, the train was worked throughout to Carlisle with one stoppage for water, again at Abington, by the Caledonian Railway.

There can therefore be no doubt, given the foregoing, that a Caledonian Railway locomotive, plus pilot engine and footplate crews, all most likely from Dalry Road shed, and with appropriate conductors, *did* enter upon NBR/E&GR hallowed ground, and worked both these Royal Trains through to Carlisle. It is also likely that Class '4' 2-2-2s of Sinclair design with tenders carrying just 800 gallons of water, of which Dalry Road had a small allocation, were pressed into Royal Service and returned some remarkably economical performances in terms of water consumption on this working, although The Queen insisted on a maximum speed of 40 mph.

The Haymarket tunnel (later Haymarket North Tunnel) was not opened until 1846, and indeed it was not until the 1st July 1848 that SCR trains commenced running between Edinburgh, Stirling and Perth, this service consisting of four trains in each direction daily. On the 28th October 1848, *The Scotsman* newspaper carried notification from the Edinburgh & Glasgow Railway Company, stating that they intended to close Haymarket station, their original Edinburgh terminus, to all passengers, horses and carriages etc., on and from the 1st November 1848. This step had obviously been long contemplated, since with the opening of the Haymarket tunnel the station had become a through station and the configuration of the 1844 terminal platforms rendered the retention of the old station as a through passenger facility well-nigh impracticable. The station, later to be rebuilt at rail level, was brought back into use in 1894, *The Scotsman* again reporting as follows on 6th July that year:

'Nothing indeed remains of the previous structure but the old booking hall ... the new station consists of an island platform over 600 feet in length, with two side platforms the same length, and on the north-west side, a small dock for special traffic. On the island platform, which is 25 feet in width, are blocks of waiting rooms, and commodious waiting and other rooms have been formed on the south platform under the newly-made road leading to the distillery. The booking hall is, as before, on street level and access is got to the platforms by broad and easy stairs and cross-over bridges. There is a luggage bridge and hoists communicating with each platform. The platforms are protected by verandah roofs, 15 feet high, carried on iron columns.

Just why this Haymarket Branch was constructed at such an early date in the company's history is open to conjecture, since the NBR had refused to consider access over their lines to Leith and Granton – the intended goal of the early Caledonian – but the saving grace was that the company was to obtain access to both the inwards and outwards traffic, including construction material, for one of Edinburgh's most highly respected and productive distilleries, the Caledonian Distillery belonging to Graham Menzies & Co. This distillery, opened in 1855, was to be noted for production of a very high quality, and much sought after, single grain whisky. From the outset it was to be served by the E&GR (later NBR) from their Haymarket Yard opposite the distillery buildings, via a trailing connection from their main line and connecting into the Caledonian Railway sidings at this facility. There was also a number of small industrial concerns along the length of this branch which were accessed by rail, producing but a modest amount of traffic for the company. The distillery itself closed in 1988 and has now been developed into housing. Rail connected traders located on this branch, from RCH records, over the years from 1892, were:

- Caledonian Distillery
- James Steel, builders
- Stuart & Co. Granolithic Works.

By 1904, as above, plus:

- Martin's Stone Siding: builders.

By 1915, the list was as above, plus:

- Stone Siding: W.G. Walker & Sons, builders
- J. Angus & Son, builders
- W. Martin, builders.

By 1925, the list included:

- Beattie's Siding.

By 1938, W.G. Walker & Sons were now trading as Asphalters, plus two additions as follows:

- John Hunter, demolition contractors
- Cruikshanks, bakery engineers.

A later addition was a rail connected scrap yard located immediately on the north side of the Wester Dalry Branch overbridge. This modest scrap yard, formerly owned by James Hunter, Demolition Contractors, passed to another noted scrap merchant, Bernard Hunter, who was originally based at Seafield. This scrap yard disappeared in, or about, 1964, with the reinstatement of the Haymarket East Junction to Slateford through main route.

In 1860, this Haymarket line from Granton Junction continued as a double line (later partly singled) towards Haymarket station (E&BR and later NBR) and Duff Street Sidings, where the Caledonian Railway continued to enjoy the physical connection (a double junction) with the E&GR main Glasgow line and the use of a double bay platform at the same Haymarket station. The purpose of this small terminal facility is shrouded in mystery. Initially the author thought that it may have been provided for use by the

A view of the original 1851 Slateford to Haymarket Branch taken circa 1960 from the Leith North Branch overbridge looking towards Haymarket and to what was a connection with the E&GR main line, which runs centre left to right; Haymarket station is just out of sight. The connections and sidings on the far right serve the Caledonian Distillery. The rail-served scrap yard on the left was operated by a well-known Edinburgh scrap dealer, Bernard Hunter and here his internal crane makes a shunt with a partly-filled 16-ton steel mineral wagon. In 1964 the original branch line would be re-instated to become a double line of passenger railway, connecting Haymarket with the WCML at Slateford once more. Donaldson's school for deaf children can be seen to the left, with Herdman's flour mills dominating the centre upper skyline. *D. Simpson/David Spaven*

Scottish Central train services, but since through services from Perth to Edinburgh and Glasgow did not commence until 1st July 1848 – with four trains per day from Perth to Edinburgh and four trains per day from Edinburgh to Stirling and Perth – and since access through to the E&GR station in Edinburgh was by now open, this was found to be highly unlikely. The E&GR had, as stated, closed Haymarket station in November that same year, and herein lies the real mystery. Work on the driving of the new Haymarket South tunnel commenced in August 1892 and the tunnel was completed in February 1895. The station facilities enjoyed by the Caledonian could not logically have survived the station closure nor construction works, yet a map showing the terminal station with sidings in situ in 1860 has been reproduced by John Thomas, an eminent Scottish railway historian, but is otherwise not commented upon.[5] This terminus appears to have been a double platform bay station lying on what later became – under the NBR scheme of widening and quadrupling of track post 1890, and upon the reopening of the rebuilt Haymarket station – the new through South Platforms, No's 3 and 4, at Haymarket station after the Haymarket South Tunnel had been constructed. From further evidence unearthed, it appears that the station and connections were never used for anything more than an exchange facility for the transfer of EP&DR general freight traffic bound for, and coming from, the Caledonian rail system and the docks at Leith, and worked by the E&GR and later the NBR over NBR and former E&GR metals.

Here, post 1865, when the Caledonian absorbed the Scottish Central Railway, which had obtained running powers over the E&GR between Polmont and Edinburgh in 1848, was a dilemma for the Caledonian. Despite having its own terminus in Edinburgh (Lothian Road), these 'running power' SCR trains were still required to use, after 1865, the metals of the NBR, which had absorbed the E&GR in that same year and was a sworn enemy. Whilst an arrangement had been agreed for the cleaning and servicing of SCR coaching stock, no such arrangements had been made for servicing the locomotives and it was unlikely that space at the early E&GR Haymarket locomotive sheds was available in any case. However, since there was a physical connection between the two companies' lines, as the map in John Thomas's book (see above) shows, and since, no doubt, the Caledonian, wanted its locomotives and those of its new acquisition, the SCR, serviced at its own Dalry Road shed, it could be assumed that they just *might* have made use of the Haymarket Branch for this purpose, but no evidence of this ever transpiring has been found.

The escape route for the Caledonian occurred on 3rd July 1876, with the construction and opening of the Wester Dalry Branch (see below) from Haymarket West Junction (NBR) to connect with the Granton & Leith Branch at Dalry Middle Junction. This new line later crossed over the Edinburgh & South Suburban Railway line and also both the Caledonian's Haymarket Branch and Granton Branch, on the north side of Granton Junction, and put paid to the Caledonian's dependency, if ever there was one, for the Haymarket station terminus. Thus the Caledonian Haymarket Branch, after

5 *The North British Railway*, Vol. 1.

Craiglockhart Cutting on the Edinburgh South Suburban Railway (NBR) looking north-west, with a Princes Street-bound express passing over to rear in 1955. The shadow of the Haymarket line bridge is just visible below the locomotive. To the left centre is Slateford with its breweries and foundries and on the skyline is an Edinburgh landmark, Corstorphine Hill. The point immediately below where the photograph was taken is where, in the next decade, a double connecting line from the Sub will be constructed on a steep, left-hand, curving gradient, passing to the south side of Slateford Yard to connect with the former CR main line at Slateford station. *Stuart Sellar*

the physical connection was broken in 1879, was to lie, largely unused, except for freight trips, for the best part of 100 years serving the aforementioned small traders. Much to the chagrin of the Caledonian Railway, the inherited running powers from the SCR did not confer upon them any rights to use NBR metals to access what would become, in the fullness of time, Waverley station, and thus that perceived door to Leith and River Forth was firmly closed in their face.

At Slateford, the double line branch diverged to left to cross over, at a later date, the Edinburgh South Suburban Railway.

Following construction of the Dalry Junction to Granton West Breakwater Branch (below), a double line junction connection was installed between the Haymarket Branch and the Granton Branch, to connect into the latter at Coltbridge Junction immediately after crossing the main E&GR lines to Glasgow (and later to Fife and the north) by the 'Caley Brig' just east of the new 1894 Haymarket MPD. The point of divergence on the Haymarket Branch was controlled by a small signal box named Granton Junction. Granton Junction signal box closed on 12th June 1937, when the double junction to the Coltbridge line in the Haymarket Branch was removed and replaced by a single line connection to the rump of the Haymarket Branch, from what became the Up Main of the Coltbridge line, controlled by a ground frame.

Between Slateford and Granton Junction, at the Slateford end, a trailing junction in the branch served the Edinburgh Iron Foundry (Edinburgh iron masters, McKenzie & Moncur). At a later point a private siding was provided to Lorimer & Clark's Caledonian Brewery (later owned by Scottish & Newcastle Brewers) in Slateford Road, and at the point where the branch crossed Murieston Crescent there was a loading platform adjacent to the Up Main Line serving a small steel fabrication yard belonging to Robertson & Ferguson, General Engineers and Welders, with an overhead gantry crane extending out to the loading facility and over the running lines. Also, close by Granton Junction, there was a private siding facility (two sidings) serving the Edinburgh City Roads Department stone yard at Tynecastle (Russell Road and McLeod Street), ground frame controlled by staff key, with the signalman at Granton Junction being custodian of the staffs.

1861, Dalry Road to Granton Western Breakwater

Apart from the Slateford to Haymarket Branch discussed above, this was to be the first major rail development carried out by the Caledonian Railway. They had already looked at the freight traffic monopoly, consisting mainly of coal, which the NBR held in the Edinburgh area, and in the Leith and Granton areas in particular; also the mineral traffic in the west of the county of Linlithgowshire, where the rich Lanarkshire coal deposits had spilled over into the west side of that county. The 5th Duke of Buccleuch had built a new harbour at Granton Western Breakwater in 1838, with an internal railway system (the Granton Harbour Lines) which connected into the earlier Middle Pier, where a new passenger station was to be provided serving the Forth ferry traffic. The Edinburgh, Leith & Newhaven Railway (EL&NR) had extended their line from Trinity to connect with the private Granton Harbour lines at that location in 1846, in addition to penetrating the docks at Leith. The EL&NR was renamed to become the Edinburgh, Leith & Granton Railway (EL&GR) in 1844.

Coal was also being shipped from Granton, but the Duke of Buccleuch was keen to break the NBR monopoly at Granton.

The Granton Junction ground frame in January 1964. The Wester Dalry Branch runs left to right centre, passing over both the Granton Junction to Granton West Breakwater Branch and the former Slateford/Haymarket Branch on the plate girder and masonry bridge spans to rear. Visible through the masonry bridge is a second plate girder span carrying the Granton West Breakwater Branch from Dalry Junction; the two Granton lines will join at Coltbridge Junction. The bridge over Russel Road can be seen to the left of the telegraph post. *Stuart Sellar*

He provided the ground for a new railway through his policies of Caroline Park, and encouraged the Caledonian Railway to build this new line of railway to Granton and to connect with the private Granton Harbour lines thus providing a physical rail connection between the Caledonian and the NBR systems.

On 28th August 1861 the Caledonian opened its single line branch from Dalry Junction to the Western Breakwater at Granton, over which it worked coal traffic for shipment. This line was constructed with a steep rising gradient of 1 in 52 over the 1½ miles from Breakwater Junction up to Pilton West Junction, a gradient which was to tax motive power throughout the days of steam and severely limit train loads between the privately-owned Granton Harbour lines and Crew Junction. Indeed, loaded wagons had to be propelled with a limit of five loads at any one time. This was a sensible safety requirement with locomotive always at the lower end in case of a breakaway. The line between the Western Breakwater was to be worked as a Yard between Pilton West Junction and Granton, with speeds of movements over same limited to 5 mph. This line was to be doubled in 1862 and extended eastwards from Crew Junction to access Leith docks (west) from Leith North Goods, opened for traffic on 1st September that same year. The line to Granton left this new branch at Crew Junction[6] and in 1864 a triangular junction opened between Pilton East Junction, Pilton West Junction and Crew Junction, giving the Caledonian direct access between Leith and Granton.

Meanwhile, the earlier Edinburgh & Dalkeith Railway (E&DR) had already constructed a branch line to Leith docks but was itself to be quickly taken over by the new NBR Company, as was the EL&GR. Coal from East Lothian was by now being worked into Leith by the E&DR for shipment and after 1845 the NBR was to be in control.

As stated in Chapter 2, this branch line skirted Craigleith Quarry lying between Craigleith passenger station and Crew Junction, and stone traffic was conveyed from the private sidings laid in for that purpose adjacent to the quarry.

Between Barnton Junction, where a new branch line to Davidson's Mains and Barnton was to diverge westwards from March 1894 (see below), and Crew Junction, a small yard was created at Crew Junction circa 1870, with seven dead-ended sidings lying to the west of the running lines and three dead-ended sidings plus an engine siding and turntable lying to the east. By 1902, the number of Down sidings had been increased to eight, and by 1905 these had been extended to form nine dead-ended sidings on the Down side. Crew Yard was to become a busy yard for freight and mineral traffic tripped up from Leith Docks and made up into trainloads for onward working, mainly to the west. The east side layout remained unchanged during this time.

This Granton & Leith line was to continue as a freight only line until August 1879, when a new suburban passenger train service between Lothian Road (Princes Street) and Leith North was introduced. The branch lines to both Leith and Granton were doubled at this time. Indeed, the chosen route of this branch from

6 The area of the town lying to the south of Granton was properly known as Crewe, but it is thought that the Caledonian Railway, fully aware of the already important L&NWR railway centre at Crewe (Cheshire), decided to rename the Scottish Crewe without the last letter 'e' in order to avoid any confusion and, thereafter, from a railway perspective, it became (quite unnecessarily) Crew! Nevertheless, OS maps and the RCH map all refer to the rail facility here as Crewe Junction.

Dalry Junction was to prove to be a winner when it came to passenger traffic. The line passed through what were then expanding, and later to be affluent, suburbs of the city; these included Murrayfield and Roseburn, where large stone, detached houses were to proliferate around the railway. Craigleith and Ravelston Dykes also saw quality housing spring up in what was ever a rather upmarket area. Thereafter, the line served the more working-class areas of Pilton and Granton. Intermediate stations were provided at Dalry Road (¾ mile), Murrayfield (1¼ miles), Craigleith (2¼ miles), East Pilton (3¼ miles), Granton Road (4 miles), Newhaven (5 miles) and Leith North (5½ miles). The line gave the company access to the western-most docks and also the later shipbuilding dock of Henry Robb & Co. (1918 to 1983) at Leith and the easternmost docks (East and West Wet Docks, Victoria Dock and Albert Dock). The increasing growth of passenger train service and carryings over the branch was testament to the sound business decision taken by the Caledonian Railway to double this line of route and commence passenger train working when it did; the passenger train service was also to speed up the growth of housing along its line of route.

This branch was also to serve the port and town of Leith at the later Leith North passenger station, lying to the south-east of the older goods yard and goods station – the former consisted of a small island platform with two faces contained within a timber-clad building and situated immediately adjacent to Lindsay Road in Leith. Nevertheless, access to the newer eastern dock area (Imperial Dock, Albert Dock and Edinburgh Dock) by the Caledonian Railway was always to be restricted to the use of a NBR owned single dock line which crossed the original Port of Leith via a swing bridge – despite the fact that the Caledonian Railway had penetrated, but never really otherwise served, the easternmost docks by means of their later Newhaven & Leith Link Line of 1903 (see below).

At Pilton East, on the north side of the branch, the then-new factory of the Edinburgh based industrial electrical engineering firm of Bruce Peebles & Co. Ltd was built and opened in 1903, and was rail connected to the Leith line. This factory employed up to 3,000 persons at its peak in the 1950s and had its own internal, electrified railway system, worked by shunting locomotives of the company's own design. This in fact was the first and only electrified railway in Edinburgh by some ninety years. The company was, between 1947 and 1954, the main sub-contractor for the electrification of the Woodhead (Manchester to Sheffield) railway line. Famed latterly for its production of giant electrical transformers, this traffic was carried mainly by road transport as exceptional loads, but in the earlier days much of the manufactured product passed to rail and was carried over this branch.

At Dalry Middle Junction, connections in the Up branch line served the rail connected premises of Colin McAndrew & Partners, construction engineers, and Alexander Mather & Son Ltd, engineers and mill manufacturers. These premises lay immediately to the north of Dalry Road station, between that location and Dalry

The Leith North Branch has closed and Crew Junction signal box is now unused and derelict, but the box structure is complete and still in situ, and still sporting its nameboard, looking north towards Pilton West Junction. *D. Simpson/David Spaven*

East Pilton station offices at street level. *David Dickson collection*

Street level station offices at Newhaven. *David Dickson collection*

ABOVE: Granton Square and the Granton Harbour lines. Here ex-NBR Class 'C16' No. 67492 pauses to allow enthusiasts to detrain from their special train in September 1958. *Stuart Sellar*

BELOW: The same Enthusiasts' Special, now topped and tailed, with Class 'C16' No. 67492 bringing up the rear, has successfully mounted the 1 in 52 gradient up to Pilton West Junction from Granton Breakwater in September. Later the 'C16' slipped badly all the way up to Dalry Junction. *Stuart Sellar*

Road proper. It is recorded that McAndrew's owned their own 'pug' locomotive.

The original Dalry Junction signal box was replaced by a completely new signal box in 1893 on a site adjoining the Fountain Brewery. This box, of Caledonian Railway 'S4' design, was constructed in timber with a slate clad hipped roof and with the operating floor oversailing the front; it was located 792 yards west of Edinburgh Princes Street signal box. This box was closed in September 1966, a full month after the closure of Morrison Street Mineral Depot (see below).

From Granton Junction on the Haymarket Branch, the Granton Branch passed over Russell Road by means of a plate girder bridge. To the south of this bridge, a trailing siding, splitting into two sidings, laid in about 1898, served the Edinburgh Corporation Stone Depot at Russell Road/McLeod Street; these sidings were removed during World War Two. The line then passed under the

Ex-L&NER Class 'B1', No. 61007 *Klipspringer*, late of Haymarket shed 64B, enters East Pilton station on a Princes Street to Leith North passenger service in June 1961. *J.L. Stevenson/Hamish Stevenson*

Fairburn 2-6-4T No. 42271 enters Newhaven station with a branch passenger train. *Stuart Sellar*

viaduct carrying the Wester Dalry Branch from 1876 until closure of same in 1964. On the approach side of Coltbridge signal box, the branch crossed the E&GR north and west main lines by another plate girder bridge – known to NBR footplatemen at near-by Haymarket MPD as the 'Caley Brig' – this method of bridge construction being adopted by the Caledonian, despite the fact that the Parliamentary Bill had specified a masonry viaduct. Coltbridge Junction signal box was constructed on an embankment and again was of standard Caledonian 'S4' design, finished in timber.

In 1903 a private passenger station was opened within Granton Gas Works and connected to this branch, to which, the Caledonian Railway ran special workman's trains (see entry below).

On 30th April 1962, the Princes Street to Leith North passenger train service was withdrawn, along with closure of all the passenger stations on the line of route; in April 1967 all freight traffic over this line was also withdrawn and the line closed.

1865/1874, The Balerno Branch

The main line from Carstairs, in running east to Edinburgh on the northern side of the Pentland Hills, was to parallel a stream (a burn in Scotland) which was to become Edinburgh's own river. This was the Water of Leith which was formed by the confluence of the headwaters of three streams at Leithhead – the West Burn, the Mid Burn and the East Burn – all of which fell sharply off the slopes of Colzium Hill in the Pentlands, where some 144 springs were to be tapped over the years to supply the city of Edinburgh with water. This small river flowed north-eastwards along the deep gorge scoured out by earlier glacial melt waters. Passing though the villages of Ballernoch (Balerno), Currie, Juniper Green, Colinton and on through the deep gorge of Colinton Dell to Slateford. From there it was to meander through the New Town via Roseburn and flow through Canonmills, Stockbridge and Bonnington before entering the River Forth at Leith. The tidal mouth of the Water of Leith afforded a safe anchorage for ships before any artificial harbours were created and was to become the original port of Leith.

The Water of Leith was to take its place in Scottish law when, in 1618, it was to play a part at a ceremony held in Edinburgh to define standard weights and measures. A jug, traditionally and widely known as the 'Linlithgow Measure', or Stirling Standard Pint Jug, was filled with water taken from the river and the volume of the contents measured and weighed and declared to be *'three punds and seven unces of French Troy Weight of clear running water of the Water of Leith'.* This was the Standard Scots Pint measure thereafter.

This narrow valley of the Water of Leith, and the fall in height of the river passing though, offered a source of power, in the form of water power, for industry. Indeed, throughout its length, traces of some eighty separate mills have been identified. The water power made it ideal for milling, and it is recorded that there were seven paper mills plus some twenty or more snuff mills, flax mills, flour mills and spice mills with glue, beer, spirits, rope, leather and wood being processed along its banks. Between Colinton and Balerno, paper making was a particularly valuable industry and it was to this commodity that the interest of the Caledonian Railway was first drawn. The possibility of a branch line to Balerno following the valley of the Water of Leith first appeared in the Minutes of the Caledonian Railway Company on 16th September 1864, with much local support. A favourable financial report of likely traffic receipts led to Board backing, and at that same time, Bills for this branch plus two other proposed railways (linking the Caledonian Railway main line with the Edinburgh & Glasgow Railway and a new line from Edinburgh to Penicuik, neither of which were ever built), were submitted to Parliament Caledonian Railway.

BR Standard '2MT' 2-6-0 No. 78046 heads an Enthusiasts' Special train of two ex-CR coaches at Balerno Junction ground frame in April 1965. The Water of Leith is in the foreground. *Stuart Sellar*

In 1865, The Caledonian Railway was empowered by The Caledonian Railway (Balerno Branch) Act to construct:

'A Railway (to be called the "Balerno Branch") commencing by a junction with the Main Line of the Caledonian Railway from Carlisle to Edinburgh near the booking office of the Slateford Station of that railway, and terminating near Balerno Bridge in the Parish of Currie, by which the road leading from Currie by Newmills, to Balerno is carried over the Water of Leith.'

This project was to be marked by start-stop progress and was mired in controversy throughout its long and difficult nascence. Planned to be a double line of railway throughout, it was a bold but very expensive project; being beset by serious financial crises from that same year onwards, the Caledonian Railway was very quickly back-pedal on starting construction of the branch and the project was deferred until 1866. The Board then planned to submit a request for Abandonment of the 1865 Act, but not until a long and bruising legal battle with the mill owners and landowners had occurred, and

Small, ex-CR Class '104' 0-4-4T No. 15155 (CR No. 167), enters Balerno station with a branch passenger train.
Graham Easton/Hamish Stevenson

No. 15205, ex-CR No. 459 Class '439' 0-4-4T, heads a passenger train on the Barnton Branch. The 4-wheeled coaches constructed for the Balerno Branch form part of the train. *J.L. Stevenson/Hamish Stevenson*

only after an undertaking by the railway company to review the original proposal and resubmit same, this time but for a single line of railway throughout, was the Abandonment Act passed.

In October 1869 a proposal was tabled that the future Balerno Branch should not in fact terminate at Balerno but should be projected beyond Balerno to connect with the main line at Ravelrig Junction, some 1¼ miles further on.

On 20th June 1870, Parliamentary Approval was given for a second Balerno Branch Act, The Caledonian Railway (Balerno Branch) Act 1870, as follows:

(1) *A Branch Railway (in this Act called the Balerno Branch) five miles and one hundred and twenty-seven yards or thereabouts in length, commencing by a junction with the Caledonian Railway leading from Carlisle to Edinburgh, near the south-western end of the Slateford Viaduct by which the line is carried over the Water of Leith near the village of Slateford, and terminating near the bridge over that river called Balerno Bridge.*

(2) *A connecting Branch Railway (in this Act called the Balerno Connecting Branch) one mile, two furlongs and sixty-six yards or thereabouts in length, commencing by a junction with the said Balerno Branch, about six chains westwards from Newmills Corn mill, and terminating by a junction with the said Caledonian Railway about seven and a half chains eastwards from the 83½ mile post from Carlisle on that line.*

This, the final configuration of the Balerno Branch, was accessed from Balerno Junction, where a connection from the West Coast Main Line led off to the south-west and was controlled by Balerno Junction signal box, lying some 484 yards west of Slateford station; this branch line, some 5 miles, 1,295 yards in length and largely composed of severe curves and steep gradients, involving twenty-eight bridges of varying sizes, a tunnel at Colinton and numerous steep cuttings, retaining walls and embankments, was not to be opened for traffic until the 31st July 1874. This difficult branch line was to be the sole preserve of the Dalry Road engines and men thereafter. The Water of Leith was to be crossed elsewhere by the Caledonian Railway at Slateford, Roseburn (Murrayfield) and Bonnington. From the outset, operation of the line demanded special locomotives and rolling stock.

Construction of the branch commenced in April 1871. A platform was to be provided at Ravelrig Junction on the main line to serve the local farming community, but usage of same was to be ever sparse and the train service serving it was dramatically pruned. This station, named Ravelrig, also carried the addition sign 'For Dalmahoy Golf Course' in an effort to attract further patronage.

The Balerno Branch was finally, after much delay, opened for traffic on Saturday 1st August 1874, ten long years after it had first been considered. The method of train control adopted for the safe working of the single line was Absolute Block Telegraph, whereby the complete line of route was split into three 'block sections' with four signal boxes being involved. The sections were:

- Balerno Junction to Currie, 3 miles, 50 chains
- Currie to Balerno, 1 mile, 14 chains
- Balerno to Ravelrig Junction, 1 mile, 18 chains.

The signalmen exchanged telegraph messages with their opposite numbers, with the aim of the system being to prevent the possibility of two trains being in the same single line block section at the same time. In fact the system was nothing more than an alternative method of One Engine in Steam working. The Absolute Block system was in use until Electric Token Block Working was introduced in 1888. After Token working was implemented, the same three block sections were retained although, in total, there were originally six signal boxes on the branch, although neither Colinton or Juniper Green were block posts and their functions were at a later date replaced by ground-frame controlled points released by the token.

In 1900 a new company, A.& R. Scott Ltd, had transferred their oat milling process from Glasgow to new grain mills (the West Mills) established at Colinton, and this was to become the home of the world-famous Scott's Porridge Oats. These mills were rail connected to the branch and were to boost Colinton's share of freight revenue quite significantly. The West Mills closed in 1947

Ex-MR Hughes '5MT' 2-6-0 No. 42807 heads a train of empty coal wagons past Balerno Junction. *John Robertson/Hamish Stevenson*

A Rail Enthusiasts' Special in the charge of Standard '2MT' No. 78046 calls at what remains of Colinton station and goods yard on 19th April 1965. This was part of 'The Scottish Rambler No. 4 Railtour' organised jointly by the Stephenson Locomotive Society and the Branch Line Society *Stuart Sellar*

when the milling operation was moved to Cupar in Fife. A new station on the branch was opened in 1908, lying between Colinton and Slateford, and named Hailes Halt. This was closed in 1943 on the complete withdrawal of all passenger train services from the branch.

Stone quarrying was another activity undertaken on the hillside above the branch (on the volcanic plugs known as Dalmahoy Hill and Kaimes Hill) and which was to swell the mineral tonnages carried by rail over the branch until closure. Originally there were three separate quarries, all connected by narrow gauge tramway to two loading banks which lay on a long siding parallel to the branch near Ravelrig Junction. These quarries were Ravelrig Quarry, Shades Quarry and Kaimes Quarry and the stone produced was invoiced through Balerno station; production peaked at 60,000 tons per annum by 1910. A public siding was also provided as one of the several goods sidings provided at Ravelrig Junction.

The original signal box at Ravelrig Junction lay to the north side of the main lines and by 1912 concerns were being voiced about the risk posed to signalmen when having to cross the main lines to exchange tokens with footplate crews working over the Balerno Branch. In 1912, the decision was taken to build a new, replacement signal box in the vee between the main line and the branch. The new brick-built box, with slated hipped roof, was opened on 3rd September 1912, when the old box was closed, and remained in situ until finally closed in April 1967.

Like the situation pertaining at Ravelrig Junction, a similar problem of risk existed with the siting of the original Balerno Junction signal box. This first box (opened 1st August 1874), controlling entry to and exit from the branch, had also been constructed on the north side of the main line. The original signal box was closed on 29th October 1914, and on the same day the new Balerno Junction signal box was brought into use, this box being, very sensibly, located between the main lines, now in front, and the branch line itself passing to the rear of the box.

The Balerno Branch was to contribute considerably to the overall freight tonnage carried by rail in and around Edinburgh, and in the early 1900s, goods traffic tonnages carried over the branch were (rounded up/down) as follows:

Goods forwarded:	20,750 tons
Inwards goods:	38,000 tons
Minerals forwarded:	61,914 tons (mainly stone traffic)
Inwards minerals:	71,100 tons (mainly coal).

Freight traffic on the branch was withdrawn completely in 1967, upon closure of the Kinleith Paper Mill.

The above-mentioned siding installed to serve Kaimes and other quarries was closed in 1959, but the connection on the main line remained in situ, unused, for the next thirty years. In 1989 Edinburgh Corporation was in severe difficulties with the disposal of household rubbish – the Powderhall Incinerator, located in the north side of the city, having been declared a health hazard, and closed. Searching around for landfill sites, Kaimes Quarry came back under the spotlight and, in conjunction with BR, a facility for unloading rubbish containers was constructed on the site of the former siding and, despite much local opposition, containerised rubbish commenced passing by rail for dumping in the abandoned quarries. Edinburgh Corporation was later taken to Court, where it was discovered that they had failed to obtain planning consent and the siding was finally closed in 1999.

1869, The Tarbrax Branch

Since all the workable main seams of oil bearing shale in the West and Mid Lothian shale field outcropped on the moorland lying to the south of Cobbinshaw Loch, it was inevitable that the mining and refining of shale oil should quickly follow once Young's Patent had expired in 1864; thus a crude oil works was established by the trustees of one E.W. Fernie of Mid Calder, who had leased the mineral rights at Tarbrax, on site at that location. Tarbrax Oil Works, which also saw a small village comprising oil workers rows (terraced houses) of the same name created alongside, was to pass through numerous ownerships. It was latterly, until closure, to be owned by the Pumpherston Oil Company, and survived to become one of the oil works contained within the 'Big Seven' oil companies. Coal from the Hurlet seam was also to be mined at Woolfords and Viewfield Colliery, Tarbrax, with much of the output being used in heating the retorting process of the oil-bearing shale, both at Tarbrax Works and at Pumpherston Oil Refinery.

The Caledonian Railway sought Parliamentary Approval to construct not one, but two branch lines, connected to their main line at Cobbinshaw (Tarbrax Junction) and in due course, under the provisions of the Caledonian Railway (Branches and Stations) Act, dated 1867, approval was given for two branch lines:

'A railway to be called the Tarbrax Branch, one mile, seven furlongs and fifty-five yards or thereabouts, commencing by a junction with the Main Line of the Caledonian Railway from Carlisle to Edinburgh, at a point where that line crosses the Boundary between the Counties of Lanark and Midlothian, and terminating near the Southern end of the retorts of the Tarbrax Oil Works in the said Parish of Carnwath.'

And:

'A railway to be called the South Cobbinshaw Branch, seven furlongs or thereabouts in length, commencing with a junction with said Tarbrax Branch about Two and a Half Furlongs northwards from Greenfield House in the Parish of Carnwath and terminating about five furlongs eastwards from the farm steading of South Cobbinshaw in the Parish of West Calder.'

The Tarbrax Branch opened for goods traffic in 1869.

At South Cobbinshaw, the initial activity was brick making, but a small oil works (South Cobbinshaw) was later to be established on the same site as the brickworks. Both shale mines and oil works were changing ownership on a regular basis at this time and the new South Cobbinshaw Oil Company decided not to carry on with crude oil production at South Cobbinshaw. The Directors of the Caledonian Railway also had a change of heart and the proposed South Cobbinshaw Branch was abandoned under the Caledonian Railway Abandonment Act of 1869; the intended South Cobbinshaw Branch was later provided by the Caledonian, but as nothing more than a long siding, at a cost of £2,000. The brickworks continued to generate traffic to rail until it too was abandoned in 1889. The South Cobbinshaw siding was finally to be recovered by the LM&SR in 1936.

There is an unconfirmed report of a special excursion passenger train being run over this branch in Caledonian days for the residents of Tarbrax village to have a day's outing to the coast, but no further information regarding this has been found. Tarbrax Oil Works was to be closed in 1925, Tarbrax Junction signal box closing at the same time. The rail infrastructure remained in situ until 1937.

In 1899, the noted Lanarkshire steel masters, Baird Brothers, commenced a mining operation for fireclay, coal and limestone at North Cobbinshaw (not to be confused with Cobbinshaw North, see below) and a private siding some 372 yards in length was laid in from the Tarbrax Branch. This operation ceased in 1910 on discovery of the same seam of limestone at Harburn and Newpark.

In about 1867 the small company of Thornton & Mungle opened a crude oil works at Cobbinshaw North lying on the moorland to the *north* side of the main line. A long siding leading from the Down Main line, close by Cobbinshaw signal box, was apparently laid in to serve both the oil works and a shale mine at Kipsyke – the latter, strangely, connected to the oil works by this standard gauge long siding – but operation ceased in 1881. Thereafter a small rump of this long siding was left in situ as a public goods siding, known as Mungles Siding, lying to the east of Cobbinshaw station on the Down side.

Whilst the Tarbrax/Cobbinshaw operation was more properly the domain of Carstairs based engines and crews, Edinburgh Dalry Road shed was also to be involved with the train working here.

As previously mentioned, another private industrial operation which was to be rail connected to the WCML, east of Cobbinshaw, was the rich and productive limestone mining operation at Harburn Lime Works. Here the Caledonian Railway main line traversed a rich, 40 feet thick, seam of quality limestone (the Burdiehouse seam), much in demand as a fluxing agent in the blast furnaces of Clydesdale, with the same seam being mined at Westfield Pit, close by Newpark station, and at Raw Camps Pit on the Camps Branch (see below). At Harburn in 1912, upon closure of the Bairds mining operation at Cobbinshaw North, a new private siding was constructed into this mining operation, with a further connection serving the lime kilns, and both controlled from a small signal box, Harburn Lime Works. Private sidings were also provided to serve the other two locations.

Midcalder Junction to Cleland

In proper chronological order, in 1869, under the authority of the Cleland and Mid Calder Railway and Branches Act 1865, the Caledonian Railway constructed a new line of railway from Midcalder Junction to Cleland, but this line of route was to prove so important to Caledonian fortunes that it is discussed separately at Chapter 4.

The Camps Branch

At Camps Junction, lying immediately to the east side of Midcalder station, a new branch was authorised under the provisions of that same Cleland and Mid Calder Railway and Branches Act 1865, when the Company moved:

> *'To construct a Branch line called Railway No. 7 (in the Act), commencing by a junction with the Company's said main line at or near the level crossing of that line, in the Parish of Kirknewton from the road leading from Kirknewton by Hillhouse towards Hatton House, and terminating about eighteen chains northwards of the Farm Steading of Burnhouse in the same Parish.'*

Approval was given to build this new branch line (Railway No. 7) to connect the main line with Raw Camps Pit and Camps Limestone Quarry, both lying east of East Calder village and working the same Burdiehouse seam of limestone as found at Harburn. The mining and quarrying operations here were both owned and worked by the Coltness Iron Company. The branch opened on the 5th November 1896. The Caledonian Company were later to establish a goods station (Camps Goods) on this site.

The NBR had in 1867, however, constructed a branch line from Uphall Junction, running southwards to serve various oil production and mining activities en route, including Pumpherston Oil Works and Roman Camps Oil Works, and terminating at East Calder Goods station, lying immediately north of the Camps complex. On the opening of the Caledonian Railway Camps branch the NBR branch was extended to pass under both the Edinburgh to Ayr trunk road and the Caledonian branch line, to serve Camps Quarry. An exchange facility was constructed to connect the lines of both companies. As will be seen when considering the freight activity involving Dalry Road engines and men at Chapter 10, from the time this Caledonian Railway, Camps branch first interfaced with the NBR Uphall Junction to Camps Quarry via the exchange line, these two branches were to form the principal and most utilised interchange facility between the two railway companies for the workings of rail-borne shale oil traffic in the area, particularly after Pumpherston was designated as Scottish Oils Ltd's central refinery for all the crude oil being produced in the Lothian shale fields. There was, however, no transfer of general freight traffic between the two companies over this route.

The limestone working had gone by 1913 and thereafter the quarry was to be used as a rubbish infill site (The Camps Shoot) by both Midlothian County Council and Edinburgh City Corporation Lighting and Cleansing Department, worked by their own internal, departmental, privately-owned engines. The waste was transported to site by rail.

The Caledonian Camps Branch, from the main line connection at Camps Junction to Camps Goods (Cal) was removed in its entirety in early 1962.

1876, The Wester Dalry Branch

As described above, under an Agreement with the E&GR in October 1845 the Scottish Central Railway Company had been assigned running powers from Larbert Junction to Edinburgh (Haymarket) via the E&G main line; the SCR trains were later to be accommodated within Edinburgh Waverley Bridge joint NBR/E&GR station on closure of Haymarket station. Running powers passed to the Caledonian Railway in 1865, when the Caledonian and Scottish Central amalgamated.

The Caledonian, with its own Edinburgh terminus at Lothian Road, was less than happy with this inherited obligation, especially one dependent upon a competing railway company (the NBR). The search for a solution led to the decision to construct a new, short connecting line of railway, running from the Princes Street–Leith/Granton line, diverging from that line at Dalry Middle Junction, then running westwards to Haymarket West Junction (NBR) where it connected into the E&G main line. This line, all of 1,408 yards in length and with an average rising gradient of 1 in 189 from Haymarket West to Dalry Middle Junction, became officially known, and referred to thereafter, as the 'Wester Dalry Branch', and for which the Caledonian Railway agreed to guarantee the NBR an annual payment of £3,000 in perpetuity. The branch was opened

Ex-CR 4-4-0 locomotive No. 14437 (CR 898) of the '900' Class ('Dunalastair III') heads a short train from Stirling and has taken the Wester Dalry Branch at Haymarket Junction to access Edinburgh Princes Street station, after running on NBR metals from Larbert. The NBR north and south main lines can be seen to the right. *CRA Archives*

for traffic on 3rd July 1876, but traffic was slow to use it. The share of traffic revenue was to be based on a mileage basis, by joint agreement; however, the Caledonian was not permitted to work any freight traffic over this branch. It appears to have been the intention of the Caledonian Railway to name the junction to the Wester Dalry Branch at the Haymarket West end as 'Damhead Junction', and this name appeared in various instructions for some time thereafter. This short connecting line passed over the Caledonian's Granton Branch and Haymarket Branch just to the north side of Granton Junction, and also the NBR's Edinburgh & South Side Suburban Railway line at a point opposite Haymarket MPD. There were conditions imposed on both companies by Parliament relating to the approval for the construction of this particular branch, with the Caledonian Railway being obliged to withdraw a total of seven railways planned under their quite ludicrous Carstairs & Larbert Junction Railway proposal (see Chapter 16). The NBR had similarly to withdraw two railways included in their equally silly Additional Working Branch Lines Bill, namely the proposed railway from Easter Inch (Bathgate) running north to terminate a mere handful of yards from the Caledonian Railway station at the Cleugh Brae in West Calder, and a proposed line from Foulshiels, south of Whitburn, on the former WM&CR line, running east to connect with the E&BR line at Livingston station, these two lines actually crossing each other at Redhouse, west of Blackburn.

By this means, all Caledonian trains to Stirling, Perth and the north could be run to and from their own Princes Street terminus, facilitated by the running powers agreement of 1845, thus avoiding Haymarket and Waverley Bridge stations; at least this was the intention. Notwithstanding the opening of this new direct route into Princes Street, the Caledonian did not immediately exercise its running powers and passengers from Caledonian Railway stations north of Larbert continued to be conveyed into Edinburgh Waverley Bridge station, probably in Caledonian coaches. It was not until 1st October 1890 that the Caledonian began to run its own trains between Larbert and Princes Street via the Wester Dalry Branch, and from that date some of these Caledonian Railway trains actually conveyed an NBR portion between Larbert and Edinburgh Waverley, this being attached or detached at Haymarket West Junction and worked by an NBR engine to and from Waverley. This NBR portion had an NBR guard who worked through to Larbert and return. The NBR portions, always on the rear of the Caledonian Railway train, numbered six on weekdays plus one on a Sunday in each direction.

Wester Dalry Branch was later to prove its worth to BR during the period when the East Coast Main Line had to be closed to traffic owing to serious flood damage in August 1948, when it became the main interchange facility for both Up and Down East Coast express passenger train services which were diverted to run via the West Coast Main Line. Its use ensured that arrivals and departures at Edinburgh Waverley station were maintained as far as possible, albeit with a very small and unavoidable increase in journey time of about 20 minutes added to the booked journey times. Indeed, during the period between 13th and 16th August 1946, a total of forty-five Up trains (to the South) and seventy-eight Down trains were transferred between the West Coast Main Line and Edinburgh Waverley by means of this facility. The operation made heavy demands on both engines and crews at Dalry Road shed. The means of achieving this diversionary working were as follows.

The 1948 diversion required that trains and their locomotives had to be formed up with the train consist reversed. On departure from

BR Standard Class '5MT' No. 73063 of Polmadie shed heads the 16.22 Edinburgh Princes Street to Perth express in February 1963 and has just passed Dalry Middle Junction signal box (in rear) and is passing over Dalry Junction on the Slateford to Haymarket branch. The signal post on the left of the photograph is on the Granton and Leith branch. *Stuart Sellar*

Edinburgh Waverley, but now travelling westwards, the diverted East Coast service drew up clear of the junction at Haymarket West on the Down North line, to be reversed at Haymarket West Junction. Here a pilot engine from Dalry Road, having come Down the Wester Dalry Branch, would couple on and draw the complete train, with train engine, back Up the Wester Dalry Branch, stopping when the train engine was standing clear of the facing main line junction points at Dalry Junction. With the pilot detached at rear, and a brake test carried out, the train, with train engine still at the head, would then depart for Carstairs and the south, with Dalry Road conductors. The same procedure was followed for Down trains, which resulted in the train engine always being at the head of the train in the desired direction of travel. Dalry Road shed had to step up to the mark, not only for the provision of pilot locomotives, but also for the provision of conductor drivers to conduct foreign crews over the WCML to Carlisle.

This branch became redundant with the impending closure of Edinburgh Princes Street station in 1965, and was itself closed somewhat earlier, on 9th March 1964. After this the ex-SCR trains to and from Stirling, Perth and beyond, and running via Polmont and Larbert, were accommodated in Edinburgh Waverley station. In 1983 the solum of this Wester Dalry Branch, held in the ownership of BR, was incorporated into the new Edinburgh Western Approach Road project and was to become an arterial roadway which followed the former Caledonian Railway line right into Lothian Road, using the same urban railway overbridges (see below).

OTHER CALEDONIAN RAILWAY DEVELOPMENTS IN EDINBURGH

SLATEFORD TO DALRY JUNCTION

In this short stretch of railway there were also to be several new private sidings laid in by the Caledonian Railway. These are included within the following developments.

In the late 1800s, the construction of new housing along the railway corridor in the Dalry/Gorgie areas was gathering momentum, as demand increased in pace with the industrialisation within the city limits. The Caledonian Railway, in response to the increasing demand, decided to construct and open a new passenger station in the Ashley Terrace/Harrison Park vicinity, in the western approaches to the city; this new station, known as Merchiston, was brought into use in 1882. Merchiston station was intended to replace the earlier 1875 ticket platform which had been provided between the Morrison Street and Grove Street overbridges on the approach to Lothian Road passenger terminal, the latter being an 'open' station (no ticket barriers), by becoming the ticket platform for all city-bound passenger services. The original ticket platform was closed in 1882. Dalry Road Motive Power Depot lay some 1,200 yards eastwards of Merchiston station on the left-hand side, immediately after the line passed under the Dundee Street overbridge.

In 1891 the Lothian Dairy Company requested that the Caledonian Railway provide a small shed or covered building at Merchiston to accommodate the considerable quantity of milk arriving by passenger train daily, and this was duly done.

On the east side of Merchiston station, four new sidings were provided in or around 1904, two of which served Allsop & Sons, a Burton-on-Trent brewery concern which had established a brewery in Edinburgh. This facility closed in 1921, when use of the siding passed to James H. Steele, an agricultural engineering company which closed in 1966. The two sidings lying at a higher level served the Edinburgh & Dumfriesshire Dairy Company, although the bulk of its milk traffic continued to be handled at the private siding within Lothian Road Goods Depot which originally belonged to the Dalbeattie Dairy Company, a forerunner of the Edinburgh & Dumfriesshire.

Alongside Angle Park Terrace, another new siding was constructed from the Down Main line to serve a new stone depot. With the ever-expanding housing market, and despite that Edinburgh had considerable quantities of quality stone available for building purposes within its boundaries, there was an ever-increasing demand for new supplies, and rail connected stone depots were established to serve the burgeoning trade of stone masons. This was to be a valuable traffic for the Caledonian.

On the Up side, what had been referred to as the 'Old Cattle Siding' was taken over by Edinburgh Corporation to establish a refuse loading bank where street refuse was loaded to rail and conveyed (it is presumed) to the Camps Branch at Mid Calder (see above).

A further siding, which served no less than three different builders yards, crossed Bryon Road via a gated crossing, but was closed by 1913.

Finally, what must have been the most malodorous of all rail connected facilities to exist in the environs of Dalry Road shed was the short siding and loading bank, located on the south-west side of the Dundee Street overbridge, and known as the Manure Siding. Horse manure (collected from the city streets and various stables in and around the city), farm animal manure and night soil were all brought here, to be loaded and conveyed onwards by rail. In the days prior to the advent of artificially produced fertilisers, this particular traffic was always in high demand by the farming community and proved to be a high value commodity for all railway companies.

On the Up side of the main line, almost directly opposite Dalry Road shed, a siding was provided to serve two customers: the West End Engine Works, and W.J. Robertson's Waverley Oil & Cake Mills where animal foodstuffs were manufactured. A second siding was laid in to serve William McEwan's Fountain Brewery, a complex with five internal sidings (see Chapter 2).

These were all sidings served and shunted by the local Dalry Road shunting trip engines (see Chapter 11).

Morrison Street Mineral Yard

East of Dalry Junction, where the 1861 Edinburgh to Granton and Leith North lines diverged, there was a major mineral yard (Morrison Street) constructed by the Caledonian Railway in the 1880s, accommodating several major Edinburgh coal merchants. In 1896 this mineral yard consisted of seventeen dead-ended sidings, but by 1906 a new fan of five sidings was added lying adjacent to the north side of the main line, bringing the total siding accommodation up to twenty-two dead-ended sidings. Caledonian cranage facilities were also provided in this yard, the boundary walls of which stretched north-westwards to finish in clear view of the original NBR Haymarket station. Morrison Street Mineral Depot was finally closed in August 1966, but Haymarket South Tunnel on the E&G main line continues to run below the erstwhile site.

Ex-MR Hughes '5MT' 2-6-0 No. 42804 heads a stopping Class 9 freight train through Merchiston station in 1958.
J.L. Stevenson/Hamish Stevenson

The main line, continuing eastwards in cutting on a falling gradient, passed under a series of overbridges carrying the streets of the West Central Edinburgh suburbs – namely Grove Street, Gardiner's Crescent and Morrison Street – over the railway. Here the company had a small ticket platform constructed in 1875, for the purposes of ticket inspection/collection on city-bound trains, situated in the cutting between the Gardiner's Crescent overbridge and the Grove Street bridge. This was necessary in revenue protection terms since the then main terminal, the Caledonian Railway Lothian Road station was an open station. To the right, and lying parallel but at a higher level on the site of the original wooden Edinburgh station, was Lothian Road Goods station, another major freight and parcels terminal, conveniently located for the city centre, lying adjacent to the Caledonian Hotel and Princes Street station in Lothian Road. Indeed, the original wooden terminus building of the Caledonian Railway's first station formed part of this goods shed, but was almost destroyed by fire in 1890. On the west side of the station throat there was, from about 1900, rail connections from the station carriage sidings to the first Edinburgh Corporation electricity generating station in Dewar Place, a small coal-fired plant. The inwards coal traffic to these sidings was normally worked in during the night hours, when the station was at its quietest. The facility was superseded and closed in 1930.

1894, Edinburgh Princes Street to Barnton Branch

At Craigleith Junction on the Granton and Leith North line, immediately north of Craigleith passenger station, the Caledonian Railway constructed a new passenger line of railway running westwards from Craigleith Junction to access what was to later become the extremely affluent, outer suburban area of Barnton, but originally serving the villages of Cramond and Davidson's Mains, both lying in the west of the city. Authorised in August 1890, this was very much a speculative initiative since housing development was slow. Known as the Barnton Branch, it opened for traffic in March 1874 as a single line of railway but was doubled at a later date. There was initially one intermediate station, Barnton Gate, renamed as Davidson's Mains in April 1903; at the same time the terminal station, originally named Cramond Brig, was changed to Barnton. A later passenger halt was provided, known as House O' Hill Halt, between Davidson's Mains and Craigleith Junction in February 1937; this was upgraded to House O' Hill station in July the following year. The branch enjoyed a frequent train service to and from town, a service which also included extra trains on Saturdays and Sundays (see Chapter 8).

1902, Granton Gas Works Station

In the city of Edinburgh and in Leith, street lighting using coal gas was being extended by 1820 and the Edinburgh & Leith Corporation Gas Commissioners (ELCGC) operated three gas production facilities, two of which were at Baltic Street in Leith and New Street in the Old Town of Edinburgh. The third gas production plant was located at Pipe Street in Portobello, although at that time Portobello was not part of the city of Edinburgh. Use of gas for domestic cooking and lighting was also making severe demands on the available supplies of gas, and since none of the aforementioned works were capable of being expanded, in 1890 the decision was taken to construct a completely new gasworks on a green field site.

The ELCGC purchased a site of some 106¼ acres, being part of the Duke of Buccleuch's Caroline Park estate at Granton, for a price of £124,000, upon which they constructed a new, modern gasworks which was opened in 1902. This gasworks was to be rail connected to the Dalry Junction to Granton Western Breakwater Railway at Pilton West Junction. An internal, private railway station was constructed within the gasworks and was served by the Caledonian Railway. The workers travelled free between Princes Street and Gas Works station, under a private arrangement between the Caledonian Railway and the Gas Commissioners. When fully operational, the new gasworks required some 200,000 tons of coal per annum, most of which was from the Lothian coalfields and was conveyed by rail from Granton Harbour by both the Caledonian Railway and the NBR. Both the NBR and the Caledonian maintained suitable locomotives for working (by propelling) the coal up the 1 in 52 rising gradient from Breakwater Junction to the Gas Works, although the NBR line was by far the more convoluted and with a more severe gradient. It was described, tongue in cheek, by one St. Margaret's driver as *'a switch-back railway which would have been as asset to Blackpool's Pleasure Beach'.* Granton Gas Works, with its never-ending demand for coal, was never the easiest place to work. Ex-MR Fowler 0-6-0T No. 47162 of Dalry Road was to be employed at Granton on this work. This portion of line from Breakwater Junction to Pilton West junction was worked as a yard.

The passenger service was discontinued in 1946.

No. 57654 of Dalry Road, a Pickersgill Class '300', ex-CR No. 298, shunts Davidson's Mains goods and coal yard in March 1960. *Stuart Sellar*

ABOVE: The grand opening day of the new Granton Gas Works station with the first workforce passengers and other invitees. The locomotive is CR No. 821, a Westinghouse fitted '812' Class 0-6-0. *The late Wallace Lockhart*

ABOVE RIGHT: Granton Gas Works station closed and out of use in 1960. *The late Wallace Lockhart*

RIGHT: Another view of Granton Gas Works station in 1934 with the Granton Breakwater Branch dropping away to the right on a falling gradient of 1 in 52. *The late Wallace Lockhart*

1903, THE NEWHAVEN & LEITH LINK LINE (THE NEW LEITH LINES)

The Caledonian Railway, in seeking to access Leith by a more direct route, came up with a very ambitious scheme to achieve this. As mentioned in Chapter 1, it was the intention that Princes Street station should not be the end of the line. The company tabled a Bill in 1890 to construct the extended line of route under the length of Princes Street and Calton Hill, in tunnel, as far as London Road, with an intermediate passenger station at Waterloo Place, in the east side of the city. From there it was seen that Leith might be accessed quite easily. Now why the Directors of the Caledonian Railway ever thought that this particular proposal would ever see the light of day, what with the conservative City Fathers and Edinburgh's ever watchful and powerful Cockburn Association, the world's oldest architectural and urban planning association, let alone the government of the day, and with the NBR sitting on the sidelines, is not known. The scheme was discussed in Parliament but was rejected, unsurprisingly, although mill owners along the length of the Balerno Branch had spoken up in support of same.

Access to the eastern side of Leith Docks was, however, still on the company's agenda and in 1903 the company was authorised to construct a completely new line of railway from Newhaven (Trinity Junction) on the 1879 Leith North branch line, striking eastwards to cross the north of the city via Bonnington, where it crossed over the former EL&GR Leith Branch, and onwards towards Leith Walk (where a goods depot known in BR days as Leith Walk West was provided above Jane Street) before crossing Leith Walk proper by a girder bridge and immediately crossing over the NBR Leith Central Branch. New passenger stations were planned for Newhaven, Bonnington (Ferry Road) and Leith Walk. In the event, although the line was constructed, it was never to be used as a passenger line but carried freight traffic only. There were to be three rail connected establishments on this line of route: a siding serving the original SCWS Chancelot Flour Mills, a small branch serving a goods depot, located between Bonnington and Leith Walk (Rosebank Goods), and another serving Restalrig Goods between Leith Walk and Seafield. The line then curved round Seafield Cemetery before diverging, with the left-hand line running to, and terminating at, what should have been its passenger terminus at Leith South (Bath Street, later a freight depot and renamed by BR as Leith East). The right-hand spur crossed to the north of the NBR South Leith Branch and terminated in a new Caledonian Leith South Yard complex alongside the sea wall to the north of the large NBR South Leith Yard at Seafield. A new locomotive shed was constructed by the Caledonian Railway at Seafield, but never was to be brought into use by them. Instead, and at a later time, alterations made in connection with the NBR Lothian Lines Project provided for a connection from Fillyside to the Caledonian line which enabled NBR locomotives to access Seafield shed.

This line was envisaged to be an integral part of the scheme for an underground railway along the length of Princes Street, as mentioned above, and the plan was to extend the line beyond Leith South (Cal) station via Salamander Street in Leith, where a new terminus was to be constructed close by the NBR South Leith station. A line leading back to Edinburgh would leave this line at a triangular junction near Lochend and involve a tunnel under Calton Hill and St. James Square, a further 'cut and cover' tunnel under George Street, and a connecting junction with the main line just outside the west side of Princes Street station. Leith Councillors were very enthusiastic and wanted even more passenger stations to be provided on this line, but one can surely understand why the very conservative City Fathers comprising Edinburgh City Council were aghast. However, some years later when a city ring road was being mooted, the City Engineer came up with an even more ludicrous set of proposals for an inner-city ring road, which were just as quickly, and quite properly, binned. Nevertheless, one must ponder just what the city transportation system might have been, in the shape of an Edinburgh & North Side Suburban Railway.

This particular New Leith Line scheme was ill-considered and over-ambitious and whilst it did give the Caledonian Railway alternative access to Leith, it brought little in the way of rewards. It was perhaps extended too far and, had it terminated in the heart of Leith Walk West, before it actually crossed the main thoroughfare (Leith Walk) which connected Leith and Edinburgh proper, then the results might have been different. The proposed stations were never to be built and the envisaged passenger traffic never materialised. Seafield locomotive shed was somewhat of an embarrassment and was never used to any great extent by the Caledonian. It was something of a relief when arrangements were made to rent it to the NBR as an overflow shed to the ever-overcrowded St. Margarets, for whom it was to become a valuable asset, becoming the main out-based shed for providing engines and crews for the many coal workings around the east and south of Edinburgh, with a link of twenty-eight crews and locomotives out-based there.

Ex-CR No. 73 Pickersgill Class '72' 4-4-0 No. 54478 of Dalry Road shed, standing at Slateford Junction in April 1960. *Stuart Sellar*

Pending completion of the new Haymarket East Junction to Slateford Junction line, WCML trains to and from Edinburgh Waverley were diverted on Sundays via the 'Sub', and here BR Standard '7MT' Pacific No. 70013 *Lightning* heads a train from the south over the 'Sub' in August 1965. The Slateford Maltings and a new housing block under construction can be seen in the background. *Stuart Sellar*

Post Caledonian Railway Developments

Slateford

In 1961, with the concentration of freight working in and around Edinburgh now being centred at the new Millerhill Marshalling Yard lying on the ex-NBR Waverley route to the south-east of the city, BR had a new connecting chord line constructed from the Up and Down Main lines at Slateford Junction via a double junction. Running on a curving, falling gradient, lying to the south of the yard area it connected into the Edinburgh & South Side Suburban Railway (the 'Sub' as known to all Edinburgh railwaymen) via another new double junction, laid in at Craiglockhart Junction. This new work required closure of the carriage sidings at Slateford Yard, although the freight marshalling yard at Slateford was to remain in use as such for several years to come. This new chord line provided direct access to Millerhill Yard for former LM&SR freight workings, and also access to Craigentinny Carriage Depot for the

Above: Ex-L&NER Class 'J37' 0-6-0 No. 64586, running tender first, brings a heavy freight train off the new Slateford Chord line and onto the Edinburgh & South Suburban Railway at Craiglockhart Junction on 24th August 1959. *Stuart Sellar*

Right: Inside the temporary Craiglockhart Junction signal box, with the block instruments arranged on the block shelf above the 10-lever signalling frame. *Stuart Sellar*

displaced coaching stock from Slateford carriage sidings, leading to a further reduction of the yard facilities at Slateford. Later, the former yard became a civil engineering depot for stabling on-track maintenance machines and ballast trains. Under the Edinburgh resignalling scheme, the connection from the West Coast Main Line at Slateford to this chord line was renewed with a new, standard single-lead junction configuration (see Chapter 4).

In October 2006, however, with Craigentinny Depot now contracted to carry out the fuelling and servicing of Inter-city, fixed formation trains belonging to the new, privatised TOC's, First ScotRail created five new stabling and cleaning sidings on the site of the former carriage sidings, for cleaning their DMU fleet, servicing of which was centred on the ScotRail DMU Depot at Haymarket.

The Slateford area was to have many rail-connected industries, with the Edinburgh iron foundry of McKenzie & Moncur perhaps being the largest. The LM&SR inherited and modernised the

What had been the junction with the CR Slateford to Haymarket branch in 1964, in preparation for the restoration of the Haymarket East Junction (also known as Duff Street Junction) scheme. The E&G main line passes from left to right across the front of what was Herdman's Flour Mills at Haymarket. To the right, work has already started on ground clearance where original CR Caledonian Distillery sidings were situated. *Stuart Sellar*

Haymarket East Junction; the track base has now been consolidated and is ready for laying the junction pointwork in July 1964. *Stuart Sellar*

Caledonian Railway's laundry at Slateford for the washing of bedding, table linen and other items from both train services and the company's railway hotels, all of which was conveyed free on rail. The laundry was a major employer of young women. The later Scottish & Newcastle brewers had a major rail-connected maltings at Slateford. There was also a complex of sidings for the Edinburgh abattoir and market located at Slateford, served by a connection to the west of Slateford station.

With the complete closure of Edinburgh Princes Street station in 1965, and to facilitate the altered operational needs for West Coast passenger traffic, BR in 1964 reinstated the double junction arrangement immediately to the east of Haymarket station (south lines) to permit direct working to and from the West Coast Main Line, bringing the 1853 Slateford to Haymarket branch line back into use. This was later electrified as part of the Edinburgh/Carstairs West Coast electrification project. The junction at Haymarket was

Haymarket East Junction; the Up direction junction and single line have now been laid in, July 1964. *Stuart Sellar*

Haymarket East Junction has now been connected up and the Slateford Branch lines are being fettled up by a P. Way relaying gang. To the right the sidings serving the Caledonian Distillery lie out of use but still in situ (as they are to this day and can still be seen amongst the heavy undergrowth which has now encroached the site). The distillery has been converted into flats. This is somewhat of a historic moment when a connection, removed in 1877, is reinstated once again. *Stuart Sellar*

Class 17 diesel/electric Clayton locomotive shunts scrap siding on the Haymarket Branch, May 1964. The P. Way material lying in the vee of the junction will be used for the restoration of the double line junction to Haymarket East Junction. *Stuart Sellar*

Dalry Middle Junction on 5th May 1964. The signal box is closed, as is Wester Dalry Branch. Track recovery has already begun with the Down line recovered between Dalry Junction and Dalry Middle Junction, and existing track layout has been so configured as to facilitate further track recoveries on the branch proper. *Stuart Sellar*

The double junction now in place, demolition work on the overbridge taking the Wester Dalry Branch over the Haymarket link has now started in July 1964. *Stuart Sellar*

Stanier 'Black Five' No. 45098 of Polmadie shed heads a ballast train working at Granton Junction during restoration of the double junction in July 1964. *Stuart Sellar*

Haymarket East Junction with the 10.20 National Express East Coast IC225 electric service from Glasgow Central to London King's Cross passing over from the now-electrified Slateford line to the Up South Main Line and bound for Edinburgh Waverley.
John Furneval

initially known as Duff Street Junction but is now, more correctly, identified as Haymarket East Junction. Since what was being provided was a double track main line, this work required that the full double junction arrangement with the Granton and Leith branch line at Granton Junction, removed in 1937, be reinstated.

CURRIEHILL STATION

The original station, opened by the Caledonian Railway on 15th February 1848, was closed by BR on 31st March 1951 but was rebuilt on the same site and reopened for passenger traffic, again by BR, on 5th October 1987, following a significant increase in new private housing at the nearby village of Currie, lying immediately to the south at a higher level. New housing has now also been provided north of the village and immediately adjacent to the station.

WESTER HAILES STATION, EDINBURGH

In the early 1980s, Edinburgh Corporation embarked on a new housing project which eventually became almost the equivalent of a large village in its own right. Lying to the south of Sighthill (an earlier post-war housing project within the city of Edinburgh boundary, lying along the line of the A71 Edinburgh to Ayr trunk road, and immediately north of the Caledonian Railway West Coast Main Line and the A70 Edinburgh to Lanark trunk road), this new housing development, a housing complex with an ever-expanding, and extremely controversial social history, added a significantly enlarged population to area but was not conveniently situated for access to the city centre. In the same year as the new Curriehill station was opened, BR constructed and opened a new passenger station almost equidistant between that station and Kingsknowe station, but centrally and conveniently located within the Wester Hailes housing complex itself. The station, named 'Wester Hailes', opened on 11th May 1987 and is now served by the Edinburgh Waverley to Glasgow Central via Shotts, Abellio ScotRail train services.

GRANTON GAS WORKS

When the Leith North Branch closed to all traffic in 1967, to ensure the continuing supplies of coal to Granton Gas Works, British Rail retained the heavily-graded Granton Breakwater Branch up to the connection to the Gas Works at Pilton West Junction. The junction box was replaced by a ground frame, with an associated headshunt to permit trains of coal to be propelled back into the gasworks sidings. Final closure of the gas works, as such, was in 1987, although the gasometers (gas holders) were to be retained and used as a gas storage facility for natural (North Sea) gas until 2001.

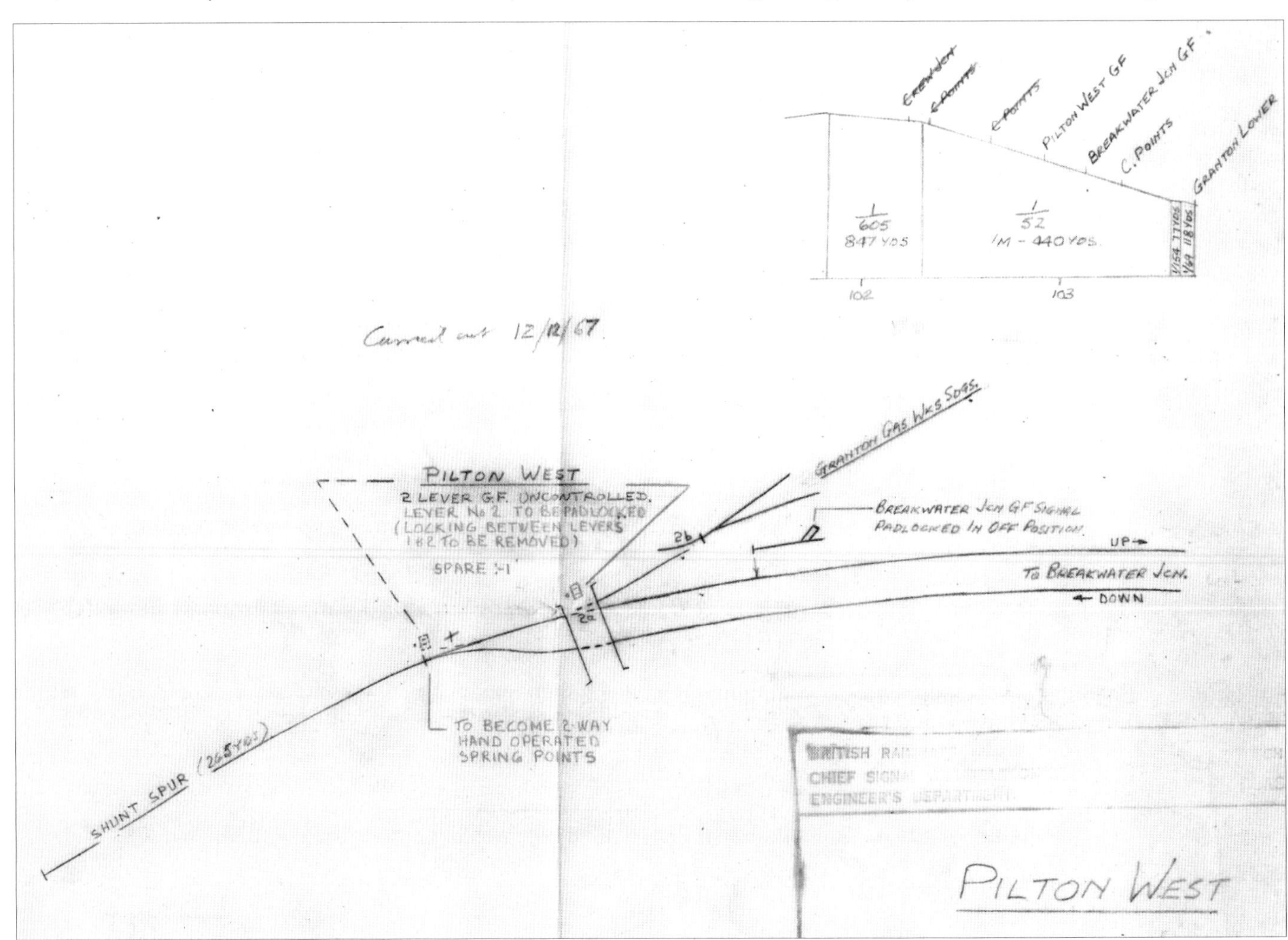

A BR signalling drawing showing the alterations at Pilton West Junction to permit coal train workings access to Granton Gas Works from Granton Harbour after the Dalry to Leith and Granton branch was closed. The work was carried out in December 1967.
Robert Dey

4 A SHORT CUT TO GLASGOW

1869, MIDCALDER JUNCTION TO CLELAND LINE

The existence of oil bearing shale seams has only been briefly touched upon so far. Following some years of experimenting in Derbyshire with crude oil obtained from canneloid coal by means of pyrolysis, Glasgow-born industrial chemist James Young and his two partners, Messrs Binney and Meldrum, in 1851 relocated their interest to Easter Insch, Bathgate, in West Lothian where they designed and constructed the world's first oil refinery. Here, crude oil was produced by retorting locally sourced canneloid coal. This crude oil was then refined into various fractions, resulting in differing oil-based products, the largest of which in terms of demand at the time, being paraffin oil, and the works were immediately to be connected to the extended (by the E&GR) former WM&CR. This was to see the expansion of Scotland's first oil boom. Bathgate town, served by both the Edinburgh & Bathgate Railway and the Monklands Railway, was at the centre of later NBR-worked territory, and that company served many of the developing new oil works. Young had patented his process in 1851, but by the late 1850s the supplies of the canneloid coal – known locally as Torbanite, from the area where it was being mined – were being worked out. Young had heard about the existence of oil bearing shales and had cleverly negotiated six shale mining concessions in and around the village of West Calder. In 1865, having bought out his partners, Young started construction of a new oil works at Addiewell (see below), about one mile west of the village, and formed Young's Paraffin, Light & Mineral Oil Company. In that same year, Young's patent expired, and a plethora of new shale oil works were to spring up, well over 120 in total, with one of the earlier oil works being at Tarbrax in North Lanarkshire, immediately adjacent to Cobbinshaw and the Caledonian Railway's West Coast Main Line to Edinburgh. Young's Paraffin, Light & Mineral Oil Company went on to be one of the biggest players in the Scottish oil industry. At the time of opening, the flagship Addiewell Oil Works, the largest oil works and refinery in the world at the time, was to be served solely by the NBR from Bathgate, but things were soon to change in the shale fields.

1869 was to be a significant year of expansion by the Caledonian Railway, for in January of that year they opened a new main line of railway for goods traffic, following in June for passenger traffic. This line ran from Midcalder Junction on the West Coast Main Line, connecting into the former Wishaw & Coltness Railway at Holytown in North Lanarkshire, under the provisions of the Cleland and Mid Calder Railway and Branches 1865 Act. This new line of route was quite inspired in concept, since it cut straight across the shale fields of West and Mid Lothian and also crossed the rich coal workings of West Lothian and North Lanarkshire around Fauldhouse. With the coming of the 1869 line, many mineral sources, formerly the sole preserve of the NBR, were very soon to be connected to the new Caledonian line and worked by engines of both companies. The safety of this method of working was enshrined in the mutually agreed 'Allocated Time Working Arrangements', whereby each company was allocated a time slot in which their engines could operate, to the exclusion of the other company's trains. Each company was obliged to be clear of a joint working line, leaving same clear for the other party, at a designated time, and it generally worked very well.

Passenger stations were provided at Newpark (14 miles from Princes Street, serving the village of Bellsquarry), West Calder (16

West Calder station in CR days with a stopping passenger train from Edinburgh to Glasgow entering the station with a goodly crowd of intending passengers (or maybe not). The locomotive is Drummond designed Class '66' 4-4-0 No. 77. This engine and five others were given higher pressure boilers; No. 77 was a long time denizen of Dalry Road. *W.D. Yuill*

miles), Addiewell (17½ miles), Breich (20¼ miles), Fauldhouse North (22¼ miles), Shotts Central (25¾ miles), Hartwood (27½ miles), Cleland (Omoa) (30½ miles) and Carfin Halt (32½ miles). This line shortened the intervening distance between Edinburgh and Glasgow to a mere 46¼ miles and this then permitted the Caledonian Railway to compete on even terms with the NBR for the lucrative Edinburgh–Glasgow passenger traffic. Much more importantly, it also gave the Caledonian Railway direct access to both the heart of the still developing Scottish oil industry, and the very productive West Lothian coal fields. However, in geographical terms it was to prove a most difficult route, climbing to cross the Fauldhouse and Polkemmet moors at Benhar Junction (813 feet above sea level) on the way.

On the west side of Newpark station, a connection (trailing) from the east to westbound line (later the Down line) gave access to a limestone pit, working the same Burdiehouse seam of limestone as was worked at both Harburn and Raw Camps Pit. This was Westfield Limestone Pit and the associated private siding was serviced by a Dalry Road Trip working. The limestone produced here was destined for the blast furnaces operating around Gartsherrie in Coatbridge. Limestone from the Levenseat limestone measure was also worked at Levenseat (see below).

By 2016, Breich station, built to serve the nearby miner's rows (houses) known as Breich Terrace, had become so remote from the new village built to the east after the demolition of the mining houses, that it was the second least used station in Scotland, with only two trains booked to call each day, one of which was by request. Whilst this book was being written in 2017, Breich topped the list of least used stations in Scotland; both Abellio ScotRail and Network Rail applied for a Closure Order, as usage amounted to less than three passenger journeys per week (October 2017), but in December 2017, despite the low use, it was announced that a Closure Order has been denied by the Scottish government.

For westbound trains from Edinburgh, the climbing started at Balerno Junction, a mere 484 yards on the west side of Slateford Junction. From Midcalder Junction, this new line initially fell away on a falling gradient of 1 in 132 before encountering a short level stretch between the 34 and 33 mileposts. From there a short rising gradient of 1 in 124 took the line through Newpark station before another stretch of level track passed through Limefield Junction and on to West Calder station (30MP). From here, an unrelenting slog faced Down trains before Benhar Summit was cleared, over a ruling gradient of 1 in 160 over the 10 miles between West Calder and Benhar. On the other side of Benhar, a ruling gradient of 1 in 130 applied from Cleland (Omoa).

Indeed, the 'hardness' of this route was commented upon at some length in the *Railway Magazine*, dated October 1906, as follows:

'*Many average speeds* [on the Caledonian Railway] *are less than 50 mph but involve great effort on the part of the locomotive. A case in point is the work involved on the Glasgow and Edinburgh direct trains, which, in the opinion of many people, is superior to any other on the system, but the average speed is only 46 miles per hour ... the nature of the line has been aptly described somewhere, as like going up the side of the roof of a house and down the other, so steep are the grades, 1 in 100 prevailing, with stretches at 1 in*

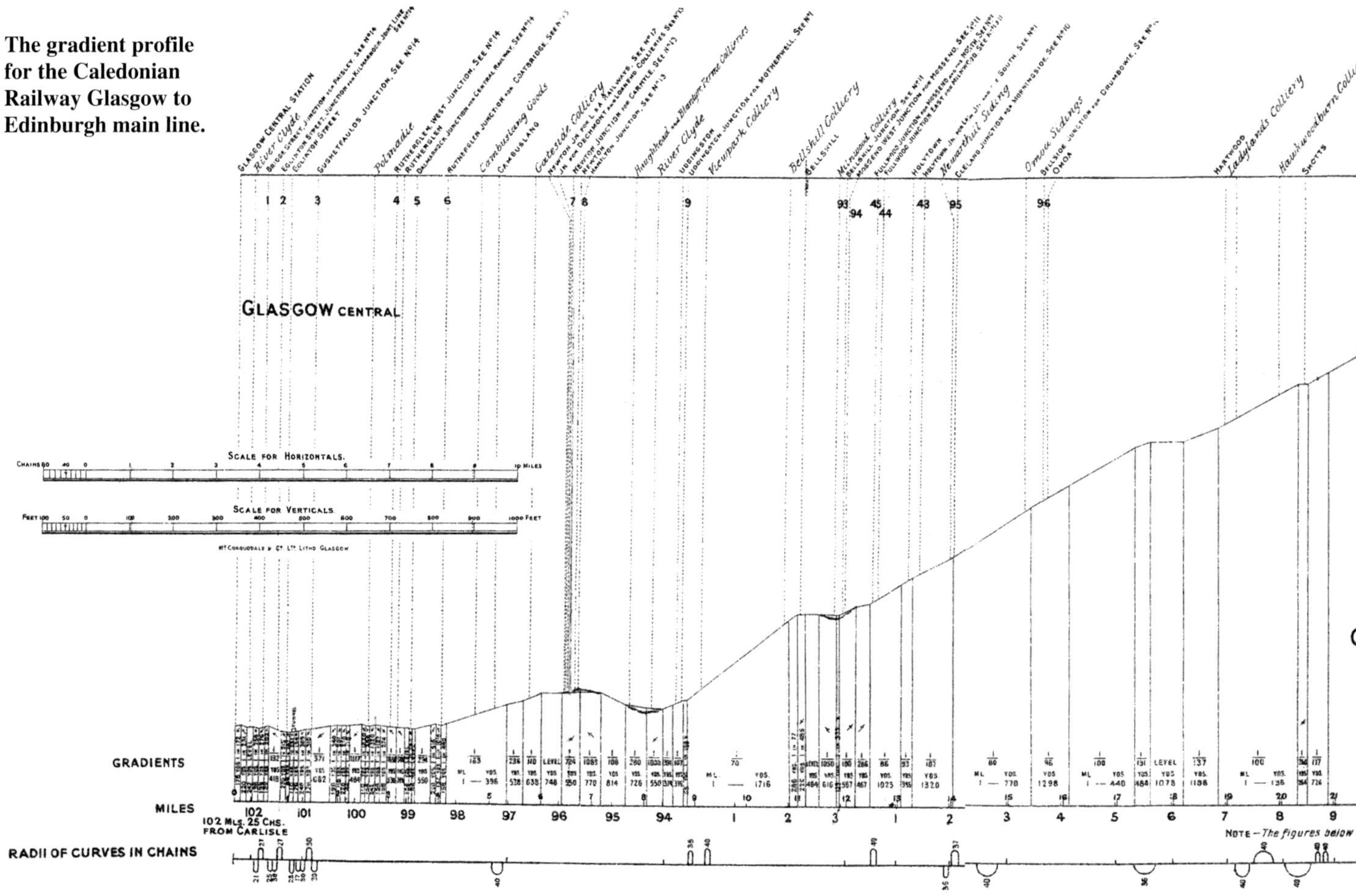

The gradient profile for the Caledonian Railway Glasgow to Edinburgh main line.

70 and 1 in 80. The summit, Benhar, 813 feet above sea level, is practically half way, and from passing here down to Edinburgh, trains are timed at nearly a mile a minute. On the western side from Benhar to Glasgow, such high speeds are impossible, on account of numerous junctions and curves. All these trains are "hard run" and it is in every way creditable that time is kept.'

Over the years, the route was to tax steam traction, on both freight and passenger workings, to the limit, and sometimes beyond, but it nevertheless permitted the Caledonian to access some of the richest coal workings containing high quality splint coal in Lanarkshire and West Lothian, plus the burgeoning shale oil industry and the mining of ironstone, limestone and fireclay, all minerals in high demand by the Lanarkshire steel masters.

The Mid Calder & Cleland line of route was to suffer badly during severe winter conditions, as did the main line between Midcalder Junction and Carstairs. The latter route, in climbing to around the 1,000 feet mark, was hit particularly hard during the very severe winters of both 1947 and 1962/63, when heavy drifting snow closed both routes for a number of days. In 1963 the main line was blocked by 20-30 feet deep snow drifts around Auchengray and an attempt to plough the route from the Carstairs side, using an independent snow plough propelled by two steam locomotives, proved fruitless when the plough ran into a very deep drift, stuck fast, and the full assembly was lost for a whole week. Dynamite had to be used by the Permanent Way Department to loosen the compacted snow before clearance could be effected. In later years, during yet another severe winter in the 1970s, the author, as Assistant Area Manager at Bathgate, spent several long and cold nights accompanying two Class 37 diesel locomotives, fitted with a double-line, nose plough front and rear, and in the hands of ex-Dalry Road men, ploughing both routes from and to Midcalder Junction in order to keep traffic moving.

Midcalder Junction signal box controlled the junction between the West Coast Main Line and the new main line to Cleland but had the potential to cause somewhat of an anomaly. This was because of the protocol of the day, observed by almost all UK railway companies in their nomenclature of the running lines, which observed the rule 'always Up to the capital (i.e. London)'. In Scotland, however, the same unwritten rule applied but with Up leading to the capital – Edinburgh, and at Midcalder Junction the Up West Coast Main from Edinburgh would, logically, become the Down Shotts line, with the Up Shotts line being that leading to Edinburgh and converging with the Down West Coast Main Line. After opening of the 1869 Mid Calder to Cleland main line, the Caledonian Railway, very cleverly side-stepped this potential pitfall by following a precedent set for their Scottish domestic routes, referring to (and publishing in the Working Timetable for the 'Glasgow and Edinburgh Direct Route') the lines not as Up and Down but merely as the 'West to East Line' and 'East to West Line'. At a later date, and most likely under LM&SR control, operating documents such as the General Appendix to the Working Timetable were standardised in presentation (as agreed at the Railway Clearing House) throughout all railway companies, and thus the nomenclature of Up and Down was applied to the 1869 Shotts line and confusion followed.

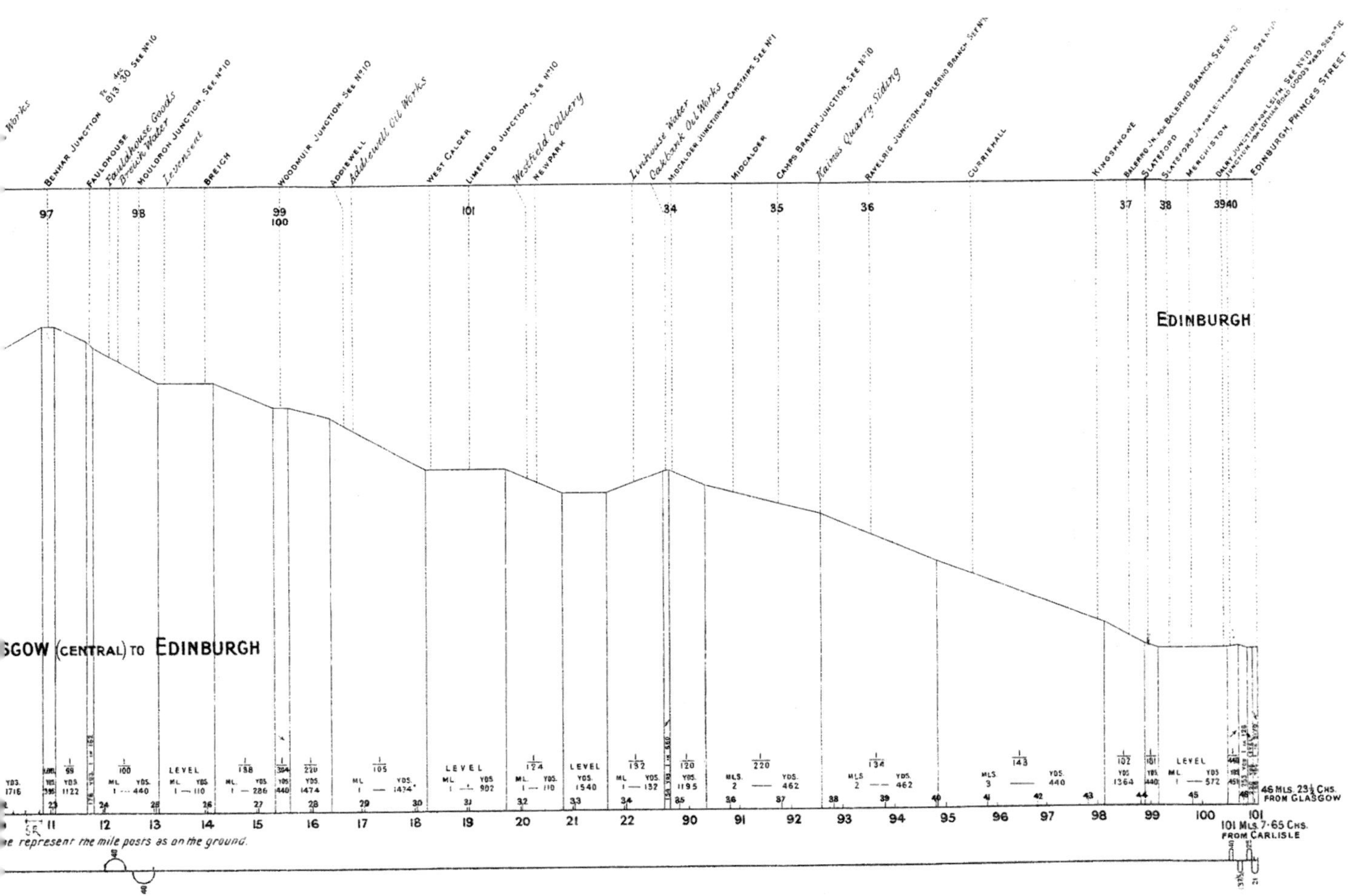

'Dunalastair III' Class '900' No. 14434 (CR No. 894) at Princes Street station on a Glasgow stopping train. *CRA Archives*

Midcalder Junction signal box was also the supervising box in respect of the automatic half barrier level crossing installations at both Midcalder station and Auchengray, the latter deep inside Carstairs-controlled territory, and the responsibility for both lay with the Area Manager at Bathgate by virtue of this somewhat odd arrangement.

The junction configuration at Midcalder Junction was renewed as a single-lead junction arrangement[1] leading to the Shotts line when renewal of the junction by BR became necessary in the 1970s, but under the most recent Network Rail electrification (EGIP) proposals for the 1869 line of route, recent rebuilding of the junction layout has seen a double line crossover junction re-instated once more, thus restoring the ability for higher speeds to be achieved over the junction leading to the Carstairs line and enabling parallel moves across the junction, thus improving train headways on the Shotts route.

Under the authority of the same 1869 Act, the Caledonian Railway moved rapidly to construct several new branch lines. A junction, facing to trains coming from the west and industrial Lanarkshire, was laid in at Benhar Junction, the highest point on the line of route, which gave access to the rich coal and shale oil workings lying high up on the Polkemmet and Fauldhouse moors via a complex plethora of single branch lines which interfaced at several points with a similar web of small single branches belonging to the NBR and coming in from Westcraigs Junction to the north. This ensured that the total output of the newest (1921) and very productive Polkemmet Colliery in Whitburn passed over Caledonian Railway lines, and those of its successors, to the steel works in and around Motherwell (see Chapter 11). Here, on the Benhar Moors, both Greenrigg Colliery and Cultrigg Colliery also produced a very high-quality steam coal, the latter being Grade 1 coal, as rated by the Caledonian, and very much in demand as a locomotive fuel. These collieries were served by both the NBR and Caledonian Railway companies.

At Fauldhouse (Muldron Junction) a new single line branch (1871), some 76 chains in overall length, running from a trailing connection in the west line, served the rich ironstone mines on Muldron Moor. This branch was closed by the early 1900s, whilst at Levenseat, lying to the east of the Muldron Branch, the Caledonian

1 Many mentions of single-lead junction configurations occur within this narrative. This is an arrangement of tracks which avoids the need for a diamond crossing whilst passing from a double line to a double branch line; instead, a series of single connections is provided. The effect is to create a section of single line between the double lines of the two routes. The benefits lie in reduced track maintenance costs and quite often higher junction speeds. However, loss of parallel running, which exists with continuous double track, inflicts a lack of operating flexibility and reduces the capacity of the line, and also introduces a degree of risk should a signal be passed at danger. The latter risk has been reduced by new techniques, but the disadvantages in timetabling and timekeeping mean that these restricted track configurations are now passé, and double junctions are being reinstated.

Railway gained access to both Handaxwood Oil Works and the limestone and sand workings at Levenseat proper, on equal terms with the NBR, and new connections were laid in at Levenseat Junction in both the East main and West main. The Levenseat Branch was worked on an allocated time basis by both railway companies (see above).

At Woodmuir Junction, the Caledonian Railway constructed a 4 miles 51 chains long, single line of railway forming a long loop known as the West Calder Loop Line, striking deep into the rich West Calder and Polbeth/Gavieside shale fields where the deepest and most productive shale pits working some of the thickest seams of shale in the industry were to be found. This loop also served, en route, the United Colliery coal mining interests at the Dykes Pit, the later Loganlea Colliery and Foulshiels Colliery (near which point it crossed, on the level, the NBR branch line from Bathgate to Addiewell Goods NBR and Addiewell Oil Works at Cuthill Crossing). Both Loganlea No. 2 pit and Loganlea No. 3 pit produced coal which was classed as the highest grade (class one) amongst locomotive coals for passenger train use by the Caledonian Railway. This Loop Line also served several smaller paraffin oil works and crude oil works before regaining the main line at Limefield Junction, lying to the east of West Calder station. Internal shale railways (Young's Addiewell and Polbeth Mineral Railway) interfaced with the Loop Line at several points. The Addiewell pugs belonging to Young's were also authorised to run through to Limefield Junction sidings via the West Calder Loop Line, from Westwood and Gavieside Oil Works, and each driver so authorised was named, along with his fireman, in the Caledonian Railway's Mineral Train Working Timetable. Each Addiewell driver was also issued with a copy of the same Working Timetable. Four Addiewell pug drivers, with firemen, were so named in Caledonian Railway documentation.

Unfortunately, this Loop Line proved to be one initiative just too far and too late for the Caledonian Railway, as the shale oil boom of the mid to late 1860s was followed by a significant downturn in the shale oil market, with many closures in this shale field occurring in the years from 1870 to 1903; as a result, the early traffic prospects on the Loop Line never materialised after such a promising start. Many of the smaller crude oil producing works served by the Loop Line were to be closed or taken over as a downturn in revenue and severe competition from the USA in the market for paraffin oil began to bite; as a result, the Loop Line, designed as a through loop and promising so much in the way of traffic, was never, insofar as can be determined, worked on a through running basis. Indeed, the line very quickly fell into disuse prior to World War One, with train working being confined largely to and from either end of the Loop, at Woodmuir Junction and Limefield Junction respectively. Coal traffic continued until the early 1960s, with NCB 'pugs' from Loganlea No. 2 Colliery and BR engines sharing the western Loop Line on an Allocated Time basis. Likewise, the shale oil traffic shared the Limefield Junction end, where oil works' 'pugs' and trip workings from Dalry Road shed could be seen on the eastern section of this Loop until the final closure of Westwood Oil Works, the newest of all the oil works, in 1962. Until the loop line was closed, BR train working between Limefield Junction, Westwood Oil Works and Hermand Agricultural Siding was conducted under the authority of a train staff (black, marked Limefield Junction and Hermand Siding), the custodian of which was the signalman at Limefield Junction.

Woodmuir Junction was also rail connected to the Caledonian Railway Woodmuir Branch, authorised under the same Cleland and Mid Calder Railway and Branches Act as was the West Calder Loop Line, to serve various mineral workings over the years. This former branch line running in a south-westerly direction served the one-time Woodmuir Quarry, and at some later time, coal workings: the earlier Rushiehill pit, in 1896 the Woodmuir Coal Company, and from 1902 the United Collieries Woodmuir, or Loganlea No. 3 Colliery. This branch ran from a facing connection in the Down side sidings at the junction, to the quarry and later pits, the latter of which was also known locally as the Blinky Pit, located on the open moorland to the south side of the A71 Edinburgh to Ayr trunk road, under which the branch passed. This branch working

Stanier '5MT' No. 45127 of Dalry Road shed, stands at the buffer stops in Glasgow Central station after arriving with the 17.18 stopping passenger service from Princes Street on 6th June 1961. *Harry Archibald*

'Black Five' No. 45469 awaits the guard's signal to start with the 17.16 all stops to Glasgow Central in May 1962. This was the author's normal evening train home whilst he was in Edinburgh. *J.L. Stevenson/Hamish Stevenson*

was controlled by train staff (black) held by the signalman in the junction signal box.

Elsewhere, on the same 1869 Mid Calder to Cleland line, a direct siding connection was laid into Addiewell Oil Works from that line, and access to same was controlled by a new Addiewell Oil Works signal box, lying immediately to the east of Addiewell station. This signal box burned down in 1936 and the former Caledonian Railway connection to Addiewell Works was never restored. At Limefield Junction, a short branch ran to the south side of the main line, serving a former crude oil works (Old Hermand) a brickworks (Louden's), and latterly, Hermand shale mine (1940-61), the shale from which was conveyed by Edinburgh trip workings to Westwood Oil Works.

At Midcalder Junction, a new siding was laid in to serve Oakbank Oil Works lying close by the junction. Initially a separate signal box (Oakbank Oil Works) controlled the access to the oil works, but later Midcalder Junction was to take over control of this access, via a new, long siding. This was yet another point where Private Owner and Caledonian locomotives shared access to the same sidings and the Allocated Time Agreement was in place to prevent confliction. Interestingly, Midcalder Junction was also to assume control of the signalling on the main line when the decision was taken to close Linhouse Water signal box. This new arrangement was to facilitate train running over both the main line and the 1869 Cleland line, since, under Linhouse Water box, Glasgow to Edinburgh services were often held at Newpark, waiting for the junction with the main line to clear.

In the late 1970s, a new rail operation was established to move block trains of spent shale (blaes) from Contentibus Bing at Oakbank to General Terminus in Glasgow on behalf of a West of Scotland road haulage concern, Malcolm's of Brookside. From General Terminus, the blaes was destined as infill and bottoming for the civil engineering industry. Two trains were run daily, worked by two English Electric Class 20 Bo-Bo diesel-electric locomotives, running in multiple, and train crews, all from Polmadie Depot in Glasgow.

Forever a route used by both freight and passenger trains, a lot of commuter traffic was generated, with the half-way point (Fauldhouse North) becoming the dividing line for traffic flows. Commuters from Shotts and stations to the west generally travelled to Glasgow Central, whilst passengers from Fauldhouse and the east travelled to Edinburgh Princes Street. Even relatively small stations like Addiewell enjoyed a very healthy passenger revenue debit, with many young girls, employed in such undertakings as the BR Slateford Laundry, Weston's Biscuit Factory at Merchiston, Wilkie & Paul tin box manufacturers, and Manclark & Son, uniform clothing manufacturers, all in the Slateford area. The girls commuted daily from Addiewell using the ever-popular half-rate weekly season tickets, and many travelled from further afield to reach Addiewell, with a large number coming from Bents and Stoneyburn. These young ladies were no angels and travelling on the 07.43 from Shotts to Edinburgh was an education for many unsuspecting young male travellers. The 17.16 ex Princes Street formed their return journey, and such was the trouble and abuse, including physical abuse, which accompanied their passage, that it led to BR substituting corridor coaching stock instead of the non-corridor suburban stock (the norm for this service), to allow the guard access to the passenger accommodation and keep the peace.

All the lines of railway described in this chapter have been addressed in some further detail in an earlier work of the author.[2]

2 *The Vanished Railways of West Lothian*, Lightmoor Press, 2017.

5 Dalry Road Motive Power Depot

Lines of railway, and railway branches, in and around Edinburgh, as described in the previous chapters, were to be the preserve of Dalry Road engines and men, but with wider horizons offered by the expansion of the Caledonian empire; the Dalry Road crews enjoyed much main line express passenger work radiating out to Carlisle and Glasgow Central, via both Carstairs and the Mid Calder to Cleland 'short cut'. Dalry Road men eventually were to work to Stirling via the NBR and Scottish Central, and in later times to places like Symington, Biggar, Peebles, Muirkirk, Lanark, Ayr and even to Heads of Ayr. The main line drivers (and many passed firemen) had impressive route knowledge cards, with many having signed for Perth, Carlisle and Dumfries – and signing for two alternative routes to the latter destination, i.e. via the WCML and Lockerbie, and also via the Glasgow, Paisley, Kilmarnock & Ayr (GPK&AR) route from Glasgow and the G&SWR, and regularly worked trains over both routes, especially the Dumfries milk trains. Much suburban and commuter passenger work was also to be their lot, but Dalry Road overall was to be a far more 'bread and butter' shed than either of its two Edinburgh rivals, with a fair mix of both express and stopping passenger work, heavy freight workings and fast, fully fitted, goods trains, plus a full share of Edinburgh District freight trip workings.

The Dalry Road Sheds

Caledonian Railway records are pretty vague on the origins of, and the various alterations to, the running shed at Dalry Road over the years, but it is recorded elsewhere that an engine house was in situ for commencement of train services between Edinburgh and Carstairs over the new main line in 1848. It has been suggested by reference to early maps that this was a very small affair, situated adjacent to the original wooden terminal in Lothian Road, but no further record of this can be found. Thus, it is thought that, from day one, the locomotive facilities were centred on the small triangular site at Fountainbridge, named Dalry Road after the main thoroughfare lying to the north of the site. To identify subsequent changes to both the shed and shed yard area, one is almost fully dependent on the OS and other maps of the time, where changes were, regrettably, anything but faithfully recorded. The only series of early maps (not OS) of Edinburgh and Leith were produced by William Horne Lizars (Edinburgh) on an annual basis, later superseded by maps from John Bartholomew & Sons (Edinburgh 1826-1989) and now owned by publishers Harper Collins, who also produced maps of the city annually – but, unfortunately, neither series of maps ever gave details of changes at the shed. Indeed, even the later 6 inches/mile OS maps are less than reliable with known changes in intervening years not being recorded. Unfortunately, there were no 25 inches/mile surveys carried out pre-1900, and no OS maps of this series of scale exist for the whole of Edinburghshire before 1900. From those OS maps available, it would appear that there were at least five different configurations of the shed layout.

Shed Location

At a point between Merchiston station and Lothian Road station (located some 792 yards west of the latter terminus), close by Dalry Junction, was to be the site of a new locomotive shed, to house the early fleet of Caledonian Railway locomotives. In this compact and cramped triangular site – bounded to the west by the delightfully and appropriately named Coffin Lane (a narrow walkway from Dalry Road to Dundee Street, running north to south and lying to the east of Dalry Cemetery), to the north by the later Granton & Leith North Branch on which lay Dalry Road station, and to the south by the West Coast Main Line and Dundee Street – the new, small, Caledonian Railway engine house known as Dalry Road shed was to be constructed and subsequently improved.

The 1848 Shed

According to a report in *The Scotsman* newspaper dated 4th December 1847:

> *'At Dalry, the road has been diverted for a short distance and the bridge over the railway is scarcely half-finished, but from the number of men employed, it cannot materially retard the opening of the line. At this point, the engine shed is to be stationed, and considerable progress has already been made on its construction. The building is to be 122 feet in length and 36 feet in breadth, and closely adjacent to it, a large water tank is to be situated.'*

Thus was the construction of the original Dalry Road engine shed described. It is known that by April 1848 a smallish, two-road, dead-ended, timber-built 'engine house' with very basic facilities and two adjacent sidings, had been provided initially, lying adjacent to the main Carstairs line, and this is shown on the early (1853) OS maps. The OS map shows no turntable in situ at the shed at this time, although coach turntables are shown at the Lothian Road terminus station and it may well have been that the engines of the time were turned on these turntables, by the time-consuming method of splitting engine and tender and turning each separately. The early main line engine allocation consisted of mainly Sinclair 2-2-2s of the 'Crewe Type'. It has also to be noted that the E&GR Haymarket engine shed, lying to the north and adjacent to Haymarket terminus, did not at this time have a turntable either. The demands for locomotive turning in these early days were most likely accommodated by the process described. It is probable that in the years following the construction of this early and basic engine shed, additional shed roads were provided to facilitate fire cleaning, and this is indeed borne out by early photographs of the shed. Messing facilities for staff were at that time, and across the board, very basic indeed, and it is unlikely that Dalry Road did any better in this respect. The mess room for a number of years to come was housed in the building lying below the water tank in the shed yard.

Aerial view of Dalry Road Motive Power Depot. The extremely cramped layout of the shed can well be appreciated from this view. Coffin Lane forms the western boundary of the shed and the entrance to Morrison Street coal depot can be seen top left; the Fountain Brewery complex lies alongside the main line centre right. *Donald Cattanach*

By 1861, with the construction and opening of the Dalry Junction to Granton Breakwater line, a triangle became available for turning purposes, running from Dalry Junction to Coltbridge Junction, and by using a section of the earlier Haymarket to Slateford line, thence to Slateford Junction.

Incidentally, the OS map referred to reveals Dalry Road to be as described above, that is, a small two-road (presumably) wooden shed. It must be said that the E&GR shed at Haymarket station is also shown on the same sheet of the map and depicted accurately in every detail. There is thus no reason to suspect that Dalry Road was in any way less than accurately depicted at the time of its construction.

The 1877 Shed

It must, in the author's view, be accepted that in the earliest days the Caledonian Railway's Dalry Road engine shed continued to be a very small facility. In the 1877 revised edition of the OS map a much-extended engine shed configuration appears, with not one, but two engine sheds now on site. In fact the newer shed, which is referred to as the secondary engine shed on the maps, was again a timber-built, double road shed (later to become a wagon repair shed and no longer used as a running shed), lying immediately adjacent to the Carstairs main line. The main two-road running shed had by this time been extended and the shed admin offices located within.

Dalry Road engine shed as shown on the OS 6 inch map of 1852. This was a very small, wooden, two-road running shed with very limited facilities with one or two sidings used for fire cleaning and loco stabling.

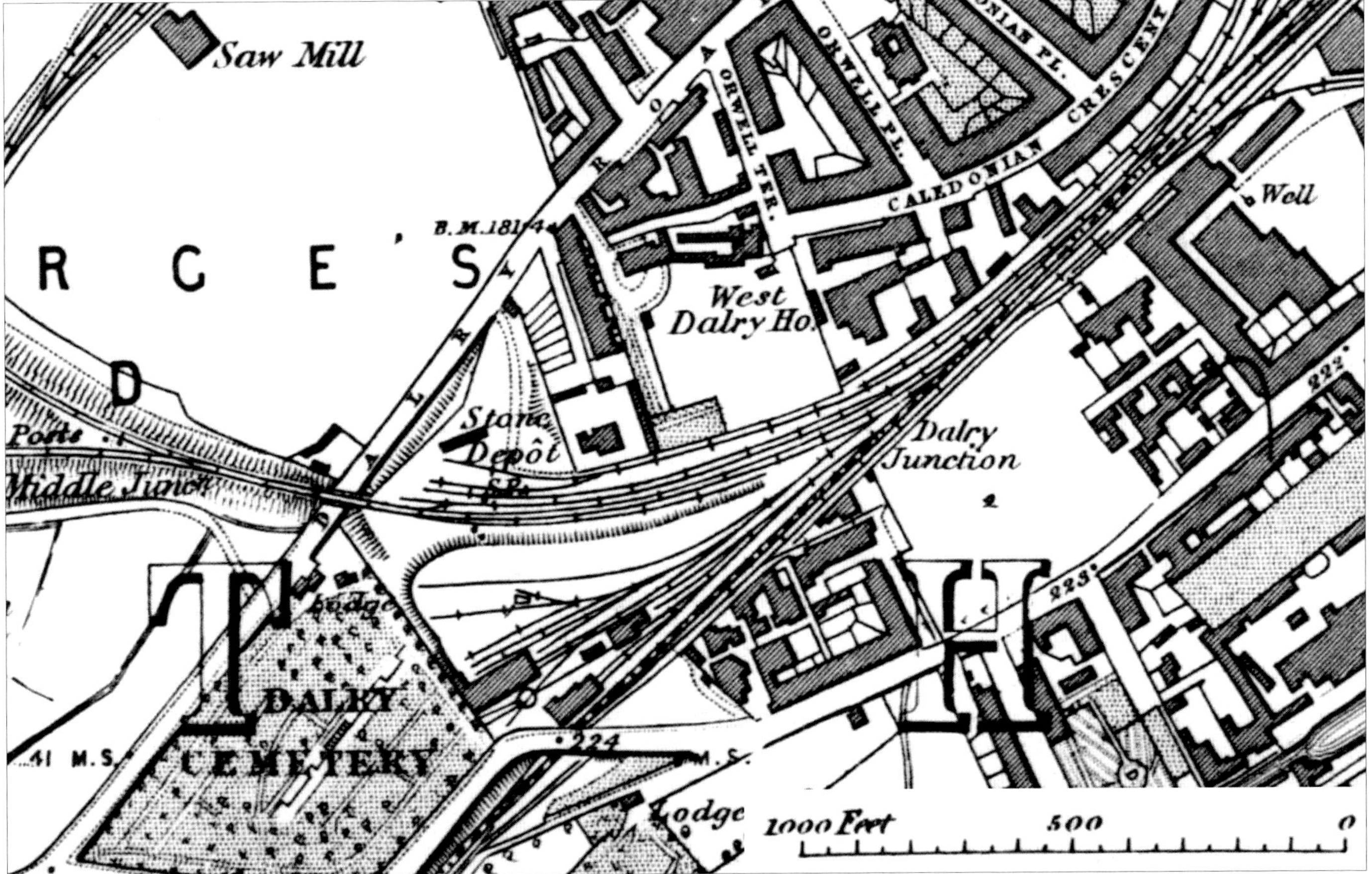

Dalry Road engine shed on the revised OS map of 1877. A new two-road running shed of timber construction has now been provided, lying alongside the running line. A water tank has been provided lying between the ash sidings and the turntable road. The turntable, a 45-foot manual table, lies between the two sheds. What appears to be a manual (hand) coaling bank lies as a short spur from the northernmost siding in the coal stocking area, which may or may not have had a hand operated crane.

Between these two sheds, a short turntable (probably 42 feet in diameter) appears for the first time, along with stabling sidings and ash pits. The Caledonian put the replacement value for insurance purposes at:

The main shed	£500
The secondary shed	£150
The engines	£1,500

The modest sum also allowed for the insurance of locomotives and would appear to suggest that the daily allocation at the shed at that time must have been in the order of five or six engines.

Three new long sidings are provided to the north side of this main shed on an area of ground which was later to be used as a coal stacking and storage area; for the first time, what could be construed as a secondary, very basic coaling facility appears. This was a short siding leading off siding No. 3 (from the shed building) and lying alongside a short loading (coaling) bank located in the coal storage area. It must be assumed that coaling by hand was still a normal means of filling tenders of engines at the shed. The area available for motive power purposes at Dalry Road was to become further squeezed when the Dalry to Granton Breakwater & North Leith Branch was constructed, passed along the northern edge of the existing shed area.

With engines arriving 'on shed', and requiring turning, coaling, and being prepared before going back out into traffic, from day one it must have become clear to the shed management that the turntable was located in the wrong place for any form of constructive service sequence to operate, Indeed, the concept of service sequence at Dalry Road shed was always to be mere hyperbole.

The 1897 Shed

A third two-road shed lying to the north side of the first two sheds appears for the first time. This map also shows, for the first time, the appearance of a new manual coaling bench, constructed to Caledonian standard wooden design, standing on a raised embankment alongside the Granton Branch on the north side of the shed; this was immediately adjacent to the Wester Dalry spur, and bounded the shed on the north side, separating the shed roads from the line to Dalry Middle Junction. The shed layout was to alter very little in the intervening years. However, at some time between 1894 and 1900, the layout of the turntable facility was improved with additional exit lines provided and a direct connecting line from the turntable to the lines leading to what, by now, appeared to be the main running shed, making 'service sequence' a possibility for the first time.

A new island platform passenger station, named Dalry Road, had been constructed immediately facing the locomotive coaling facility and opened in 1900. It had earlier been used as Dalry Road Middle Junction ticket platform but is not shown on this OS map of 1897.

This shed turntable was gone by 1910, superseded by the provision of a larger 60 feet diameter turntable at Edinburgh Princes Street station, built by Cowans Sheldon of Carlisle, which was located on the west side of the signal box there. An engine holding siding, with watering facilities, was also provided running to the east side of the signal box at the Princes Street terminal and upon which engines which had been turned could be held pending their next outward working. This facility was provided to minimise as far as possible the number of light engine movements required between shed and station. At Dalry Road proper, an additional ash pit and locomotive stabling roads were laid in on the site of the former turntable at the shed at this time. By 1906, a third shed road had been provided in the northernmost shed and by 1908 this shed had been rebuilt as four-road running shed, but still of timber construction.

At some point in time, the early two-road shed became a two-road wagon repair shop, lying alongside the Down Main line. The 1877 centre-most shed, formerly a small two-road running shed, was converted into a fitting shed and also contained the shed admin offices. A water tank and sand kiln were located between the shed roads and the ash pits with the staff messroom located below the former (see below).

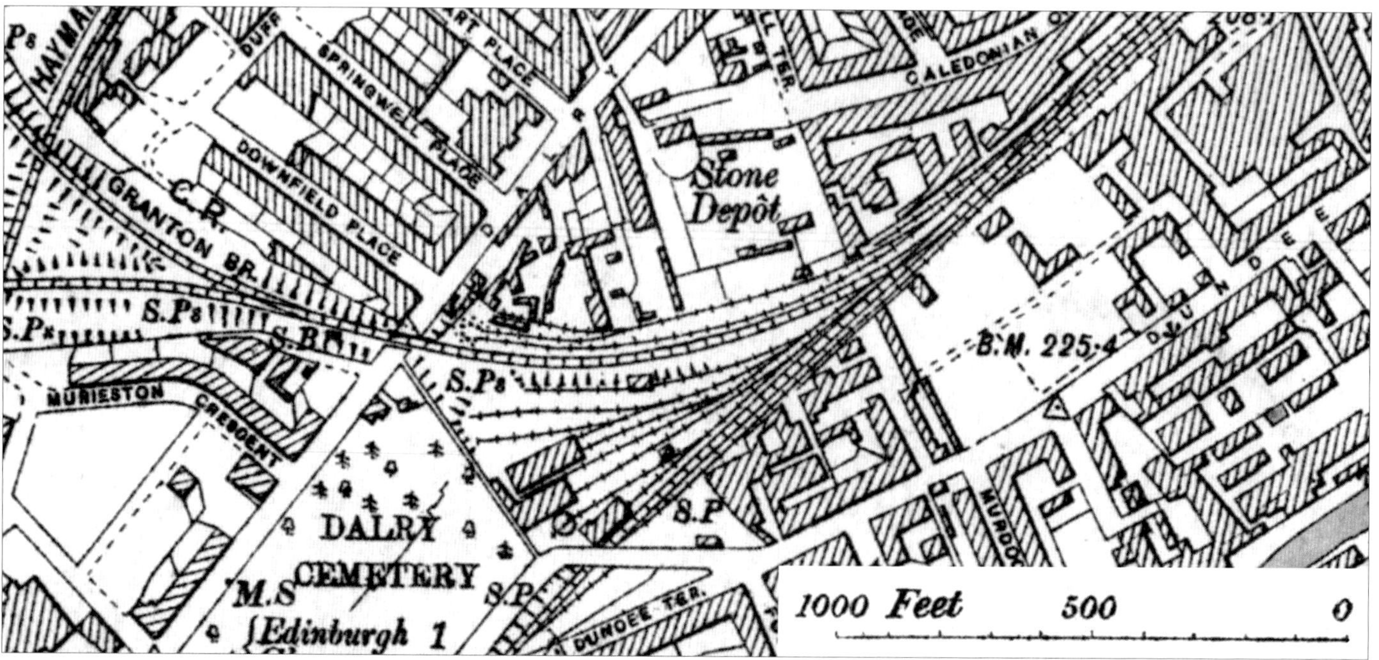

Dalry Road shed as shown on the OS 6 inch map surveyed in 1894 and published in 1897. A new third running shed, again containing two roads, has been constructed on the northernmost part of the shed area. The 45-foot turntable is still in situ.

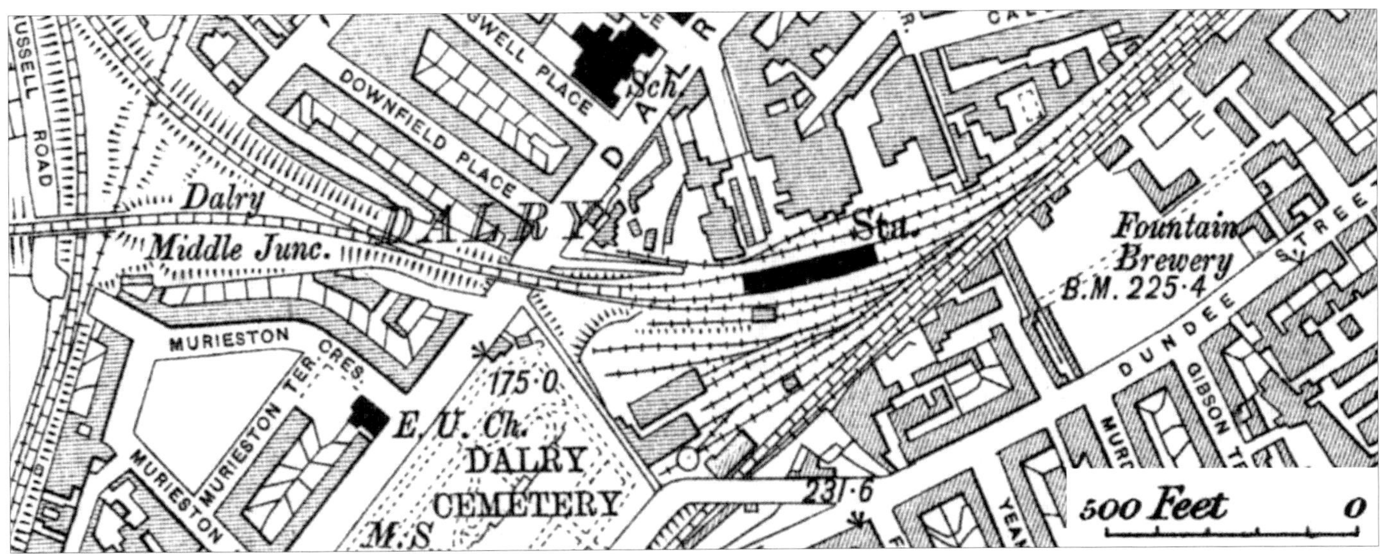

Dalry Road shed, resurveyed in 1906. This turntable will have gone by 1910.

The Proposed Replacement for Dalry Road Shed

Just before the 19th century was out, the Caledonian Railway, fully aware of the cramped and limited space and facilities at the shed, and the inherent problems this posed to engine working and servicing; it thus, drew up a grandiose plan for a completely new running shed to replace the existing Dalry Road shed, planning to locate this at Slateford Junction, a mere 2,222 yards to the west. This new shed, measuring 300 feet by 165 feet, was planned to be a brick built, ten-road shed with an eleventh road terminating in a small adjacent workshop, and with a mechanical coaling plant and 60-foot turntable provided. The running shed was to be equipped by a north-light, saw tooth pattern roof, similar to the design adopted on the L&NWR – but, oddly, the workshop lying alongside was shown as having a conventional, longitudinal ridged roof. This plan was considered by some to be over-ambitious and thus the drawings lay gathering dust until June 1899, when a further alternative site was considered, at Gorgie, but NBR objections to the required bridging works over their lines (the Edinburgh & South Side Suburban Railway) associated with this suggestion, quickly put paid to that particular line of thought.

Dalry Road: The Final Engine Shed on Site (circa 1912/13)

The company, thwarted in their bold plans, had to choose, and choose quickly, just how to take this matter forward. Five different plans had been drawn up and two were eventually short-listed, these being Plan No. 2 with an estimated cost of £3,000 and Plan No. 5 costing £4,000. Having come to a decision to adopt scheme No. 2, the company determined merely to rebuild the existing shed in situ, with an improved shed yard layout from an operating perspective, albeit still in the same cramped space,

CR McIntosh Class '104' 0-4-4T No. 169, stands at the coaling stage at Dalry Road with coalmen getting in on the act in this undated photograph. This engine worked the Balerno Branch although the CR 'bow tie' route indicator appears to have slipped in this case.
Hamish Stevenson collection

55229

A 1955 panoramic view over Dalry Road MPD. The brick-built building (centre) is the sand kiln with water tank to rear. The original, wooden coaling stage is left rear. Over the city skyline, the spires of St. Mary's Episcopal Cathedral dominate. The two Dalry Road tool vans stand alongside. *Stuart Sellar*

and firm estimates were compiled in 1911. A tender for carrying out the work was invited and despite the higher final cost was duly accepted, from one contractor, James Kinnear of Edinburgh, for a cost of £5,190 19s 8d. This contractor could not, however, provide the company with a firm completion date, and the latter, parsimonious to the last, accordingly reduced the monthly payments being made by 10%, as compensation. Despite Kinnear's perceived problems with timescale, the works were all completed more or less on time and the new shed was finished in early 1912. McIntosh, Locomotive Superintendent of the Caledonian, approved the provision of a new water column in front of the reconstructed shed, at a cost of £65.

The new shed comprised of a brick-built, four-road (dead-ended) shed with a nine-pitch, transverse, slate finished roof, fitted with smoke vents and eighteen glazed side windows. It measured 153 feet by 52 feet. The larger of the former running sheds was converted into a locomotive fitting shed and provided with a 30-ton hoist. This latter building also housed the shed administration offices.

An interesting photograph at Dalry Road. LM&SR No. 15151 0-4-4T (ex-CR Class '104' No. 108) stands ahead of 4-4-0 No. 14359 (ex-CR No. 150, a non-superheated McIntosh 'Dunalastair IV' Class '140'). The 0-4-4T, probably just going out on a Balerno Branch working, is having the roof cleared of coal spillage after an over exuberant visit to the coaling stage and is giving some cleaners (see cleaning materials alongside on the ground) a source of innocent amusement. No. 14539 is having some attention carried out on the smokebox. *Hamish Stevenson collection*

Class '782' 0-6-0T No. 56312, ex-CR No. 434, stands in front of the tool vans at Dalry Road on 16th August 1960. *Stuart Sellar*

Dalry Road shed, resurveyed in 1913. Seen in its final configuration as rebuilt on the same site by the CR in 1911. Running shed accommodation has been improved, as have staff facilities, but it is still a case of a 'quart in a pint pot'. A proper, manual coaling bench with a single coal drop only has, by this time, been provided alongside the northern edge of the shed adjacent to the new Leith & Granton Branch.

Above: LM&SR Compound 4-4-0 locomotive No. 919, one of a batch from Vulcan Foundry in 1927, was allocated new to Dalry Road shed, seen at the coaling plant waiting to be coaled.
CRA Archives

Right: A view over the shed in BR days showing the very cramped conditions. A McIntosh 0-4-4T of the Caledonian Railway Class '19' of 1895, No. 55124 (ex-CR No. 28) with railed coal bunker, stands in the foreground in Dalry Road shed yard, stored out of use and awaiting withdrawal. In front are two ex-Caledonian 6-wheeled coaches converted into depot tool vans. Alongside are Fairburn 2-6-4T No. 42272, a long-time habitué of Dalry Road, Stanier 'Black Five' 4-6-0 No. 45355 of St. Rollox shed, and a further three, unidentified, locomotives. *John Lambie*

The fitting shed was a throwback to earlier Caledonian Railway days, as described, around 1877 and was a long-term feature of the site. A new sand kiln was provided in 1915, at a cost of £450. Further improvements were authorised over the ensuing years, such as enhanced lighting (electric) and new storage sidings. The staff messing facility continued to be located below the water tank in the centre of the shed yard. The wagon repair shop was closed and demolished in the 1930s and the free area created was given over to additional locomotive holding sidings. Further improvements at the shed were to come in 1923 when the existing timber-built latrines were replaced by a brick-built facility. In 1947 the LM&SR were to spend £2,000 upgrading the messroom, lavatory and washing-up facilities. It was to be all downhill after that time. Even the office accommodation at Dalry Road, still in the former 1877 running shed, now the fitting shed, was to be cramped and basic, right up until the final closure.

Even with the new shed up and running, life was never to be easy at Dalry Road and the site was never conducive to well-ordered shed operation; the bulk of engine preparation continued to take place in the open in the outside shed roads, and in all weathers.

The later LM&SR Stanier Class '7P' Pacific locomotives, no strangers to Dalry Road, could not even be turned on the Princes Street turntable because of their sheer overall length, and had to turn via the triangle of lines formed by the Granton line, at Dalry Junction, Coltbridge Junction and Slateford Junction.

Dalry Road Motive Power Depot was closed on 3rd October 1965, but the actual site of the running shed, marked by the brick walkway floors and the remains of the four pits, stayed in view on the left of passers-by when city-bound on the new Western Approach Road (constructed 1983), at the point where the new road swung left to join the grade separated road junction with Dundee Street.

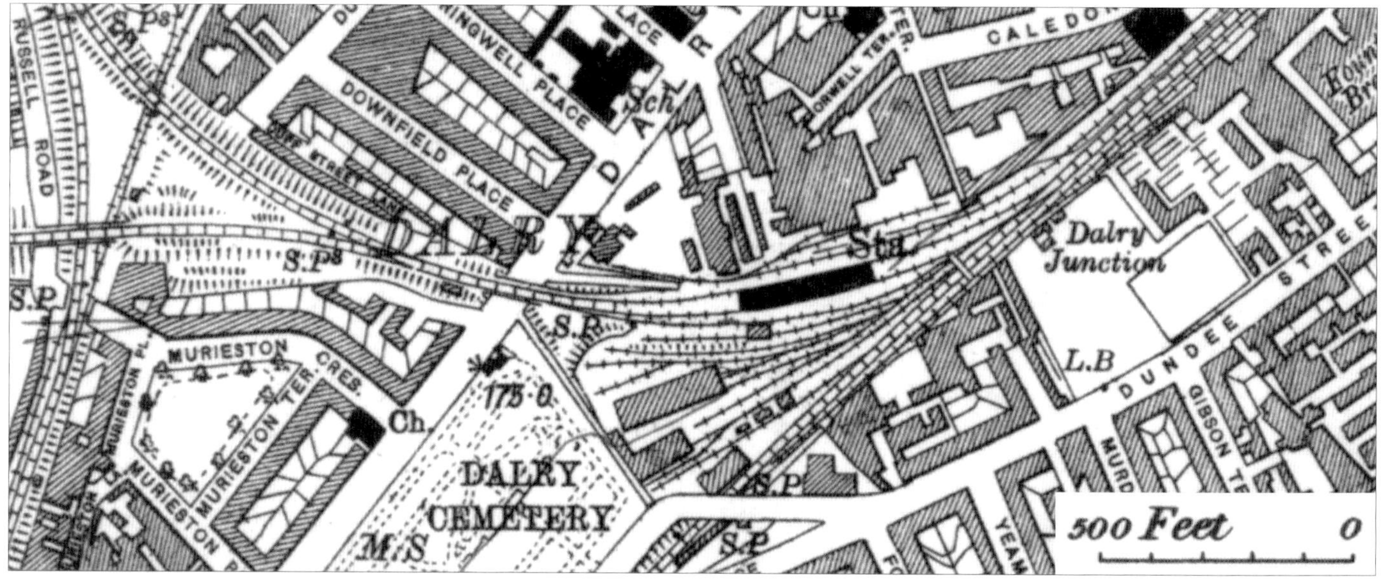

Above: Dalry Road shed, circa 1932. The shed is seen as it was in the early days of the LM&SR and without any significant alterations.

Left: An unusual visitor at Dalry Road, BR Standard '5MT' No. 73036 of Polmadie shed receives attention in the running shed on 13th September 1953.
David Anderson

The handsome lines of the final Caledonian Railway McIntosh 4-4-0 design are in no way diminished by age. Out-shopped in 1913, the locomotive is by this time 42 years old; displaying reasonably clean BR black lined livery and numbered 54452, it seen here alongside Dalry Road shed in June 1955. *Stuart Sellar*

'Black Five' No. 44994, in very clean condition, stands alongside the shed wall at Dalry Road shed. *J.L. Stevenson/Hamish Stevenson*

Above: 'Black Five' No. 45183 makes a shunt in the shed yard at Dalry Road whilst the fireman rides, illegally, on the loco front footsteps. *J.L. Stevenson/Hamish Stevenson*

Right: Dalry Road running shed immediately after closure in 1965. *Author's collection*

Left: Seen on a cold winter's day, when even the weather is depressing with sleet falling. The Leith North Branch has closed completely, as has Edinburgh Princes Street station and a deserted and forlorn Dalry Road station stands out of use and somewhat overgrown, waiting demolition. In the left centre background is Dalry Road shed, equally forlorn, with the wooden coaling stage in the centre of the picture. The site itself will be cleared to make way for the new Western Approach Road scheme. *D. Simpson/David Spaven*

6 Locomotive Engineers and Dalry Road Shed

For the 117 years of its existence, Dalry Road Motive Power Depot was to be influenced by the works of no fewer than fourteen different Locomotive Engineers and Chief Mechanical Engineers as they were later to become. The major influence lay with the Caledonian Railway Engineers, but advances in locomotive design in both LM&SR and BR years were also to impact on the shed. With Nationalisation of the railways in 1947, Scotland became a single entity, known as the Scottish Region of the new British Railways, made up of two former constituent companies, resulting in engines of one company suddenly being found at work on what had been foreign soil. Dalry Road was to fall into this category, with both ex NBR engines and L&NER engines being employed there.

In what follows, the work of such great steam locomotive engineers will be examined, along with their impact, however great or small, on the subject of this book, Dalry Road shed.

The Caledonian Railway Years

In the annals of Caledonian Railway locomotive history, one name appears with unfailing regularity in the early days, that of Alexander Allan. Allan was never to be employed by the Caledonian Railway in any capacity but has been quite erroneously credited with making one significant contribution to the early Caledonian Railway locomotive fleet – the 'Crewe Type' two-cylinder, outside-framed locomotives. The truth is that these 'Crewe Type' locomotives most likely came about as a result of collaboration between Locke, Buddicom and Trevithick. Allan was apprenticed to a millwright in Montrose before joining Robert Stephenson & Co. at Newcastle in 1832. He then moved to George Potter of Liverpool, where he was involved in the construction of two, outside cylinder, double-framed engines for the Liverpool & Manchester Railway.

After several axle breakages on locomotives of Stephenson's design, William Buddicom, Locomotive Superintendent of the Grand Junction Railway and located at Edge Hill Works, had been charged with devising the use of straight axles on new locomotives, a feature which required the use of inclined outside cylinders, and thus two locomotives similar to those of L&MR were ordered by the GJR. At Edge Hill, the locomotive works were to be reorganised under William Buddicom. Buddicom subsequently resigned in 1841 and was replaced by Francis Trevithick. It may have been that Allan, as Workshop Foreman at Edge Hill, had suggested the use of outside cylinders to Trevithick, but it was the latter who continued development of the 'Crewe Type' locomotive at the new L&NWR Crewe Works when it opened in 1843.

Allan continued to serve under Francis Trevithick at Crewe, as Works Manager, but in 1863 he was obliged to resign, or be dismissed, for a serious misdemeanour of removing pages from the Works Meetings Minutes Book. Fortunately for Allan a vacancy arose on the SCR a few weeks later and he duly became Locomotive Superintendent of that company. His major contribution to locomotive design was in fact his straight link valve-gear, which he designed and introduced in 1854, and which incorporated elements of both the Stephenson and Gooch valve-gear designs. This was compact valve-gear giving excellent steam distribution, and which was widely used by the L&NWR, the Highland and other railway companies for the next fifty years.

Allan resigned from the Scottish Central upon its amalgamation with the Caledonian Railway, to become chief engineer of the Worcester Engine Company. Robert Sinclair, recalled by Locke from France, thereafter assumed responsibility as General Manager (unconfirmed) and Locomotive Superintendent for both undertakings until December 1856.

Robert Sinclair, 1847-1856

In 1841, Robert Sinclair of the Grand Junction Railway (GJR), an employee in the office of William Buddicom, went to France to assist Buddicom's new railway engineering company, Allcard, Buddicom & Co., in establishing a new locomotive works at Les Chartreux, where he became Works Manager, and later an even larger complex at Sotteville lès Rouen, on the outskirts of Rouen, for the Paris & Rouen Railway Co. In 1847, Sinclair was recalled by Locke to take over the post of Locomotive Superintendent of the Glasgow, Paisley & Greenock Railway at Greenock, following the accidental death of Edward Griffith Illbery. In addition, he became at that same time, Locke and Errington's 'Mechanical Superintendent' for both the Caledonian Railway and SCR.

In the years prior to 1850, the types and allocation of locomotives in use on the Caledonian Railway were largely unrecorded, and it is most likely that the early locomotives in use at Dalry Road, were based on the 'Crewe Type' 2-2-2 and 2-4-0 types, as first designed by William Buddicom for the Grand Junction Railway. No less than fifty-eight locomotives of the Class '4' 2-2-2s, and with some rebuilt 2-4-0s, as designed by Robert Sinclair, were at work on the Caledonian Railway by 1850. The 2-2-2s, notoriously difficult to balance, suffered from somewhat of an imbalance of weight distribution owing to the weight of the double-frames, smokebox and cylinders all being grouped over the front axle. Sinclair was not afraid of weight and indeed his obituary read as follows:

> *'It is only those familiar with locomotive details some forty years ago who can fully appreciate the influence of Mr. Sinclair's work on modern practice. In those days, Locomotive Engineers generally were far more afraid of a little weight in their engines as they now are, and there was hence a tendency towards excessive lightness. Mr. Sinclair did not share these views. He was an advocate for large wearing surfaces and ample strength and did not fear a little extra weight if he thought it necessary to give efficiency and durability. Nowadays the proportion of valve gear and cylinders which Mr. Sinclair used would not appear unusual, but forty years*

ago they provided areas of bearing surfaces far in excess of general practice.'

However, fourteen of these 2-2-2s were converted to 2-4-0s by extending the wheelbase by one foot and fitting a second set of driving wheels. No. 45, a Sinclair 2-2-2, is known to have been a casualty in an accident on the main line between Edinburgh and Glasgow via Carstairs whilst working an Anglo-Scottish passenger train, with perhaps the earliest ever casualties suffered by Dalry Road shed (see Chapter 14). The later 2-4-0s, built at Greenock in 1854/55, had very little Crewe influence other than the framing, being much larger than their English counterparts and it is quite likely that these engines were to become the mainstay of motive power at Dalry Road shed.

Sinclair was very much his own man, and whilst his engines had 'Crewe Type' framing, his designs owed little to the L&NWR and were generally much larger. He was a prolific designer, being responsible for 168 locomotives in all. He designed and had built some useful 2-2-2 locomotives with 7ft 2ins driving wheels (the Class '65'). Dalry Road had three engines of this class, No's 67-69.

In the later post-1870 days, all train working was most likely in the hands of the later Connor 7ft 2ins Class '42' 2-4-0s (see below). These engines proved to be incapable of maintaining time on the then new Edinburgh/Glasgow via Shotts services and were eventually replaced by four locomotives of the '88' Class of Connor 7ft 2ins 2-4-0s, No's 88-91, which had been originally transferred across to Glasgow from Greenock in 1875, ostensibly to work the main line trains between Glasgow and Carlisle. With the introduction of the four new Connor Class '113', 8ft 2ins singles later that same year, the four Class '88' engines were replaced on main line duties by the Class '113' engines and joined the Sinclair 7ft Singles, being allocated between Dalry Road and Carstairs sheds.

On the Caledonian Railway, where outside framed engines had been in the majority, Sinclair also introduced an inside framed design, based on engines of this type that he had encountered in France. These included outside cylinder 0-4-2s and 0-6-0s, the latter being practically unheard of in Britain, but on which he had been involved in 1846 before returning from France. Indeed, until the appointment of Dugald Drummond in 1882, the early Caledonian Railway was to be most unlike other British railways of the time, in having many locomotives in the fleet which were fitted with two outside cylinders, when the norm for the time was for inside cylinder engines. Caledonian passenger engines of the time were normally 2-2-2 Singles, and goods engines were either of 0-4-2 or 2-4-0 types, with the wheel configuration 0-6-0 being quite rare.

Amongst the earliest Sinclair locomotives were fifty-five Class '4' (between 1847 and 1850) and six Class '59' 2-2-2, locomotives (1848/52); thirty of the former were built at the Caledonian Railway workshops, Greenock, twelve at Vulcan Foundry, ten by Jones & Potts at their Viaduct Foundry, Newton Le Willows, and the final three by Scott, Sinclair Shipbuilding & Engineering at Greenock. These pioneer, double-framed, Caledonian Railway 2-2-2s, with two 15ins × 20ins outside cylinders and 6ft diameter driving wheels, were to be the mainstay of all the main line express passenger trains of the time between Glasgow and Carlisle, and would have been familiar as they were the only passenger locomotives to be allocated at the early Dalry Road shed. Sinclair followed this 'Crewe Type' design of 2-2-2 passenger engine faithfully, but he chose an 0-6-0 inside frame design of locomotive for an order to Jones & Potts for fifteen goods engines of a Class '96' which were built in 1849/50. They were not a success and after a short time he had them rebuilt, quite strangely for the time, but they proved to be one of the most useful mixed traffic designs in use. Subsequent enlargement of boilers and cylinders to 17ins × 24ins, and with 5ft 2ins driving wheels, they continued their good work.

Robert Sinclair tendered his resignation to the Caledonian Railway Board on 7th July 1856, having by this time held at least two senior positions – as Engineer of the Line (Chief Civil Engineer), and Locomotive Engineer. Anecdote also has it that Sinclair was, in addition to the foregoing, General Manager of the Caledonian Railway but that has never been confirmed. Caithness-born Sinclair, after a productive career with the Caledonian Railway, went on to be Locomotive Engineer for the Eastern Counties Railway until 1862, when he became the first Locomotive Superintendent of the newly-formed Great Eastern Railway. During his long tenure of office he became noted for introducing the Joy valve gear to the Caledonian Railway, using steel for axles and fitting roller bearings on coaching stock. Sinclair retired to Italy where he died in October 1898.

Benjamin Connor, 1856-1876

Sinclair was succeeded by Benjamin Connor (often alternatively spelt as Conner), another prolific locomotive designer and an experienced Locomotive Engineer, who came to the Caledonian Railway via the marine engineering works of Smith & Rogers in Govan, which he managed from joining that company. He joined Smith & Rogers in March 1854, having earlier been with Neilson & Co. Hyde Park Engine Works (later to become one of the major constituent companies which formed the soon to be world-famous North British Locomotive Company). During Connor's tenure of office, Neilson's obtained permission to construct an 8ft Single locomotive for the Great Exhibition in 1862, after which it was agreed that it would join the Caledonian Railway locomotive fleet. Neilson's reneged on this agreement and sold the locomotive to the Pasha of Egypt; the Caledonian sued for breach of contract and Neilson's paid them £500 in compensation. The locomotive, one of the most beautiful and distinctive of all 19th century locomotives, was to be the forerunner of Connor's own 2-2-2, outside cylinder, 8ft 2in driving wheel, double-framed, passenger locomotives, of the '76' and '113' classes of locomotives, always known as the 'Connor Singles', with the smokebox elegantly flaring out to meet the curve of the two outside cylinders.

Later, a number of the Class '76' locomotives (No's 76 to 87), twelve in all, were built at St. Rollox Works. Main line passenger train workings between Carlisle and Glasgow were to be the preserve of these twelve fine engines over the following years, but following the construction of an additional four similar Class '113' engines (see below) the sixteen engines of the combined two classes were split almost evenly in allocation between Carlisle (seven engines) and Glasgow (eight engines), with the unaccounted one being destined for Dalry Road shed. The four Class '113' engines displaced the four Class '88' engines on main line workings. It is known that Dalry Road had just one of the 8ft 2ins Single 2-2-2 engines allocated there, this being No. 78, which regularly worked over the heavily-graded line between Edinburgh and Carstairs with portion trains from Edinburgh to the south. The work of the 8ft Singles on the main line was largely unspectacular and pilot assistance was frequently required, but they remained relatively

CR Connor 8ft 2-2-2 No. 78 of the '76' Class and the only member of the class allocated to Dalry Road shed for working West Coast expresses between Edinburgh and Carstairs, seen here at the original Carlisle shed, as in use before 1872 when the construction of Kingmoor was authorised. *CRA Archives*

Connor 7ft 2ins 2-4-0 No. 111 of the '98' Class, allocated to Dalry Road shed in February 1869. This engine was scrapped as No. 111A in February 1900. *CRA Archives*

unknown in Edinburgh until 1886, apart from the single example mentioned above, when they were superseded on the main line duties and transferred to the Edinburgh and Glasgow route.

As mentioned above, a further four engines of the '113' Class were built in 1875, No's 113-116, and locomotives No's 88, 90 and 91 of the '76' Class, were accordingly moved to Dalry Road where they joined the Sinclair Class '88' 7ft 2ins Singles No's 67 and 69 for the working of the portion trains between Princes Street and Carstairs/Carlisle and over the Shotts route to Glasgow. It was on this latter route that two engines, No's 80 and 85, were written off after an accident (unspecified) on the Edinburgh/Glasgow line.

Within the Caledonian Railway of Connor's time there were no 'mixed traffic' locomotives as we know them but rather, from 1860 onwards, Connor designed and had put into service a long series of 2-4-0 engines, albeit that the driving wheel was as large as 6ft 2ins diameter. Within four classes he had constructed 107 engines

CR Connor 7ft 2ins 2-4-0 No. 117 of the '463' Class. Built by Neilson's as CR No. 466, it was renumbered in 1876 and withdrawn in 1923. The handsome, workmanlike lines of the engine are seen to advantage in this photograph, seen as rebuilt in 1894. *CRA Archives*

of this type, plus a further class of 2-4-0 locomotive with 5ft 2ins driving wheels numbering seventeen in all.

Between 1867 and 1874, a further five classes ('30', '42', '98', '466' and '472') of 2-4-0 locomotives with 7ft 2ins driving wheels were constructed, and Dalry Road had No's 99, 111 and 112 from around early 1869, followed by No. 47, a Connor 7ft 2ins passenger class 2-4-0 in May 1874. The 6ft 2ins 2-4-0 Class '615' locomotives successfully worked main line goods trains. Between the years 1878 and 1883 all these locomotives designed by Connor, displayed, down to each nut and bolt, the influence of the earlier 'Crewe Type' engines. Taken into the Caledonian fleet, they were to survive and be very successfully reboilered by no less than the great Dugald Drummond himself. Apart from local passenger workings, Dalry Road's allocation were used to pilot heavy West Coast express trains from Edinburgh as far as Cobbinshaw.

Connor was also responsible for designing and having built, by Neilson's in 1873/74, four special 0-4-4T passenger bogie locomotives (Class '488') to work branch lines, based on the American 'Forney' design where a large water tank was built into the rear section of the coal space. Numbered 488-491, they were later renumbered 167-170; No. 170 was assigned to the Balerno Branch, No's 168 and 169 worked the Leith Branch, and No. 167 was the spare engine, utilised on shed shunting duties. They were at a later time to appear on other branch lines within the Caledonian system.

George Brittain, 1876-1882

Connor was not a well man on his appointment and died in harness in 1876. He was succeeded by George Brittain, who was Operating Superintendent for the complete system, but as Locomotive Superintendent he did not exactly set the heather on fire. The long-standing influence of Allan in Caledonian locomotive matters continued into Brittain's days. As primarily a 'running' man, Brittain was to contribute very little to the Caledonian Railway locomotive stock during his tenure of office. He did, however, design a useful passenger engine, the 'Crewe Type' Class '130' 2-4-0 locomotive with 6ft 2ins driving wheels.

Brittain also designed a further 0-4-2 tender goods engine (Class '670'), thirty of which were built by Dübs. The class was known at Dalry Road, with the last of the class, LM&S No. 17020 (Caledonian No. 717, built in 1881) surviving there until 1932, having latterly been used as stationary boiler. This engine and a further one of the same class, No. 673, were allocated to Dalry Road shed and both made appearances on freight workings over the Balerno Branch. These engines ran with a mix of 4-wheeled and 6-wheeled tenders, with 4-wheeled tenders being the norm post-grouping.

As a matter of interest, in 1909 the Oakbank Oil Company considered purchasing one of these Class '670' 0-4-2 locomotives from the Caledonian Railway Co. at a cost of £1,200, in order to have a more powerful locomotive in their fleet, but even an 0-4-2 engine, plus tender, would have proved unsuitable for the private shale railways of the time, and the plan came to nought.

Dugald Drummond, 1882-1890

In 1882, the Caledonian Railway appointed Dugald Drummond, the doyen of Scottish locomotive engineers of the Victorian era and fresh from his successes with the North British Railway Company, as their Locomotive Superintendent at Cowlairs. By August of that year, Brittain, already a sick man, was effectively demoted in his post of Locomotive Superintendent by virtue of a 're-adjustment of his department' and he was required to work alongside Drummond after his appointment to the post. In November of that year, Brittain intimated to the Board that he wished to retire and left the service of the Caledonian Railway in December.

By Drummond's arrival at St. Rollox, locomotive affairs on the Caledonian Railway were less than satisfactory. Passenger workings

CR Brittain 6ft 2-4-0 No. 130 of the Class '130', built by Dübs in 1878. Seen here at Dalry Road shed in the company of what appears to be an unidentified Connor 7ft 2ins 2-4-0 engine plus an unidentified 4-4-0. *CRA Archives*

were more or less in the sole hands of the Connor's 8ft Singles and 2-4-0s, but these were increasingly proving unsuited to current requirements and frequently required pilot assistance. The new builds, numbering 257 over the previous twenty years, fell into four basic types:

107 × 6ft 2ins 2-4-0s formed of four separate classes
17 × 5ft 2ins 2-4-0s in one class
94 × 5ft 2ins 0-4-2s in two classes
39 × 5ft 2ins 0-6-0s in one class.

Drummond immediately set about designing a new 0-6-0 goods engine for the company. However, due to the reorganisation of the shop floor at St. Rollox on and from the 26th December 1882 – a 'reorganisation' which saw the demolition of the original works, apart from one section of the old north wall which was retained, and a complete new and larger works constructed on the site – construction of these new locomotives could not be carried out in-house. As a result, tenders for construction for the first fifteen of these new engines were invited from outwith the company, and the contract was awarded to Neilson's in mid-1883. By 19th January 1884, the first fifteen engines entered service. These engines of the '294' Class were the forerunners of the ubiquitous 'Jumbos', and Dalry Road was initially to receive a small allocation of one or two engines. They were to be the real workhorses of the Caledonian, with many surviving to see service into BR days.

At the same time, Drummond had designed a 4-4-0 passenger locomotive (Class '66') based upon his very successful '476' Class of 1876, designed for the North British Railway. Ten of these engines were included with the original tender documents for the '294' Class. Neilson again won the contract and the first engine arrived at St. Rollox on 22nd February 1884. By April, all locomotives of this new '66' Class had been delivered, bearing Caledonian Railway running numbers 66 to 75. A further batch of six engines was ordered in that same month. Initially Dalry Road was not to have an allocation. These fine engines had a very quick impact on Caledonian Railway train working and by the 1887 the success of Drummond's 'big engine policy' was obvious when, in the official analysis of locomotive expenditure, it was recorded that a requirement for sixty-nine pilot engines in 1883 had now been reduced to twenty-four, with further reductions being in the pipeline.

Drummond at this time designed a tank engine for use on the Caledonian Railway, and these were to be the very first 0-4-4T Caledonian Railway locomotives fitted with side tanks, known as the '171' Class. A total of twenty-four locomotives of this class were constructed at St. Rollox between 1884 and 1891, numbered 171-178, 228-231, 222-227 and 189-194; these were based on the earlier 4-4-0T Class '72' locomotives which he had designed for the NBR, but in this case the class was for light branch work. Dalry Road was allocated several engines of this class, which were employed on the Balerno Branch passenger services until 1899. These he followed with ten saddle tank engines, two built as 0-4-2STs (No's 263 and 264 for the Killin Branch) and the remaining eight as 0-4-0STs for general shunting use; all had outside cylinders.

By the end of 1884, Drummond had also had larger boilers fitted to the Connor 6ft 2ins '420' Class goods engines, along with Stirling cabs, and with some success. The rebuilt Class '420' engines went on to do some good work although no amount of rebuilding could enhance the tractive effort of the other Connor engines.

Now, there was what proved to be a momentous event in Caledonian locomotive design. In 1886 an International Exhibition was held in Edinburgh, and two entirely new Caledonian Railway locomotives – one, a 4-2-2 designed and built by Neilson's, and

CR Drummond Class '66' 4-4-0 No. 1062 (originally No. 62), seen in this photograph after rebuilding with a 'Dunalastair' boiler; it was duplicated in 1916 to make way on the capital list for the new Class '60' 4-6-0s at Dalry Road shed and was finally withdrawn in 1931 as LM&SR No. 14304 after 46 years of service; it was the last of the Drummond Class '66' in service. *CRA Archives*

ABOVE: Home again. Ex-CR No. 123 sits in Dalry Road shed yard, seventy-eight years after the exploits in the 1880 'Races to the North' when she was a Dalry Road locomotive. *Stuart Sellar*

RIGHT: The log of the outstanding running of CR No. 123 on the 16.08 Carlisle to Edinburgh Princes Street on 9th August 1888 during the East & West Coast Races to the North.

AUGUST 9th, 1888

CALEDONIAN RAILWAY · 4.8 p m CARLISLE–EDINBURGH

Load: 4 bogie coaches, 80 tons
Engine Drummond 4-2-2 No. 123

Miles		Time min. sec.	Speed m.p.h.
0·0	CARLISLE	0 00	—
4·1	Rockcliffe	5 35	62
8·6	Gretna Junc.	9 38	72
13·1	Kirkpatrick	14 07	57
	Brackenhill		54½
16·7	Kirtlebridge	17 46	65½
20·1	Ecclefechan	21 04	57
	Castlemilk		57
25·8	LOCKERBIE	26 46	64½
28·7	Nethercleugh	29 22	70
31·7	Dinwoodie	31 54	72
34·5	Wamphray	34 26	65/72
39·7	BEATTOCK	39 13	60
42·0	*Milepost 42*	41 44	52
44·0	,, *44*	44 20	43
46·0	,, *46*	47 17	39
48·0	,, *48*	50 23	38½
49·0	,, *49*	51 58	37½
49·7	*Beattock Summit*	53 04	36½
52·6	Elvanfoot	56 05	70
55·3	Crawford	56 42	64
57·8	Abington	59 52	70/64
63·2	Lamington	65 35	71½
66·9	SYMINGTON	69 04	62
68·5	Thankerton	70 29	73
70·0	*Leggatfoot*	71 45	65
72·0	*Milepost 72*	73 28	72
73·2	*Strawfrank Junc.*	74 44	slack
74·8	Carnwath	77 16	
78·0	*Milepost 78*	80 51	64
79·1	Auchengray	8 55	61
80·0	*Milepost 80*	82 51	58½
81·0	,, *81*	83 54	56½
82·2	Cobbinshaw	85 13	54½
85·3	Harburn	88 16	74
89·3	*Midcalder Junc.*	91 45	60
95·1	Currie Hill	96 58	70
98·4	Slateford	99 58	60
99·4	Merchiston	100 55	64
100·0	*Milepost 100*	101 28	66
100·6	PRINCES STREET	102 33	

the other, a 4-4-0 designed and built by Dübs – were specially constructed to be put on show. The general design and all the detail drawings for engine No. 123 were prepared by Neilson's without any intervention from Drummond. This engine had 7ft driving wheels and was modelled on Drummond practice; it appeared from Neilson's works in a full, new, special livery of Caledonian Blue and carried the Caledonian coat-of-arms on the tender. No. 124, the Dübs engine, was basically a '66' Class 4-4-0 and again carried full Caledonian Railway livery. Both were awarded Gold Medals and were highly acclaimed by the technical press of the day. After the Exhibition, both were purchased by the Caledonian and taken into St. Rollox Works. When No. 123, emerged, it was allocated to Dalry Road shed to work the 10.00 Edinburgh to London Express passenger train and other Edinburgh to London trains.

A Dalry Road star for several years, this was to be the only Caledonian Railway locomotive used between Carlisle and Edinburgh in the 1888 Races of northbound trains. No. 123 was, most likely, in the hands of Driver J. Dick of Dalry Road, although this has never been confirmed in any of the accounts of the racing days. No. 123 put up extraordinary times over the heavily graded line between Carlisle and Edinburgh, not just by fast downhill running but by sheer excellence in the uphill work. A log of the fastest time (9th August 1888) is included. No. 123 remained a Dalry Road star for several years, post racing days, and was employed mainly on the 10.00 London Express which it worked through to Carlisle. Fitted originally with a non-standard Neilson six-wheeled tender, limited water capacity (2,850 gallons) was to be an inherent problem until around 1888 when No. 123 received a new Drummond six-wheeled tender with a 3,130 gallon water capacity.

No. 124 proved to be less of a success. After the Exhibition it went to Polmadie where the early performance was marred by serious failures. Rebuilt in 1887, No. 124 went on to earn a high reputation on the Carlisle main line.

The '66' Class 4-4-0s had proved an immediate success, but coincidentally a need for further express passenger locomotives was to lead to Drummond, keen to determine for himself whether the claims being made regarding the economies of compounding could in fact be effected by simple engines working with a higher boiler pressure than usual for the time. Six new engines of the class were constructed in 1888/9, numbered 76-79, 84 and 87, for use on through trains between Carlisle and Aberdeen. In 1889, Drummond arranged a series of trials using four of the six new locomotives, No's 76, 77, 78 and 79, all fitted with higher pressure boilers and, once again, as with the 1888 Races, the 10.15 Edinburgh Princes Street to London express via Carlisle was the chosen working, returning with the corresponding Down train departing Carlisle at 16.30. Despite poor coal (there was a miners' strike at the time) the results were nothing short of brilliant. Dalry Road crews were in charge for all the runs and were running with trailing loads varying between 237 to 257 tons, to schedules demanding average speeds of 51.35 mph in the Up direction and 50.1 mph in the Down. Since the chosen train was the regular turn for Driver J. Dick of Dalry Road it is highly likely that he may have been the only driver involved. After the trials, the boiler pressure on the six locomotives was reduced to the standard boiler pressure of 160 psi. The last batch of the Class '66' locomotives (built in 1891) was also fitted with the standard 160 psi boilers. No. 77, along with No's 60 and 62 of the earlier Class '66' engines, and No. 113, one of the later 1891 engines of this class, were all to become a long-time favourite resident at Dalry Road shed.

Hugh Smellie, 1890-1891

In April 1890, Drummond resigned his position with the Caledonian Railway and was initially succeeded by Hugh Smellie, Locomotive Superintendent of the Glasgow & South-Western Railway on 1st September 1890, but unfortunately Smellie was dead within the year.

John Lambie, 1891-1895

Smellie's successor in June 1891 was John Lambie, who was an out and out running man with an intimate knowledge of Caledonian Railway locomotives and the men who worked them. It was Lambie who was to give the crews cab doors, longer handrails and additional footsteps, little things in themselves perhaps, in the greater scheme of locomotive design, but of great importance to easing the lot of his drivers and firemen. Lambie was to lean heavily on Drummond designs for new engines, but he did design and have built the very fine Class '13' 4-4-0 locomotive in 1894. These engines, six in all, worked with the same boiler pressure (160 psi) as the Drummond's and proved to be fast running and economical. In the 1895 Railway Races to the North, with the Drummond engines No's 79 and 90 working the more difficult Carlisle to Perth leg of the journey, and the Lambie 4-4-0 No. 17 running the final Perth to Aberdeen leg, new standards of high performance were set. Lambie was also responsible for the Class '211' 0-6-0STs and,

CR 4-4-0 No. 14, of the '13' Class, at Princes Street station. A Lambie version of Drummond's '66' Class, built with a Smellie boiler, these locomotives were introduced in 1894. This is an extremely handsome locomotive of a class which were to feature large in the Railway Races of 1895, to and from Aberdeen. Dalry Road had an allocation of four of the original '66' Class, No's 60, 62, 77 and 113. *CRA Archives*

CR McIntosh 4-4-0 No. 721 of the '721' ('Dunalastair I') Class runs into Princes Street on 20th September 1910 at the head of a Glasgow to Edinburgh working. *CRA Archives*

still closely following the Drummond principles, both classes of the condensing tank engines for the new underground Glasgow Central Low-Level Railway, these being the Class '19' 0-4-4Ts, numbering ten in all, and also the Class '29' 0-6-0Ts. These engines were to be the prototypes respectively of the 5ft 9ins passenger tanks and the 4ft 6ins mineral tanks, both of which were built in large numbers for the Caledonian Railway Company. Lambie was to establish a system of boiler interchange to reduce the time engines were in works for major overhaul. Still in harness, John Lambie died on 1st February 1895.

It is interesting to note from G.P. Neele's writings that over his years with the L&NWR and regularly accompanying Royal Train workings north from Carlisle, he specially commented that the Caledonian Railway always employed locomotives carrying *'the Splendid Royal Blue'* for working these Royal Trains. Neele also remarked on enjoying the company of the following Caledonian Railway Locomotive Engineers on various Royal Train workings over time, namely: Mr Connor, Mr Brittain, Mr Dugald Drummond, Mr Smellie and subsequently Mr Lambie, and all of them *'confident in the power of their respective engines to run well with the allocated burden, right up the Beattock Incline, and to keep time to a second'.*

JOHN FARQUHARSON MCINTOSH, 1895-1914

Another running man, McIntosh had been Assistant Locomotive Superintendent under Lambie and was appointed Locomotive Superintendent in the same month as Lambie died. He was an extremely practical man and set about making his mark by developing his own ideas about improving the Drummond breed of locomotives even further. Speed was the all-important watchword on the Caledonian Railway of that time, but instead of preaching the cult of expansive working, as had Drummond, McIntosh set about giving his drivers bigger boilers and marginally larger fire grate areas. Thus, in 1896, out of St. Rollox Works emerged the first of the immortal class of what were to become known as the 'Dunalastair' 4-4-0 locomotives; locomotives which, although not initially superheated, could be driven hard for hours on end and responded to any style of driving. They had an almost unlimited capacity for generating steam. In all, McIntosh, one of the greats in Caledonian Railway locomotive history, was responsible for the design and construction of some 627 locomotives, spread over twenty-seven different classes, during his tenure of office as Locomotive Superintendent.

In the first instance, fifteen engines of the '721' Class were turned out, later to be known as 'Dunalastair I', with No. 731 being allocated to Driver J. Dick at Dalry Road for use on his long time, single, daily booked working. This was the very demanding 10.15 from Princes Street to Carlisle, returning with the 16. 30 ex Carlisle, both stages of the journey requiring non-stop running over what was a very heavy road indeed and featuring average speeds in excess of 52½ mph in each direction.

McIntosh oversaw the completion of the order for the Lambie, 0-6-0 'Jumbos', but saw to it that the final two, No's 709 and 710, were fitted with the Westinghouse continuous, air-braking system, thus ensuring that the engines could be utilised on passenger train working. He also at that time ordered a further eighty-one engines of that class fitted with Westinghouse brakes as standard. The first three engines of this order, No's 711-713, were still essentially Lambie engines with the true McIntosh design locomotives commencing with No. 714. That and all subsequent engines of the class were fitted with inside brake rodding and other McIntosh innovations.

Between 1895 and 1900, McIntosh built a number of 0-4-4T tank engines, falling into three distinct types, including condensing 5ft 9ins 0-4-4Ts, non-condensing Class '439' 5ft 9ins 0-4-4T locomotives for suburban and branch line work throughout the Caley system, and Class '104' 4ft 6ins 0-4-4Ts for the Glasgow Cathcart Circle line and the Edinburgh Balerno Branch workings. Dalry Road received No's 104-109 and 167-170 from new, with the balance being shedded at Glasgow Polmadie, although allocations were to vary. These engines all carried the Caledonian Blue livery. In 1912, the first engines of Class '498' 0-6-0T with outside cylinders were out-shopped. Known in the west as the 'Braby Pugs', 'Wee Cuddies' or 'Beetlecrushers', they were designed by McIntosh in 1912 for dock work. Only two engines (Order No. Y100) were initially built, but Pickersgill, his successor, completed the build of twenty-one engines in total. Dalry Road was later allocated three engines of this class, one of which, No. 531 (later No. 57157), transferred across from Balornock shed in 1921 and transferred back to Greenock Ladyburn shed by 1945, was used at Leith North for working in the docks there; the other two, No's 514 and 515 (later 57172 and 57173) were used on unspecified duties. They were outstandingly good and versatile locomotives, capable of

CR Class '766' 'Dunalastair II' 4-4-0 No. 775 at Dalry Road shed. Dalry Road had but one of this class, allocated to Driver Dick in the top link. Although the locomotive is still in its Caledonian livery the photograph was taken post 1923 as indicated by the LM&SR livery on the 30-ton coal wagon on the coaling stage. *CRA Archives*

CR 4-4-0 Class '900' 'Dunalastair III' No. 887 at Dalry Road shed. *CRA Archives*

CR McIntosh Class '140' 'Dunalastair IV' 4-4-0 No. 923 of Dalry Road shed, cleaned to perfection, starts the 14.00 'Corridor' West Coast express train out of Edinburgh Princes Street. The burnished edges of the smokebox wingplates and burnished smokebox door hinges, personalisation features of many Caledonian locomotives, are particularly well illustrated here. *CRA Archives*

working over severely curved lines, down to a minimum radius of a three-chain curve.

In 1897, McIntosh ordered a further fifteen 4-4-0 passenger locomotives with larger cylinders than those carried by the fifteen Class '721' 'Dunalastair I's; numbered 766 to 780, these were to be known as 'Dunalastair II's (Class '766'). Edinburgh Dalry Road was allocated two locomotives, Nos. 768 and 769, for a short time and the former, No. 768, becoming the regular engine of Driver Will Stavert, an up and coming star of the shed. Indeed, so successful were these engines that the Belgian government approached McIntosh to supply similar locomotives for the Belgian railways. However, on the Caledonian Railway lines, drivers seemed not to like the Class '766' locomotives as much as the earlier Class '721' and later Class '900', claiming heavy coal consumption as the reason. On tests, the class had returned coal consumption figures of 49.6 lbs/mile, although inferior quality coal was cited in defence of this rather high figure.

In 1899 came a class of further improved and more powerful Dunalastairs, the '900' Class, soon to become known unofficially as the 'Dunalastair III's. Dalry Road was allocated No's 896 and 899. At this time the attentions of McIntosh and St. Rollox Works were turned towards construction of even larger locomotives for the Caledonian Railway, and in 1903 two large but experimental 4-6-0 locomotives, No's 49 and 50, designed to handle the heaviest express trains between Glasgow and Carlisle, emerged from St. Rollox Works. With these turning out to be less than an unqualified success, in 1904 construction of new 4-4-0 locomotives was commenced once more with the building of a new class of 4-4-0, the '140', known as the 'Dunalastair IV's. These proved to be extremely capable machines. Dalry Road received No's 140 and 141. Once again, Driver Will Stavert was to be privileged and was allocated No. 140, with No. 141 going to his counterpart, Driver W. Watts (see Chapter 14). A total of sixty-five engines of the four classes comprising the 'Dunalastairs' were constructed at St. Rollox and, of these, four of the 'Dunalastair II's, four of the 'Dunalastair III's and three 'Dunalastair IV's were later rebuilt with superheaters.

Dalry Road was also to have a further two locomotives of the '140' Class, as built new in 1908, allocated – No's 923 and 924.

In 1906 the '903' Class 4-6-0 locomotives emerged, known as the 'Cardean' Class, of which No. 905 was initially allocated to Dalry Road shed (see Chapter 7).

Between 1906 and 1907, McIntosh designed and built a further fifteen engines with the 4-6-0-wheel configuration comprising his Class '908' engines (ten) and his Class '918' engines (five). One engine of the '918' Class was allocated to Dalry Road shed from new, this being No. 921, whilst the shed was also to have two engines of the former class, No's 916 and 917. These Class '918s' were basically an extended version of his Class '55' locomotives, with a lengthened trailing overhang and outer firebox, and built for fast freight workings. The Class '908' was a larger wheeled version of the Class '918'.

Though a running man like his predecessors, McIntosh was prolific designer and between 1895 and his retiral in 1914, he had a hand in designing and building twenty-eight different classes of

Ex-CR McIntosh 4-6-0 No. 14752 (CR No. 903), the famous *Cardean*, makes an impressive sight at the head of a stopping passenger train for Glasgow Central, at Edinburgh Princes Street. This was a Polmadie locomotive and the driver, obviously proud of his charge, rests a nonchalant arm on the running plate as he takes a break from some oiling up before departure. *CRA Archives*

Ex-CR Class '714' 0-6-0 No. 17432 (originally CR No. 333) one of the very last of the class built in 1897 as a Westinghouse fitted Passenger/Goods engine (the CR did not use Mixed Traffic designation) stands waiting its next turn of duty at Dalry Road shed. *CRA Archives*

An unidentified ex-CR Pickersgill Class '60' 4-6-0 heads an Edinburgh District trip working, E107, past Midcalder Junction and takes the Down Glasgow via Shotts line. *Author's collection*

Caledonian Railway locomotives, many of which saw service at Dalry Road. His Standard Passenger Tank engine, the Class '439' 0-4-4T, was well represented at Dalry Road and continued in service well into BR days, as did the very useful Class '714' 0-6-0s, known as 'blue Jumbos'. The latter, although heavy goods engines, also appeared on the odd passenger working around Edinburgh. His later Class '812' 0-6-0s, with 'Dunalastair I' boilers, cylinders, valve chests and exhaust pipes but based on his 'Dunalastair II' Class, were to prove the outstanding heavy goods engines of the Caledonian Railway. The first seventeen engines of the class, being used mostly on passenger train working, were Westinghouse fitted and painted Caledonian Railway blue, and were still to be seen, hard at work, well into BR days.

William Pickersgill, 1914-1923

McIntosh retired in 1914 and was succeeded by William Pickersgill, Locomotive Superintendent of the Great North of Scotland Railway (GN of SR). Pickersgill took over the reins at St. Rollox on 4th May 1914 and was to be faced with the single biggest crisis since 1882 – the period when Brittain, not a well man, had been at the reins as Locomotive Superintendent at St. Rollox but had failed to rejuvenate the Caledonian Railway's ailing locomotive fleet – when World War One broke out later in the year, with the consequential loss of many skilled men to the Armed Forces, locomotive maintenance suffered and the availability of suitable motive power became critical.

But in these critical days the Caledonian Railway was to receive a most welcome windfall when in October 1915 it were able to purchase the six 4-6-0, ill-fated, Highland Railway 'River' Class locomotives, as designed by F.G. Smith and built by Hawthorn, Leslie of Hebburn, Tyneside. Upon purchase, these locomotives were identified as the Caledonian Railway Class '938' and were numbered by the Caledonian as No's 938-943. Of these, four were shedded at Glasgow (Balornock), whilst the remaining two were allocated to Perth. The Balornock engines worked, in the main, Glasgow to Carlisle freights, whilst the Perth duo were to spend most of their time working fitted goods trains between Perth and Glasgow and Carlisle. Unfortunately, there has been nothing found to suggest that these engines ever visited Edinburgh.

The construction of twelve new '944' Class 4-6-2T engines was authorised in November 1915 and two engines were allocated to Polmadie shed for use on passenger workings between Glasgow Central and Edinburgh Princes Street. They proved to be very heavy on coal.

Between 1916 and 1917 the new Pickersgill Class '60' 4-6-0s emerged, six in all, and numbered 60-65. They were allocated to Glasgow Balornock, Polmadie, Carlisle and Perth, but the Carlisle engines worked through to both Glasgow and Edinburgh, so the engines were known at Dalry Road and were often seen working Edinburgh District Trip Diagrams. At a later time, one or two were actually allocated there. These locomotives became known as 'Greybacks', a nickname related to the Scottish term for the common woodlouse.

It was to be 1918 before Dalry Road was to be allocated new locomotives. These came from the first batch of a two-part order for express passenger 4-4-0 locomotives, with the first engines emerging from the North British Locomotive Company Atlas

Ex-CR Pickersgill 4-4-0 No. 14471 (CR No. 932) of the '113' Class, a Dalry Road engine, awaits departure from Edinburgh Princes Street with an express passenger train. *CRA Archives*

Works, numbered 928-937, whilst the second batch of locomotives, plus all the tenders for the whole class, were built at St. Rollox. No's 932 and 933 were quickly allocated to Dalry Road shed. Very similar in design to McIntosh 4-4-0s, they maintained the Caledonian distinctiveness. They were to prove somewhat sluggish when running downhill but did display a certain liveliness when running uphill.

Pickersgill also built further McIntosh Class '498' 0-6-0T engines (see above), three of which went to Dalry Road for dock and Balerno Branch working. He also had a further batch of 0-4-4T engines constructed (four initially, No's 159, 161-163), but an additional nine engines of the same class were to follow thereafter, numbered 418, 425, 426, 430-36. His final contribution to the Caledonian Railway fleet of locomotives was to be four large, Class '956', 4-6-0 three-cylinder locomotives, all fitted with derived valve gear, numbered 956-959. Performance was to be disappointing in the extreme, with the derived valve gear being a constant source of trouble.

The reasons for their construction and the subsequent implied criticism have been fully explored in an excellent book written by Donald Peddie,[1] a noted member of the Caledonian Railway Association.

1 *William Pickersgill and the Caledonian Railway '956' Class Locomotives: An Objective Assessment*, by Donald Peddie, published by Lightmoor Press and the Caledonian Railway Association, 2016.

THE LONDON, MIDLAND & SCOTTISH RAILWAY YEARS

GEORGE HUGHES, 1923-1925

George Hughes, the final CME of the L&YR, was upon its amalgamation with the L&NWR on 1st January 1922 to become the last CME of the L&NWR. He was faced with a most difficult task of overcoming the influence of, primarily, the Midland Railway's Derby Works on locomotive design, an influence which was to plague the early LM&SR after the Grouping of 1st January 1923. A new single company formed by the integration of no less than six companies was inevitably a challenge, but the dominant influence of the Midland had saddled the new company with rather small passenger locomotives, mainly of 4-4-0 design and inappropriate for the heavier trains, both freight and passenger, of the time.

Hughes' main contribution to the motive power at Dalry Road proved to be his well-liked Class '5MT' 2-6-0 design of 1926, but built under the direction of Fowler, forever to be known as 'Crabs' because of their large outside 21ins × 26ins cylinders and the peculiar side to side oscillation which developed when working hard or in running. Pairing with Fowler straight-sided tenders which were narrower than the cab width on the engines gave the footplate an exposed feel as it was possible to sit on the seats provided and have a clear view back along the train. With 5ft 6ins driving wheels and boiler pressure of 180 psi, they developed 26,580 lbs of tractive effort.

Dalry Road were to have a maximum of three examples of this class in BR days, with two having been allocated there from new in 1926.

Hughes, and Fowler who followed him, perpetuated construction of 4-4-0 three-cylinder compound locomotives, with a further series of based on the 1924 ex-Midland Railway Deeley design. The new build compounds had modified dimensions and reduced boiler mountings, and Dalry Road enjoyed a number of these fine locomotives in both LM&SR and later into BR days, with No's 919 and 920 allocated there from new.

SIR HENRY FOWLER, 1925-1931

Fowler was deputy to Hughes and on taking over the reins as CME was to be no more successful in co-ordinating the design, building and repair practices of the former constituent companies. He did, however, introduce both a production-line system for locomotive repairs, which reduced the 'in works' down time, and a policy of standardisation which eliminated many of the smaller locomotive classes. He was noted for his three-cylinder 'Royal Scot' Class 4-6-0 '6P' locomotives, introduced in 1935. The class was deemed to be *'more than adequate'* when introduced, giving power with excellent economy, until steam leakage problems with the wide ringed pistons resulted in ever increasing coal consumption. They were also prone to hot axlebox problems. The whole class were later rebuilt and transformed by Stanier, becoming Class '7P' engines. Stanier replaced the problematic axleboxes with his own design of steel box, with oil entering from the keep rather than from the crown. The 'Royal Scots', original and rebuilt, were no strangers to Dalry Road shed although none were ever allocated there.

Fowler had also been responsible for a fleet of sturdy Class '4F' 0-6-0 freight locomotives based on standard Midland design. Post-grouping, in 1924, there was a development of more of these very useful engines which benefitted Dalry Road shed, for it was to have four in BR days for some time. He also designed a very useful class of parallel boiler 2-6-4T engines, some of which were to dominate the Glasgow Central to Gourock and Wemyss Bay services. 2-6-4T locomotives were to become commonplace at Dalry Road in later years, but these were of a later Fairburn design, of which Dalry Road was to have a welcome and highly regarded allocation.

In 1930, Fowler was to rebuild a number of ex-L&NWR 1912 'Claughton' 4-6-0 passenger locomotives as parallel boiler Class '5XP' 4-6-0s and known as the 'Patriot' Class, followed by a further fifty new builds in the same class. The 'Patriot' Class was to become well known at Dalry Road, working into Edinburgh, typically on both through Anglo-Scottish express workings from the industrial north-west of England and Welsh Rugby Specials (see Chapter 9). In 1928, Fowler designed and introduced a Class '2F' 0-6-0T, short wheelbase, outside cylinder, engine for shunting in dock areas, the build totalling ten in all; Dalry Road were to receive, in the fullness of time, two engines of this class, No's 47162 and 47173. No. 47162 was employed at Leith and Granton docks before moving, along with the diagrammed working, to St. Margarets shed upon closure of Dalry Road shed, whilst No. 47163 was dedicated to the daily goods workings over the Balerno Branch.

In 1930 Fowler was promoted to a research and development post within the LM&SR, and his former post was covered by E.H. Lemon, the company's Carriage & Wagon Engineer, but merely as a temporary measure, pending a new appointment.

Fowler '2F' tank No. 47163 shunting at Colinton on 30th January 1954. *Stuart Sellar*

Un-rebuilt Fowler 'Royal Scot' 4-6-0 locomotive No. 46137 *The Prince of Wales's Volunteers (South Lancashire)* of Crewe North shed, at Dalry Road having worked the morning express to Edinburgh earlier in the day. The engine will remain on shed until it takes up its return working on the morning Birmingham the next day. *Stuart Sellar*

Ex-LM&SR Fowler Class '2F' 0-6-0T with outside cylinders No. 47162, designed for dock working, is seen here standing outside St. Margarets shed, Edinburgh, to where it had been transferred upon closure of Dalry Road shed in 1965 and from where it was employed in shunting duties at Leith and Granton docks. *Author's collection*

Ex-LM&SR un-rebuilt 'Patriot' Class 4-6-0 No. 45503 *The Royal Leicestershire Regiment* of Crewe North shed enters the ashpits at Dalry Road after working north on the morning Birmingham New Street to Princes Street express, 15th July 1955. *Stuart Sellar*

SIR WILLIAM A. STANIER, 1932-1944

The choice for the new appointment was to be an inspired one for the LM&SR. William Arthur Stanier was a GWR, Swindon-trained locomotive engineer. Headhunted (to use modern parlance) by the LM&SR in the year following Lemon's elevation, he was appointed CME of the LM&SR on and from the 1st January 1932, with a mandate to design and produce a range of standard locomotives having the least number of separate classes. Such locomotives were to be economical in fuel and maintenance charges, and capable of working long, through turns. In short, the Chairman of the LM&SR sought a significant reduction in the total locomotive stock of the company. Stanier was faced with a Herculean task on two fronts: firstly to weld together a strong team from the previous disparate, warring factions from the former Midland Railway at Derby and the L&NWR at Crewe in particular, and, thereafter, to deliver a modern locomotive fleet to meet exacting standards. This he was to do in no small measure.

Over the West Coast Main Line on the former Caledonian Railway stretch between Carlisle and the north – very much familiar ground to Dalry Road crews – there was a growing need for engines which could handle passenger trains loaded up to 500 tons tare without any assistance over the gruelling climb of Beattock Bank, and still having the capacity to cope with accelerated timings. So in the early 1930s came Stanier's first new Pacific locomotive, the 'Princess Royal' Class '7P'. With 6ft 6ins driving wheels, four 16¼ins × 28ins cylinders and a boiler pressure of 250 psi, these engines developed a nominal tractive effort of 40,285 lbs. Only two engines appeared from Crewe Works initially, No's 6200 *The Princess Royal* and 6201 *Princess Elizabeth*, both of which were put to work between London Euston and Glasgow Central. Never noted as free steaming engines, they were re-boilered in 1935 and their performance was transformed. A further ten engines followed in the summer and early autumn of 1935, all carrying names of ladies of the British Royal Family. In November of 1936, No. 6201 worked a special test train of 225 tons from London to Glasgow non-stop in 5 hours 53 minutes and 42 seconds (353.7 minutes); it returned south on the following day, with the same load, in a mere 344.1 minutes. As a class they were not entirely unknown at Dalry Road but were to appear far less frequently than their soon-to-appear bigger sisters.

In 1934 there came what was to be perhaps Stanier's finest design of Mixed Traffic ('5MT') 4-6-0 locomotive, soon to be known everywhere as the Stanier 'Black Five'. Based on a GWR Swindon Churchward boiler, but with the safety valves mounted on the Belpaire firebox, these locomotives with two 18½ins × 28ins cylinders and 6ft driving wheels were soon to be seen working heavy mineral trains, express freight trains and express passenger trains, and all with inordinate ease. A total of 842 were built and post-nationalisation they were to be found at work in every corner of every region across British Railways. Dalry Road had a modest allocation which they used indiscriminately on both heavy mineral and express passenger trains alike.

Also in 1934, further locomotives of Stanier's planned Standard fleet were to emerge in the shape of a tapered-boiler version of the 'Patriots', known as Stanier Class '5X' ('6P') 4-6-0 or the 'Jubilees'. Fitted with small superheat, domeless boilers, three 17ins × 26ins cylinders and 6ft 9ins driving wheels, a total of 113 new locomotives were ordered straight off the drawing board – but these at first

Ex-LM&SR Stanier 'Black Five' No. 44994 of Dalry Road shed brings a Princes Street branch passenger train into Murrayfield station in February 1961, whilst a Leith North train has just departed. *Stuart Sellar*

Ex-LM&SR Stanier 'Jubilee' Class '5X' No. 45714 *Revenge* of Carlisle Kingmoor shed, fitted with small, straight-sided tender, prepares to leave the shed yard at Dalry Road in July 1952. *J.L. Stevenson/Hamish Stevenson*

failed to live up to expectations, with early steaming troubles being prevalent. The fault lay in the small fourteen-element superheater, which was incapable of preventing the carrying over of water if the boiler water level was too high when the engine was starting, let alone providing a sufficient degree of superheat in running. Also, the draughting arrangement was not ideally proportioned, but a simple alteration to the blast pipe orifice and the provision of a larger superheater system soon put matters right, and they settled down to give reasonably good work on fast passenger services and, again, were to be widely distributed across the LM&SR system. In retrospect, the inherent problems outlined above must surely have cost the LM&SR much, in all the alterations required, and indeed some may well argue that the problems were never completely resolved. These engines, numbering 190 in total, were as a class to be regular visitors to Dalry Road shed.

In 1937, Stanier outlined his plans for a super-Pacific locomotive to be known as the 'Princess Coronation' '7P' Class. With larger boilers than the earlier Princesses and offering a large increase in heating surface, four 16½ins × 28ins cylinders, 6ft 9ins driving wheels and developing some 40,000 lbs of tractive effort, the earliest of the engines of the class emerged from Crewe with streamlining, following L&NER practice in what was the Coronation year of King George V. The early finish was in blue with silver stripes, the blue being chosen to represent the former, splendid Caledonian Railway blue of yesteryear, though later streamlined members of the class carried the LM&SR crimson lake with gold stripes. In all, a total of thirty-eight locomotives of this class were constructed, twenty-four of which were streamlined (No's 6220-6229 and 6235-6248), and the final two of the class, which did not emerge until 1947, fitted with roller bearing developments and detail alterations to the design of H.G. Ivatt. This class of locomotive was a regular daily visitor to Dalry Road shed.

In 1943, Stanier set in motion the redesign and rebuilding of Fowler's parallel boilered 'Royal Scot' Class 4-6-0s. This rebuilding was to leave very little of the original locomotives, as they acquired a new taper-boiler with double chimney, new cylinders and altered valve settings. After rebuilding, these engines proved very capable, free steaming machines and, as a class of locomotive, were also to be regular visitors at Dalry Road shed.

Charles E. Fairburn, 1944-1945

Stanier was transferred to the Ministry of Production as a full-time Scientific Adviser in 1944, and it thus fell to Fairburn, an electrical engineer, to oversee the rebuilding of the 'Royal Scot' Class although the day-to-day detail was to be addressed by H.G. Ivatt.

In 1935, a Stanier-designed three-cylinder 2-6-4 '4MT' engine entered service, followed by a two-cylinder version of same constructed at Crewe. Some ten years later, in 1945, Fairburn also introduced a two-cylinder 2-6-4T, which was a development of the earlier Stanier version, and whilst these engines are credited to C.E. Fairburn, it is safe to assume that Ivatt had had significant input. Dalry Road was to receive an allocation of six of these fine locomotives and they were much loved by their crews. Employed mainly on fast inter-city services, local passenger workings and piloting duties, they were a mainstay of the shed for many years and became very popular with the operating authorities because of the flexibility they offered in train working.

Ex-LM&SR 'Princess Coronation' Pacific locomotive No. 46249 *City of Sheffield* awaits departure from Edinburgh Princes Street station with a stopping passenger train bound for Glasgow Central, via Shotts. Ease of road access to platform level is clearly shown to fore. *Stuart Sellar*

Fairburn 2-6-4T No. 42269 of Dalry Road shed brings an Edinburgh to Glasgow stopping passenger service into Merchiston station on 4th May 1955. *Stuart Sellar*

H.G. IVATT, 1945-1951

Ivatt was destined to oversee the LM&SR locomotive matters through the period of Nationalisation. His influence at Dalry Road was largely confined to his rebuilding of some fifteen of the Fowler 'Patriot' Class with large taper boilers, new cylinders and double chimneys, duly re-classed as '7P' engines and, again, as such, fairly regular visitors to the shed.

THE BRITISH RAILWAY YEARS

R.C. BOND, 1951

After Nationalisation, R.C. Bond was given tenure of office as Chief Officer (Mechanical Engineering), with E.S. Cox as Executive Officer (Design). R.A. Riddles was an L&NWR trained locomotive engineer with an impressive war-time record of producing steam locomotives for military use overseas, exemplified in his ex-WD 2-8-0 and 2-10-0 heavy freight locomotives which numbered around 1,000; most were returned to work on BR and were to be frequent visitors to Dalry Road shed. Riddles, as Executive Member with responsibility for Mechanical Engineering and the Chairman of the BR Standards Committee, was more or less given free rein to work with Bond and Cox to design and introduce a series of new, robust, standard steam locomotives, with optimum route availability for BR in the post nationalisation period. As a result, he went on to design and build some 999 new locomotives of varying power classifications, and this took place *after* more than 1,500 new steam locomotives, to the designs of former railway companies, had been constructed in BR days. This duplication was an unnecessary complication. All Riddles Standard engines, with the exception of '8P' No. 71000 and the whole of the Class '9F' 2-10-0s, were classed as Mixed Traffic engines with power classification ranging from 7 down to 2, and whilst these engines certainly met the criteria of 'standardisation', they were in the main based on ex-LMS practice and design. A few designs, such as the '6MT' 4-6-2 'Clans' in particular, were not really necessary and never were to prove either popular or successful, whilst the '5MT' 4-6-0, a mere copy of the Stanier '5MT', proved a useful engine, as were the '4MT' 2-6-4Ts, a class which again echoed earlier Stanier and Fairburn design. Not only were few of the Standard range of locomotives really necessary, even fewer could match the designs of the old company locomotives as built by BR. The exception was the Class '9F', of which 251 were constructed. Known to enthusiast as 'Spaceships', they proved their worth on both freight and fast passenger workings.

BR Standard locomotives were known at Dalry Road, with the shed latterly being allocated one or two Standard '4MT' 2-6-4T engines, while Standard Pacifics of both the '6MT' 'Clan' and '7MT' 'Britannia' classes, and of course the Standard '5MT' 4-6-0s, appeared on an almost daily basis.

7 DALRY ROAD SHED: LOCOMOTIVE ALLOCATION OVER THE YEARS

Dalry Road shed was fated always to have a modest allocation of locomotives, especially when compare with the two neighbouring NBR depots of St. Margarets (64A) and Haymarket (64B), the former having in excess of 220 locomotives allocated and the largest engine allocation in Scotland, and the latter some eighty-five locomotives including no less than thirty-seven Pacific engines. The Dalry Road allocation hovered around forty-five to sixty locomotives and peaked at seventy engines in the mid 1930s, with all being wholly appropriate to the traffic needs of the areas served by the shed. No Pacific locomotives were ever allocated; indeed, no locomotives with a higher power classification than a '5MT' were allocated to the shed. In June 1906, and for a very short period of time only, No. 905, one of the magnificent McIntosh '903' Class 4-6-0 engines, known to all as the 'Cardean' Class, was allocated to the top link (Driver Will Stavert) at the shed. Sadly, as it was not being used to its full potential there it was quickly transferred away to Perth, later being replaced by two locomotives of the '140' Class. These 'Dunalastair IV's, proved more than adequate for the traffic needs of the shed, becoming long time denizens, still in use in the 1950s. And so, the scene was set.

That is not to say that larger and more powerful locomotives were strangers to Dalry Road, or that its footplate crews were not proficient in handling the larger classes of both Caledonian and LM&SR passenger locomotives. From their earliest introduction, and in their latter guise, the Stanier Class '7P' streamlined 'Princess Coronation' Pacific locomotives were to be well known in Edinburgh Princes Street and to Dalry Road crews, as will be discussed in full later.

Equally, in January and February, when the Five Nations international rugby competitions were held, and when either England or, more so, Wales were playing against Scotland at Murrayfield, a regular procession of Rugby Special trains arrived from south of the border, hauled by a selection of 'Patriots', 'Royal Scots' and 'Jubilees', all of which were coaled and serviced (and frequently stabled) at Dalry Road pending back workings. At this time of year, Dalry Road became a veritable Mecca for railway enthusiasts (see Chapter 8).

With many frequent local passenger branch workings in and around Edinburgh, Dalry Road enjoyed a selection of the ubiquitous ex-Caledonian 0-4-4T locomotives, including those specially constructed for the Balerno Branch. All performed a lot of hard work and gave good service over the years.

For heavy freight working, Dalry Road shed was allocated the early Drummond and Lambie 0-6-0 tender engines known to all and sundry as 'Jumbos'. However, a trend developed in LM&SR days, continuing afterwards, of lumping the McIntosh Class '812' 0-6-0s into this same soubriquet. This no Caledonian driver or fireman would ever have done, but it became common elsewhere to see McIntosh's great freight engines being referred to as 'Jumbos'.

A welcome return to home territory for CR 4-2-2 No. 123. Taken from store in St. Rollox Works, Glasgow, and returned to full working order, here No. 123 in immaculate and utterly splendid CR blue livery pauses at Slateford with two restored ex-CR coaches on 18th March 1955. *Stuart Sellar*

EARLY DAYS

Caledonian Railway locomotives allocated to Dalry Road in the early days post 1848 have already been mentioned, ranging from the Class '4' 2-2-2s of Sinclair design, through the magnificent Connor 8ft Singles and 7ft Singles to his fine 2-4-0s. Indeed, the early Sinclair Class '4' 2-2-2s were to be the mainstay of early express passenger workings allocated to Dalry Road shed, being required to work what were the fastest trains of the day – the passenger services over the 27½ miles between Edinburgh and Carstairs and return in a mere 32 minutes, involving an overall average speed of 51.25 mph, with trains consisting of four coaches and weighing 35 tons. Not surprisingly, time was often lost.

Caledonian Railway No. 123, the Neilson 4-2-2, is known to have been at Dalry Road shed during the 1880 'Races' and beyond. The six higher-pressure 4-4-0s, No's 76-79, 84 and 67, designed and built by Drummond, and based on his '66' Class, all ran out of Dalry Road shed during the comparative trials between Edinburgh Princes Street and Carlisle. Then came the great days of the inspired McIntosh 'Dunalastair' 4-4-0s, with Dalry Road having a representative of each of the four versions plus, for a short time, one engine of the 4-6-0 'Cardean' Class. The 'Dunalastairs' – both Class III and Class IV versions, were to be used for Royal Train workings by Dalry Road over many years. Dalry Road also had much freight work and was duly allocated locomotives which were entirely suited to that purpose.

LEFT: CR Connor 6ft 2-4-0 No. 127 of the '583' Class of goods engine; built by Dübs it originally carried the number 586. It is seen here at its home shed of Dalry Road, standing amongst what appears to be an ever-increasing pile of ashes. This locomotive was retrospectively fitted with Westinghouse brake equipment to work passenger trains. *CRA Archives*

BELOW: A finely turned out example of the CR '721' Class ('Dunalastair I'): No. 722 enters Edinburgh Princes Street with a portion of a Down West Coast express, which may be the Down TPO. *CRA Archives*

Superheated 4-4-0 No. 14434 (ex-CR No. 894) of the '900' Class 'Dunalastair III' heads an Edinburgh to Glasgow service at Princes Street station. The engine is in very clean condition with attractive smokebox embellishments, maintaining a long Caledonian tradition. This locomotive had been superheated in 1916. *CRA Archives*

There were also four quite unique locomotives allocated to Dalry Road after the opening of the Balerno Branch in August 1874; these were the Connor Class '488' bogie 0-4-4WT locomotives, built by Neilson & Co. – No's 488, 489, 490 and 491, later renumbered 167, 168, 169 and 170. The first two were sent to Stirling and Perth for a time, but when the Balerno Branch finally opened the four engines of the class were transferred back to Dalry Road, where No. 170 was assigned to the Balerno Branch. No's 168 and 169 frequently worked the Leith Branch, and No. 167 was the spare engine and shunting pilot at Dalry Road shed. No. 170 was withdrawn in 1900, 1168 and 1169 in 1907, and 1167 in 1915. In short, Dalry Road shed could be said to have had a custom-built allocation of appropriate motive power for all occasions.

At the Grouping

Despite becoming part of the new London, Scottish & Midland Railway Company (LM&SR) in January 1923, it was not to be until a full year later that the former Caledonian territory of the LM&SR, Northern Division, finally accepted the reality of the grouping and started painting engines in the new company livery, having continued to paint locomotives in Caledonian blue during 1923. Continuance of the use of blue livery could well be ascribed to the fact that the Caledonian Railway was to be a somewhat later member than the other constituent companies of the group because of a legally disputed reason. The first Caledonian locomotives to be seen in the new LM&SR livery and numbering at the shed were Class '812' 0-6-0s No's 17245 and 17399. No firm allocation for Dalry Road shed is recorded for the year 1923, but it is known that ex-Caledonian Railway locomotives were in the majority.

Dalry Road engines observed on shed in January 1924 and continuing to carry 'Caley' blue were:

- Class '812' 0-6-0s No's 822, 870 and 873
- 'Dunalastair III' No. 889
- 'Dunalastair IV' No. 141
- Class '918' 4-6-0 No. 921
- Class '104' 0-4-4Ts No's 109 and 167.

An evening shed visit by an enthusiast in 1923 revealed the following twenty engines 'on shed'.

- Class '728' 0-6-0T No. 489
- Class '812' 0-6-0 tender goods engines, eight in total as follows: No's 333, 822, 858, 838, 869, 872, 873 and 876
- Class '264' 0-6-0T No. 615
- Class '66' No. 1062 (formerly No. 62)
- Class '900' No. 889
- Class '294' No. 323
- McIntosh 'Pug' No. 1162
- Brittain '670' No. 1672
- Unknown. No. 1577
- Class '488' No's 167/170.

Earlier that same day, Dalry Road had turned out 'Dunalastair III' 4-4-0, No. 889 for the 10.00 Princes Street to London, piloted over Cobbinshaw and Beattock summits by Class '66' 4-4-0 No. 62; both engines then worked home from Carlisle, and both were on shed by the time of the visit. Indeed, the 'Dunalastair' Class engines (all variations) continued to be used on West Coast expresses both as train engines, and later as pilot engines, giving very good service for the duration of their days at Dalry Road shed.

The ubiquitous 0-4-4T engines, of which there were many, were conspicuous by their absence, being at the time of this visit still going about their normal daily duties on the many Edinburgh suburban passenger services.

One significant benefit of the grouping for the rail enthusiast was the advent of through workings of 'foreign' locomotives, and as early as 1923 the following 'strangers' were noted in Edinburgh:

- Ex-G&SWR 4-6-0 Class '18' No. 344 on a special from Ayr
- Ex-G&WSR, 4-6-0 No. 501 on a special from Ayr
- Ex-MR '4F' 0-6-0 No. 3943 on a freight working from the south
- Ex-L&Y 'Pug' 0-4-0ST, No. 1286.

Caledonian Railway Allocation

- Brittain 0-4-2 Class '670' Goods.
  Two engines: No's 717 and 252.
- McIntosh 4-6-0s.
  Two engines: No. 916 ('908' Class) and 921 ('918' Class).
- McIntosh 4-4-0 Class '140' ('Dunalastair IV').
  Five engines: No's 140, 141, 143, 923, and 924.
- McIntosh 4-4-0 Class '900' ('Dunalastair III').
  Two engines: No's 889 and 899.
- Pickersgill 4-4-0 Class '113'.
  Two engines: No's 932 and 933.
- Drummond 4-4-0 Class '66'.
  One engine: No. 124 (renumbered 1124).
- Drummond 4-4-0 Class '80'.
  One engine: No. 81 (renumbered 1081).
- McIntosh 4-4-0 Class '721' ('Dunalastair I').
  One engine: No. 732.
- Lambie 0-6-0 Class '294' 'Jumbo'.
  One engine: No. 201.
- McIntosh 0-6-0 Class '714'.
  Two engines: No's 330 and 333.
- McIntosh 0-6-0 Class '812'.
  Twelve engines: No's 287, 288, 290, 661, 820, 821, 838, 862, 869-71 and 873.
- Pickersgill 0-6-0 Class '300'.
  Four engines: No's 306, 321, 672, 673.
- Lambie 0-6-0 Class '294'.
  One engine: No. 548 (renumbered 1548).
- McIntosh 0-4-4T '104' Class.
  Four engines: No's 106, 109, 167 and 170; the latter two built for the Balerno Branch.
- McIntosh 0-4-4T Class '439'.
  One engine: No. 384.
- McIntosh 0-6-0T '782' Class.
  Seven engines: No's 254, 474, 434, 516, 634, 810 and 811.
- Drummond 0-6-0ST Class '323'.
  One engine: No. 506.
- Drummond 0-6-0T Class '272'.
  One engine: No. 509.
- Pickersgill 0-6-0T Class '498'.
  Two engines: No's 514 and 515, with a third, No. 531, shedded there between 1912 and 1945.
- McIntosh 0-4-0ST.
  Four engines: No's 613, 621, 622 and 625.

No's 923 and 924 were engines of the 1908 new builds of the McIntosh Class '140' 'Dunalastair IV'. The four Pickersgill 0-6-0

Ex-CR 4-4-0 No. 14433 (CR No. 772) of the '766' Class 'Dunalastair II' entering Merchiston station whilst working an Edinburgh Princes Street to Glasgow Central passenger train. This locomotive had been superheated in 1914. *CRA Archives*

Above: Ex-CR McIntosh 4-4-0 No. 14342 (CR No. 892) of the '900' Class enters Merchiston station on the Up main line with a stopping passenger service for Edinburgh Princes Street. *CRA Archives*

Below: Ex-CR McIntosh 4-4-0 No. 14348 (CR No. 899) of the '900' Class in the shed yard at Dalry Road. The LM&SR style of visible smokebox riveting, in comparison to the flush finish used by the Caledonian, is clearly visible. *CRA Archives*

CR McIntosh Class '104' 0-4-4T No. 167 in CR livery is seen at Dalry Road in this undated photograph. Note the unidentified CR saddle tank loco sitting alongside. *Hamish Stevenson collection*

CR Drummond Class '272' outside cylinder 0-6-0ST No. 1509 at its home shed of Dalry Road. These engines were six-coupled versions of the 0-4-0ST engines, retaining the Stirling cab and bunker configuration. The longer wheelbase rendered these engines less useful than their 0-4-0 brethren. *CRA Archives*

Class '300' engines allocated to Dalry Road shed, No's 306, 321, 672 and 673, were dedicated to one turn from Edinburgh to Aberdeen and one turn to Forfar nightly, with the four engines covering the return workings each night. It is not known whether Dalry Road crews worked throughout and lodged, or exchanged footplates on route, but the former is most likely since it is known from discussions with Haymarket Charge-hand Cleaner, Jimmy Blake, an ex Dalry Road fireman and driver (see Chapter 13), that in earlier times Dalry Road crews did work through to Aberdeen.

The SLS Journal of January 1933 contained an updated allocation for Dalry Road shed as at December 1932, which showed some seventy locomotives to be on hand:

- Ex-MR Hughes/Deeley 4-4-0 (3-cylinder compound) '4P'.
  Two engines: No's 919 and 920.
- Ex-MR Fowler 0-6-0 '4F'.
  Four engines: No's 4103, 4104, 4319 and 4320.
- Ex-LM&SR 0-6-0T '2F'.
  Three engines: 11272, 11273, 11275 (unidentified although numbers indicate locomotives of the former L&Y Railway).
- Ex-LM&SR Hughes 2-6-0 'Crab' '5MT'.
  Two engines: Nos. 13214 and 13215.
- Ex-CR McIntosh Class '900' ('Dunalastair III').
  Three engines: Nos. 14337, 14347, 14348.
- Ex-CR McIntosh Class '140' ('Dunalastair IV').
  One engine: No. 14349.
- Ex-CR McIntosh 4-4-0 superheated Class '139' '3P'.
  Three engines: No's 14445, 14450, 14451.
- Ex-CR Pickersgill 4-4-0 Class '928' '3P'.
  Three engines: No's 14465, 14472 and 14491.
- Ex-CR McIntosh 0-4-4T Class '19' '2P'.
  One engine: No. 15119.
- Ex-CR McIntosh 0-4-4T 'Class '104' Balerno 2P'.
  Six engines: No's 15149-14152, 15155, 15158.
- Ex-CR McIntosh 0-4-4T Class '438' '2P'.
  Two engines: No's 15169 and 15202.
- Ex-CR McIntosh 0-4-0ST 'Pug'.
  Three engines: No's 16030, 16031, 16034.
- Ex-CR McIntosh 0-6-0T Class '498'.
  One engine: No. 16157.
- Ex-CR McIntosh 0-6-0T Class '782 '3F'.
  Eight engines: No's 16253/282/283/288/312/313/329/372.
- Ex-G&SWR 0-6-2T Class '1'.
  One engine: No. 17020.
- Ex-CR Drummond, Lambie & McIntosh Standard Goods engine) 0-6-0 '3F' ('Jumbo').
  Seven engines: No's 17247, 17358, 17375, 17429-32.
- Ex-CR McIntosh 0-6-0 Class '812' '3F'.
  Ten engines: Nos. 17559/60/76, 17600/07/08/09/22/23/25.
- Ex-CR McIntosh 0-6-0 Class '652' '3F'.
  One engine: No. 175545.
- Ex-CR Pickersgill 0-6-0 Class '300' '3F'.
  Three engines: No's 17562, 17577, 17586.

Amongst the larger types of locomotive to be seen at Dalry Road shed in pre-war days were a small allocation of McIntosh designed 4-6-0s, including Class '908s' No's 916 and 917, the former being withdrawn in 1931 and the latter in 1935. The third such 4-6-0 was No. 921 of the '918' Class.

The two Hughes Class '5MT' 2-6-0s, No's 13214 and 13215, both of the 1930 Crewe build, were additions, from new, to the Dalry Road locomotive allocation. Two Aberdeen engines, No's 13212 and 13213 of the same class, were diagrammed to work fast freights into Edinburgh Lothian Road Goods on a nightly basis. In addition, two Carlisle Kingmoor engines of the same class and build date, No's 13216 and 13219, were similarly diagrammed to work through to Edinburgh overnight. These six engines were then all used on a daily basis by the Running Foremen at Dalry Road shed,

Ex-CR McIntosh 4-4-0 No. 14451 (CR No. 44) of the '43' Class at Dalry Road shed. This was a sometime Aberdeen engine.
CRA Archives

Ex-CR 0-4-4T No. 15151 (CR No. 108) of the '104' Class of 1899 stands on the Balerno Branch in a beautifully clean condition and with attractive embellishments on the smokebox. The front buffers are brightly polished, as is the front drawbar and coupling, and all together shows the care and attention lavished upon it by its crew. This engine and the rest of the class were long time denizens of Dalry Road shed and were always well cared for. *CRA Archives*

Ex-CR Pickersgill Class '498' 0-6-0T No. 16157 at Dalry Road shed. One of three engines of the class allocated to Dalry Road shed in 1912 for dock workings, this engine was transferred away to Greenock Ladyburn shed in 1945. This class of CR locomotive is very similar in looks and style to the later LM&SR Fowler design of 0-6-0T dock tank, which was also represented at Dalry Road shed. *J.L. Stevenson/Hamish Stevenson*

filling-in on passenger turns on both express and stopping services between Edinburgh Princes Street and Glasgow Central via Shotts. This filling-in usage was included in the official engine diagrams and was quite the normal procedure with ex-LM&SR locomotives, which were all classed as 'common user' engines (see below). The Aberdeen and Carlisle engines worked back to their home sheds later that same evening on overnight fast freight workings.

In later LM&SR days, Dalry Road was equipped with Stanier 'Black Five' 4-6-0s, as recorded above, and what useful workhorses they turned out to be. Equally at home on fast passenger workings or heavy mineral trains, they were highly regarded by Caledonian crews and did some sterling service over the years. They were supplemented by earlier '5MT' engines – the ex-LM&SR Hughes 2-6-0s, the ubiquitous 'Horwich Crab', another class of engine equally capable of proper mixed traffic duties but somewhat more uncomfortable at higher speeds. Passenger duties were covered largely by Fairburn 2-6-4Ts (also much-loved, but at times sorely-abused by their crews, see Chapter 15) of which Dalry Road had six of the class, and these were used equally on express and stopping passenger turns and also as pilots for heavier WCML trains over the heavy Cobbinshaw Road.

At Rail Nationalisation, 31st December 1947

Inevitably, on the Caledonian Railway becoming one of the many constituent companies of the largest of all new railway companies at the Grouping, known as 'The Big Four', foreign locomotives from other constituent companies were to filter, albeit fairly slowly, into Dalry Road's inheritance of pre-grouping locomotives, with additions from new builds of the LM&SR. Some of these 'new' engines, falling into the latter category, had become a valued asset to the shed. In particular, the Fairburn 2-6-4T engines were highly regarded by Dalry Road Caledonian crews, as were the ubiquitous but much-loved Stanier 'Black Fives'.

- Ex-MR Hughes/Deeley 4-4-0 3-cylinder compound '4P'.
  Three engines: No's 911, 1177 and 1178.
- Ex-MR Fowler 0-6-0 '4F'.
  Five engines: No's 4103, 4104, 4318, 4319 and 4320.
- Stanier 4-6-0 '5MT'.
  Two engines: No's 4931 and 5029.
- Fairburn 2-6-4T '4MTT'.
  Six Engines: No's 2268, 2269, 2270, 2271, 2272 and 2273.
- Hughes 2-6-0 '5MT'.
  Two engines: No's 2804 and 2807.
- McIntosh 4-4-0 Class '140' superheated 'Dunalastair IV' '3P'.
  Two engines: No's 14451, 14452.
- Pickersgill 4-4-0 Class '72' '3P'.
  Two engines: No's 54478 and 14507.
- Unknown 4-4-0 '4P'.
  One engine: No. 14644.
- McIntosh 0-4-4T Class '92' '2P'.
  One engine: No. 15125.
- McIntosh 0-4-4T Class '439' '2P'.
  Eight engines: No's 15165, 15166, 15177, 15189, 15202, 15210, 15229 and 15233.
- McIntosh 0-6-0 Class '29' '3F'.
  Six engines: No's 16236,16253, 16283, 16312, 16313 and 16329.
- Ex-LM&SR Fowler 0-6-0T Class '2F'.
  Two engines: No's 14162 and 14163.
- McIntosh 0-6-0 Class '81' '3F'.
  Five engines: No's 17550, 17553, 17559, 17565 and 17576.
- Pickersgill 0-6-0 Class '9' and Class '294' '3F'.
  Four engines: No's. 17578, 17645, 17654 and 17674.

Compound No. 911, usually turned out in sparkling condition, had been a regular performer on the Edinburgh Princes Street/Glasgow Pullman services.

Fairburn 2-6-4T No. 42272 stands in the shed yard sidings at Dalry Road shed. *J.L. Stevenson/Hamish Stevenson*

British Railways Days

After the peak of seventy engines in 1932, locomotive allocation at Dalry Road was to continue to hover around fifty to fifty-five engines, but now with ex-NBR engines appearing amongst the ranks. In August 1952 the allocation consisted of:

- Stanier 4-6-0 '5MT'.
  Nine engines: No's 44994, 45022, 45023, 45030, 45036, 45086, 45127, 45161 and 45183.
- Hughes 2-6-0 '5MT'.
  Three engines: No's 42804, 42807 and 42830.
- Ex-NBR Reid 0-6-0 Class 'J37' '5F'.
  Three engines: No's 64536, 64547 and 64591.
- Ex-MR Hughes/Deeley Compound 4-4-0 '3P'.
  Three engines: No's 40911, 41177 and 41178.
- Fairburn 2-6-4 '4MTT'.
  Six engines: No's 442268, 42269, 42270, 42271, 42272 and 42273.
- Pickersgill 4-4-0 '3P'.
  One engine: No. 54478.
- Ex-LM&SR Fowler 0-6-0T Class '2F'.
  Two engines: No's 14162, 14163 (renumbered 47162, 47163).
- McIntosh 4-4-0 'Dunalastair IV' '3P'.
  Two engines: No's 54451 and 54452.
- Ex-NBR Reid 0-6-2T Class 'N15' '3F'.
  One engine: No. 69187.
- Ex-NBR Reid 0-6-0 Class 'J35' '3F'.
  Two engines: No's 64495 and 64500.
- McIntosh 0-6-0T '3F'.
  Four engines: 56253, 56283, 566312 and 56313.
- Pickersgill 0-6-0 '3F'.
  One engine: No. 57679.
- McIntosh 0-6-0 '3F'.
  Seven engines: No's 57550, 57553, 57559, 57565, 57576, 57603 and 57645.
- McIntosh '2P' 0-4-4T. Five engines: Nos. 55165, 55166, 55177, 55202 and 55210.
- Pickersgill 0-4-4T '2P'.
  Two engines: No's 55229 and 55233.
- McIntosh 0-4-4T Class '879' '2P'.
  One engine: No. 55139.
- Ex-NBR Holmes 0-6-0 Class 'J36' '2F'.
  Two engines: No's 65271 and 65311.

By 1951, in the Scottish Region of British Railways the use of 'foreign' locomotives was happening to a far greater extent than in any other region of BR, mainly because the Scottish Region was a geographical entity formed by only two of the former post-Grouping railway companies. Hence, ex-Caledonian engines could be seen in all sorts of odd corners of ex-L&NER lines and vice versa. Dalry Road was a case in point, with ex-NBR engines featuring in the later allocations, and ex-L&NER Gresley and Thompson products also being no strangers. Members of the Riddles Standard classes were to become familiar sights at Dalry Road, with Standard '4MTT' 2-6-4s actually allocated there. BR Class '5MTs', the Class '6MT' 4-6-2 'Clans' and Class '7MT' 4-6-2 'Britannias' were soon to be almost daily visitors.

A smoky Stanier '5MT', No. 45030, heads a stopping passenger service out of Edinburgh Princes Street. *Hamish Stevenson*

Ex-Midland Hughes Class '5MT' 2-6-0 No. 42807 on shed at Dalry Road on 20th March 1955, with ex-NBR/L&NER Class 'N15 '0-6-2T in background. Both engines were allocated to Dalry Road at the time. *Stuart Sellar*

Ex-NBR/L&NER Class 'J37' 0-6-0 No. 64591, recently transferred to Dalry Road, stands in the shed yard. *Stuart Sellar*

Ex-MR Johnston 4-4-0 compound No. 40911, allocated to Dalry Road, stands in the shed yard. *J.L. Stevenson/Hamish Stevenson*

Fairburn 2-6-4T No. 42273 clears Kingsknowe with an Edinburgh to Carstairs and Lanark stopping passenger train. This was one of six of a much-loved class of engines at Dalry Road and they were to do sterling work on local (and not so local) passenger services. In the Down sidings on the left are the coaches for a Kingsknowe to Edinburgh Princes Street local service, normally allocated to an 0-4-4T. *David Anderson*

ABOVE: Ex-CR Pickersgill 4-4-0 of the '72' Class, No. 54478 on shed at Dalry Road in 1955. This engine was the regular Slateford Carriage Sidings Pilot. *David Anderson*

RIGHT: Ex-LM&SR Fowler Class '2F' 0-6-0T Dock tank engine, one of two allocated to Dalry shed. This engine, No. 47163, was normally used on the Balerno Branch freight workings. *David Anderson*

Ex-NBR/L&NER Class N15 0-6-2T No. 69187 of Dalry Road shed shunts across Granton Square in February 1953. *J.L. Stevenson/Hamish Stevenson*

Despite being painted in unlined BR black, this ex-CR McIntosh superheated Class '43' 'Dunalastair IV' No. 54451 still shows its Caledonian Railway lineage to good effect when photographed in the early summer sunshine at Dalry Road in May 1955. Built as No. 44 at St. Rollox in 1913, these locomotives retained the elegant CR curved valences along the running plate above driving wheels and coupling rod. *David Anderson*

In 1954 the allocation of Class '5MT' freight engines was swelled by three ex-NBR/L&NER Class 'J37' '5Fs', No's 64536, 64547 and 64591 plus four Class 'J35' '3Fs'. By 1960 three ex-L&NER, Thompson Class 'B1' 4-6-0s, had been added to the complement. The author had the privilege of riding on the footplate of many of the Class '5' engines, both ex-L&NE and ex-LM&S, working the 01.40 Crew Junction to Clyde Iron Works (see Chapter 14). It was an interesting interlude, but the ex-NBR 0-6-0 '5F' (Class 'J37') engines proved to be every bit as powerful as the Stanier '5MTs' on these heavy iron ore trains, though perhaps not as comfortable. They certainly always, steamed to perfection.

By April 1960, the three ex-LMS Hughes/Deeley 4-4-0, compound locomotives which had languished in storage at Dalry Road for a number of months were transferred away to Stranraer and put back into service. Despite both diesel locomotives and rail cars coming onto the scene, ex-Caledonian Railway locomotives were still to the fore in the final decade of the shed's existence, and the allocation at 64C (at April 1960) was as follows:

- Stanier 4-6-0 '5MT'.
  Eight engines: No's 44994, 45022, 45023, 45030, 45036, 45086, 45161 and 45183.
- Ex-L&NER Thompson 4-6-0 Class 'B1'.
  Three engines: No's 61007, 61244 and 61260.
- Hughes 2-6-0 '5MT'.
  One engine: No. 42807.
- Ex-L&NER Gresley 0-6-0 Class 'J39' '5F'.
  Four engines: No's 64794, 64946, 64963 and 64986.
- Ex-NBR Reid 0-6-0 Class 'J37' '5F'.
  Three engines: No's 64554, 64561 and 64569.
- Riddles BR Standard 2-6-4T '4MTT'.
  One engine: No. 80006.
- Fairburn 2-6-4 '4MTT'.
  Two engines: No's 42272 and 42273.
- Ex-L&NER Gresley 2-6-2T Class 'VI' '3P'.
  One engine: No. 67668.
- Ex-NBR Reid 0-6-2T Class 'N15' '3F'.
  One engine: No. 69187.
- Ex-NBR Reid 0-6-0 Class 'J35' '3F'.
  Three engines: No's 64500, 64501 and 64507.
- McIntosh 0-6-0T '3F'.
  Two engines: No's 56312 and 56313.
- McIntosh 0-6-0 '3F'.
  Five engines: No's 57550, 57559, 57560, 57565 and 57645.
- McIntosh 0-4-4T '2P'.
  Three engines: No's 55165, 55202 and 55210.
- Pickersgill 0-4-4T '2P'.
  Two engines: No's 55229 and 55233.

A stranger in the camp. Here ex-L&NER Class 'B1' No. 61007 *Klipspringer*, late of Edinburgh Haymarket shed, working tender first pulls out of Murrayfield station with a Leith North passenger train and is entering the elegant stone arched viaduct at Roseburn which carries the branch over the Water of Leith. *Stuart Sellar*

Fairburn 2-6-4T No. 42272 heads a Leith North passenger train past Leith High Depot in February 1961. *Stuart Sellar*

- Fowler 0-6-0T '2F' dock tanks.
  One engine: No. 47163.
- BR Diesel 0-6-0 '0F'.
  Eight engines. No's D3560, D3561, D3736, D3737, D3739, D3741, D3742 and D3877.
- BR Diesel 0-4-0 '0F'.
  Three engines: No's D2745, D2754 and D2755.

In 1962, Lambie Class '19' 0-4-4T No. 55124 of Dumfries shed (68B), having been withdrawn from service, was stored at Dalry Road, pending preservation, but nothing more came of that initiative and the engine was scrapped. Another 0-4-4T was later to be save for preservation (see Chapter 13).

In BR days, another incumbent of Dalry Road shed was an ex-L&NER Class 'D11/2' 4-4-0 No. 62685 *Malcolm Graeme*, a

Ex-CR Lambie Class '19' 0-4-4T No. 55124 of Motherwell shed (68B) stands at the head of a special train at Symington platform, once the venue for splitting and joining Edinburgh and Glasgow portions of West Coast express trains. *J.L. Stevenson*

hors de combat member of the class of 'Scottish Directors', based on the ex-Great Central Robinson design of 4-4-0. This locomotive had been transferred over from Haymarket shed. Although not in running order, this locomotive nevertheless entered the Dalry Road books, but in the capacity of stationary boiler for the Caledonian Hotel. It spent the remainder of its days standing against the south-eastern wall of the station and hotel, in the 'Horse Box Siding' in Lothian Road Goods Yard. There, it provided unending supplies of hot water for the baths of the privileged classes.

A unique feature of Dalry Road shed was the fact that the average locomotive enthusiast could be sure of spotting foreign locomotives of interest on an almost daily basis, not least of which were Crewe North (5A) 'Princess Coronation' Pacifics. The use of engines from other sheds on a filling in turn had a history starting away back in

Class 'J35' No. 64554 in Dalry shed yard, April 1958. *Stuart Sellar*

Ex-NBR/L&NER Class 'N15' 0-6-2 No. 69187 brings a train of coke out of Granton Gas Works in May 1956. *David Anderson*

ABOVE: Ex-L&NER Class 'D49' No. 62712 *Morayshire*, withdrawn from service and seen here acting as stationary boiler to provide hot water for the BR Slateford Laundry in August 1961. This engine is now in running order once more and can be seen on the SRPS Bo'ness to Manuel railway. *Stuart Sellar*

LEFT: Ex-L&NER Class 'D11/2' No. 62685 *Malcolm Graeme*, out of revenue earning service and relegated to act as stationary boiler for the Caledonian Hotel, stands hidden out of sight along the east wall (the horse loading bank) of Princes Street station in 1961. *Stuart Sellar*

Ex-LM&SR Fowler Class '2F' 0-6-0T No. 47163 and ex-CRMcIntosh 0-4-4T '2P' No. 55210 stand in the shed yard at Dalry Road in March 1958. Identifiable in the background is McIntosh 0-6-0 '3F' No. 57565. *Stuart Sellar*

1937, when the prestigious 'Coronation Scot' express passenger train between London Euston and Glasgow Central was first introduced by the LM&SR, worked by the new Stanier streamlined Pacifics that had been constructed specially for this working. Five of these engines were allocated to London (Camden) shed, of which four covered the working on a weekly cyclic diagram, with two engines always being at the Polmadie end, one for the Up 'Coronation Scot' and the second for a diagrammed southbound spare working (the 23.25 from Glasgow to Carlisle, returning on the 03.30 Carlisle to Glasgow). Two engines were similarly always on hand at Camden shed also, with one diagrammed to work the northbound 'Scot' whilst the other worked the 21.25 London to Crewe, returning with the 03.46 Crewe to London, leaving one engine available for maintenance or other spare work. In the latter part of 1937 the Camden-based train engine of the day, allocated to the northbound service, after arrival at Glasgow Central was also diagrammed to work the 18.45 train from Glasgow to Edinburgh Princes Street, returning with the 21.30 ex Princes Street and ready to work the Up 'Coronation Scot' next day from Glasgow. However, the author could find no evidence of Stanier's earlier 'Princess Royal' Class '7P' engines ever having worked into Edinburgh but would be pleased to be corrected.

At the time of Grouping. the new LM&SR Company, unlike the others in the 'Big Four', did not have a General Manager but was headed by a Chairman, one Sir Josiah Charles Stamp, tax expert, economist and ex-director of a large industrial concern. He (quite correctly) questioned all expenditure, demanded economies and improved performance, right across the board. From this policy arose a drive to maximise locomotive availability and utilisation, and the concept of making all engines 'common user' emerged. Instead of perpetuating the Caledonian Railway practice of allocating one engine to one or two drivers and one turn of duty, the LM&SR, in this drive to achieve maximum performance, decreed that no longer would engines be allocated to individual crews, but were there for any running foreman to appropriate and utilise on any working as seen fit. It was, in fact, a seriously flawed policy. Locomotives could be, and were, lost to owning sheds, sometimes for many days on end, and any system of planned preventative maintenance by fitting staff at the owning shed had to go by the board. Engines suffered in terms of cleanliness and mechanical condition. Failures abounded and staff morale plummeted. This policy was diametrically opposed to that pertaining on the L&NER for instance, where the Gresley Pacifics (and later variation of thereof) were allocated to individual drivers, and worked out and home daily in dedicated, rotating links.

This common user policy was extended by Polmadie shed to the Class '8P' Pacifics from Crewe North shed on arrival at Glasgow Central on overnight workings, as well as engines of Polmadie's own allocation of Class '8P' Pacifics; these were regularly being used on daytime 'filling in' turns. Two of the regular turns were the 08.15 Class 'B' Glasgow to Edinburgh Princes Street stopping train and the 08.40 Class 'A' fast on the same route. The 08.15 was shunted at Holytown to enable the following fast to overtake, with arrivals in Princes Street being 09.53 and 10.35 respectively. These Class '8P' engines were too long for the Princes Street turntable and thus there was the daily sight of Pacifics running around the triangle formed by Slateford Junction, Coltbridge Junction and Dalry Middle Junction, before being coaled at Dalry Road. The return workings to Glasgow were the 11.30 ex Princes Street and the 13.35 ex Princes Street. Over the years, Class '6MT' 4-6-0 'Royal Scots', BR Standard '6MT' 4-6-2 'Clans' and '7MT' 4-6-2 'Britannias' could also be seen on these workings, all adding a *je ne sais quoi* to the day for the loco spotting fraternity in and around Dalry Road shed at that time.

Modern times! An English Electric 350hp 0-6-0 diesel shunting locomotive shunts the shed yard at Dalry Road and has ex-CR Pickersgill 4-4-0 No. 54478 and McIntosh 0-4-4T No. 55165 in tow. *Hamish Stevenson*

A three-coach portion train for a London Midland Region destination, headed by BR Standard 'Britannia' Class '7MT' No. 70009 *Alfred the Great*, is diverted round the 'Sub' to avoid Edinburgh Princes Street station having to be opened on a Sunday, in May 1964; it will regain the WCML via the Craiglockhart Junction chord line to Slateford. This portion will be joined to the train from Glasgow at Carstairs Junction. *Stuart Sellar*

In the late 1950s, dieselisation affected Dalry Road shed. The initial introduction of diesel multiple units (DMUs) was in the shape of Gloucester two-car (Twin) units which had been drafted in to work the Leith North passenger services. Many Dalry Road drivers and passed firemen were trained to drive these units and the DMUs soon displaced many of the old faithfuls, such as the ex-Caledonian 0-4-4T locomotives. Before long, the Edinburgh & Glasgow via Shotts services were similarly dieselised with, firstly, the Gloucester 'Twin' units, followed by Metro-Cammell three-car DMU's, all running in multiple as four or six-car trains.

In the later days of Edinburgh Princes Street there was to be an interesting development, when Swindon-built three and six-car DMUs of the 1956/7 vintage, similar to those first introduced in August 1956 to takeover passenger services between Edinburgh Waverley and Glasgow Queen Street, appeared at Edinburgh Princes Street to work the Edinburgh and Glasgow passenger services running over the 1869 Cleland & Midcalder route. A three-car version, formed by two Driving Motor Brake Second (DMBS) coaches and a First Corridor coach (FK), the latter containing seven First Class compartments (forty-two seats), worked the 08.00 ex Edinburgh Princes Street to Glasgow Central on weekdays and the 16.30 return. This curiosity came about because there was quite a well-known Glasgow businessman (name not now remembered) who travelled daily from Merchiston station to Glasgow Central, and he held an Annual First Class Season ticket. Glasgow Queen Street was not so convenient for his place of business and thus he eschewed the option of using the E&GR route and, having friends in high places within BR, he made loud complaint about lack of private First Class accommodation on the new Gloucester 'Twin' DMU units. This new, and somewhat unique arrangement, caused its own inherent problems, the least of which was the imbalance created between First Class accommodation and the availability of Standard Class seating. This factor posed problems for the Edinburgh guards, with regular out of class travel becoming the norm. This in turn led to some regular confrontations for guards, one of whom was a senior Lothian Road Goods guard, and a regular and most punctilious stand-in at Princes Street, who worked these trains fairly regularly. The preferred option for many of the young female commuters returning home in the early evening to North Lanarkshire (Shotts), was to travel in First Class comfort, and this resulted in out of class travel being their normal. All attempts by the guards to extract Standard Class to First Class excess fares were met with derision. This specially adapted three-car set ran these trains for some years, but if memory serves correctly, this particular set had an additional Standard Class Trailer coach (TS) inserted into the consist, to correct the imbalance of Standard Class accommodation, running thereafter as a four-coach unit.

It was, largely, the ill-considered introduction of the DMUs which was to hasten the end of commuter traffic in and out of Edinburgh Princes Street (and other suburban routes). These trains lacked the comfort and privacy of the BR non-corridor coaching stock, were prone to overheating (both in summer and in winter) and featured the ingress of noxious fumes to the passenger accommodation. They were but glorified buses, but considerably less successful, and passengers voted with their feet.

On Sunday 8th February 1959 many of the Gloucester 'Twin' DMUs were suddenly withdrawn from service, 'for special examination'. Dalry Road shed was required to find, at very short notice, five suitable, serviceable locomotives, with ten footplate crews to work the replacement steam services on the Leith North Branch. The locomotives provided were Fairburn 2-6-4T No. 42270, ex-Caledonian McIntosh 4-4-0 'Dunalastair IV' No. 54478, ex-Caledonian Class '812' 0-6-0s No's 57559 and 57572 and ex-NBR Class 'J37' 0-6-0 No. 64636. This group ran the North Leith Branch, with replacement train sets each consisting of three non-corridor coaches, very efficiently and effectively for the duration of the Gloucester crisis.

In terms of shunting locomotives, Dalry Road acquired a few English Electric 350 HP 0-6-0 diesel shunting locomotives. Very powerful locomotives indeed, but when it came to trip workings their top speed of 27 mph proved a bit of a hindrance. Nevertheless, they were to see the demise of the two-remaining ex-LM&SR Fowler 0-6-0Ts, No's 47172 and 47173.

Main line diesel electric locomotives, mainly in the shape of English Electric 1-Co-Co-1 diesel electric Type '4' locomotives (later to be BR Class 40s), were, by the early 1960s, making a regular appearance on West Coast passenger services, such as the Manchester, Liverpool and Birmingham trains, working through from places like Crewe. Dalry Road drivers were trained to drive these and handled them on a regular basis. Dalry Road itself had no allocation of main line diesel engines, but was supplied on an as required basis from Haymarket which, by 1964, had become the main diesel locomotive stabling and maintenance facility in Edinburgh. What it supplied was, in the main, the quite dreadful Class 17 Claytons. These engines were soon displacing the Stanier '5F' 4-6-0s on the heavier mineral workings to the west, and not doing a very good job in the process! The author remembers one evening in Benhar Junction signal box, when one such train made a painful approach on the rising gradient from the east, hauled by one of the Class 17s (re-engined with a Rolls Royce engine). The exhaust manifold glowed a bright cherry red, visible because the engine compartment side doors, obviously opened to assist the cooling air

The last passenger train to operate over the Princes Street to North Leith route, formed by a two-car Gloucester DMU, departs for Leith North on 30th April 1962. On the right-hand side can be seen vanfits standing in Lothian Road Goods sidings whilst Edinburgh Castle overlooks this railway moment. *Author's collection*

flow, swung open and shut as the train literally crawled past the box. The Class 17s, consumed sump oil in vast quantities and frequently fell victim to high water temperature problems when required to work 'against the collar'. With a very conveniently located and comfortable centrally-mounted driving cab, this was a class of diesel-electric locomotive which promised so much, but delivered so little. Like so many other diesel-electric locomotives in that sad chapter of BR history, they were ill-thought out and just not fit for purpose. However, during their short time at Dalry Road the Class 17 Claytons, although not fitted with steam heating boilers, could be seen on summer passenger workings, with a regular turn being the 14.05 Edinburgh Princes Street to Manchester portion train, which a single locomotive worked as far as Carstairs.

In the final two years of Dalry Road shed's existence, it became a temporary depository for some of the Gresley Class 'A4' Pacific locomotives, displaced by English Electric Type '5' 'Deltics' at the following sheds on the ECML: Haymarket 64B, Gateshead 52A and London King's Cross Top Shed 34A. It had been the intention to transfer all these Class 'A4' engines to Edinburgh St. Margarets 64A, but space was always at a premium at that overcrowded shed, and thus, pending a final decision on the fate of these engines, the members of the class listed below came to Dalry Road. In September 1963, on the very day its home shed was closed to steam traction, ex-Haymarket Top Link 'A4', she of the long nameplate, No. 60012 *Commonwealth of Australia* was officially transferred to Dalry Road and took up residence. Then in 1964 two former denizens of Top Shed arrived, No's 60007 *Sir Nigel Gresley* and 60034 *Lord Farringdon*. All three engines were finally, and officially, transferred on to Aberdeen Ferryhill shed 61B, where they re-entered revenue-earning service on the new three-hour Glasgow–Aberdeen express workings. Happily, No. 60007 was preserved for posterity.

On the final day before closure of the shed (Saturday 4th September 1965), six Clayton Class 17 diesel-electric locomotives were noted, stabled in the shed yard: No's D8568/69/72/75/80 and 84. Standing alongside were the following steam locomotives:

- 44975 (withdrawn)
- 45053
- 45127
- 45357 of Stirling shed
- 45360 (withdrawn)
- 45469
- 45477
- 45483
- 61134
- 61245 (withdrawn)
- 61308 (withdrawn).

Come final closure of the shed in 1965, many of the Dalry Road drivers and passed firemen transferred to Leith Central, home of all the DMU workings in and around Edinburgh, as drivers, and remained there when this depot was created a Promotion, Transfer & Redundancy (PT&R) Motive Power Depot in its own right (64H) at the end of 1959. Some men, however, opted to stay with main line diesel traction, as opposed to rail cars, and were taken on to the strength at Haymarket Diesel Depot (64B) in 1965.

Above: Strangers in the camp! No's 60007 *Sir Nigel Gresley*, one of the pair of Class 'A4' Pacifics, late of King's Cross Top Shed and transferred to Edinburgh St. Margarets shed, a shed where space to accommodate yet another two Pacifics was sadly lacking, so into storage at Dalry Road they had to go. *Ian Musgrave*

Right: Dalry Road shed on 4th September 1965. Locomotives in the shed area are: six Class 17 Clayton D/E locos; eight Stanier Class '5MT' 4-6-0s, four of which were withdrawn, and three Thompson ex-LN&ER 4-6-0 Class 'B1s', two of which were also withdrawn. *Harry Archibald*

8 Dalry Road Shed: Passenger Train Workings

The Caledonian railway was not slow to make the most of the fact that it was the first Scottish railway to provide a direct service from Scotland to England *'without change of carriages'* as the advert of the time was to boldly declare. The constituent companies of the East Coast Main Line route, whilst running through services, required that passengers changed trains at the Tyne (Newcastle) station, and also were transferred to coach at Tweedmouth in order to negotiate the other unbridged gap of the River Tweed at Berwick.

What was known as 'The Edinburgh Branch' of the Caledonian Railway main line from Carlisle, being the line of route from Carstairs Junction to Edinburgh, was ready for traffic on 15th February 1848 but, following the opening of Lothian Road passenger station, as described in Chapter One, there were to be no express passenger trains at first, the company explaining that *'it was waiting until the line was a little more consolidated'*. However, in March 1948, the Post Office, in a rare show of confidence, transferred its London–Edinburgh mail service from the East Coast to the West Coast route and the first train services to operate over the line, according to the timetable dated March 1848, were the daily Anglo-Scottish services (three in each direction), the mandatory Parliamentary train to Carstairs and the south, as listed below, plus a further four daily trains in either direction running between Edinburgh and Glasgow, via Carstairs, but this was soon to change.

Thus, in March 1848, the four daily departures from Lothian Road passenger station were:

06.50 Mixed train to London. Conveying First, Second and Third Class passengers through to London.
11.15 Mail train. Conveying First and Second Class passengers.
17.00 Parliamentary train. Conveying First, Second and Third Class passengers; all stops to Carlisle.
21.15 Mail train. Conveying all classes to Carlisle, and First Class only to London from Carlisle.

There were two Sunday services, both being the Mail trains, at 11.15 and 21.15 as shown above, and with the same weekday conditions for passengers.

Very soon a new Anglo-Scottish train was introduced between Edinburgh/Glasgow and London, and vice versa; this was a 09.00 departure (see below). By the April of 1848, the Caledonian Railway felt the need for a timetable revision after introducing the additional train service, and this amended timetable was duly published in the *Scotsman* newspaper, advertising the daily passenger train service between Edinburgh and Glasgow (running over the 56¼ miles via Carstairs) and vice versa, comprising of a mere four trains in each direction on weekdays, with two Sunday services, plus the introduction of a new, local 'all stops' service running between Edinburgh and Carstairs, departing at 13.30; these were in addition to the other Anglo-Scottish trains bound for Carlisle and south thereof (except for the 17.00 departure). Speeds were moderate, and the daily departures were:

06.50 Mixed Train. Conveying First, Second and Third Class (First Class through to London only).
09.00 Mixed Train. Conveying First, Second and Third Class.
11.15 Mail Train. Conveying First and Second Class only.
13.30 Local. All stops to Carstairs.
17.00 Parliamentary train. Conveying all classes and taking up all stops to Carlisle (the obligatory train stopping everywhere on the line of route, with a journey time to Carlisle of 4½ hours.
21.15 Mail train. Conveying all classes to Carlisle, and First Class only to London from Carlisle.

From April of that first year, after the Caledonian Railway had secured the Royal Mail traffic, the last departure was the Mail Train. However, the Caledonian line of route was quickly to become a popular choice, when, by the month of May 1849, the company was offering through trains to London, Birmingham, Manchester and Liverpool, from both Edinburgh and Glasgow. All these express passenger trains, on departing from Edinburgh, were in the hands of both Sinclair 2-2-2s and later his 2-4-0s, supplied from the modest shed at Dalry Road.

Historically, pre-1846, there had been a mid-morning northbound departure from London Euston, forming part of a train-to-stagecoach configuration for passenger transportation to Scottish destinations. Following the completion of the Lancaster & Carlisle Railway in 1846, the stagecoach journey was confined to north of Carlisle and in September 1847, when the Caledonian Railway opened its new line from Carlisle to Beattock, the form of stagecoach/train transport was restored to favour, with the remaining 50 miles north of Beattock being run by stagecoach. With the opening of the final stretch of the WCML over Beattock, the mid-morning departure from Euston meant that rail passengers could be in Edinburgh by 01.30 and Glasgow by 01.40 the following morning. With the rail link now being completed between London and Edinburgh/Glasgow, faster through travel by train became a possibility and in March 1848, a new morning service was introduced, leaving both Glasgow and Euston at 09.00 respectively, with a journey time northbound of 12 hours 10 minutes to Glasgow and, by means of portion working, reached Edinburgh in a time of 12 hours exactly. In October 1849 this schedule was extended to 12½ hours, which was to become the standard journey time for some time to come. Incidentally, it was the Edinburgh portion of this train which was involved in the Auchengray accident (see Chapter 14).

The overnight train for general 'Scotch Traffic' left Euston at 21.00 and took 12½ hours to reach Edinburgh and 13 hours to arrive in Glasgow. The night 'Limited Mail' was limited to three First and Second Class coaches – one for Edinburgh, one for Glasgow and the last for Perth – and was timed to reach Edinburgh at 07.10 and Glasgow at 07.22. This train was to be the precursor of the West Coast Travelling Post Office (TPO) train, the well-known 'Night Mail'. Originally, in 1847, terminating in Carlisle, with mail traffic for Scottish destinations being taken forward by stagecoach, or post-1848 by service trains, but it was to be 1885 before the TPOs were run as portion postal trains, solely for the conveyance of mails, this being done at the behest of the Post Master General himself in order to improve reliability of Anglo-Scottish Mail. In 1894 there was a daily Edinburgh to Carstairs TPO train conveying one of two special mail carriages, No. 2 (built 1863) and No. 1 (built 1872); these carried one net each, on one side only, and were used for letter sorting between Edinburgh and Carstairs. The return working for the Dalry Road men and the coach was via the Down Mail Special from Carstairs. In 1902 these coaches were replaced by two ex-WCJS gangway-connected mail coaches, No's 196 and 197, fitted with one net and two delivery arms each.

In 1862, a new 10.00 departure from both Glasgow and Edinburgh for London Euston was introduced, with the respective southbound portions initially combining at Beattock. In the Down direction there was the corresponding northbound departure at 10.00 from Euston, now a through train, which split at Beattock and arrived in Edinburgh at 22.00 and in Glasgow at 22.10. This 10.00 Edinburgh departure was to become the most important express working allocated to Dalry Road shed, one which the Dalry Road crews were soon working through to Carlisle non-stop, and was not combined with the Glasgow portion until Crewe (see below). In 1927 the LM&SR conferred the title 'Royal Scot' upon this service, with the train engine carrying a headboard displaying the name. The overall journey times of this train were later reduced to 8½ hours from and to Edinburgh, and 8¾ hours between Glasgow and London, as a consequence of the Railway Races of 1888, of which more below.

On 9th July 1869, the opening of the Mid Calder to Cleland line to passenger traffic offered a far shorter and more direct route between Edinburgh and Glasgow (46¼ miles). By now seven trains ran in each direction daily over this new route, whilst a further six Glasgow-bound services continued to run via Carstairs. The Lothian Road terminus was under severe pressure, since all passenger train arrivals and departures had to use the same single line of railway on the approach to the platform line from the junction in the vicinity of Grove Street overbridge. It was a classic quart into a pint pot scenario. The second line was operated as a single goods line only. This situation was to lend urgency to the construction of the new Lothian Road station, which was opened on 2nd May 1870. By this time, sixteen trains were running in each direction daily between Edinburgh and Glasgow, with all now running via Shotts.

In the early days of the Caledonian in Edinburgh, and up to the time shortly before the first of the East Coast and West Coast 1888 Railway Races, the most important Scottish destination in respect of the early express passenger train working over the West Coast Route was Edinburgh itself and this was reflected in the importance placed upon, and preferential treatment afforded, the Edinburgh train by the L&NWR. These early through trains, whilst running as whole trains over Caledonian metal to Carlisle, were in fact to be 'portion' trains north of Crewe, where the L&NWR chose to split or combine the trains, probably to ease the working of same over the heavily graded Westmorland and Cumbrian Fells; it was always the Edinburgh portion which was allowed to precede the Glasgow portion through to Carlisle, and onwards to Carstairs Junction. The Up and Down 'Corridors' between Edinburgh, Glasgow and London were combined southbound, or split northbound, at Crewe, with the Edinburgh train taking preference.

In the mid to late 1800s, Princes Street had two through London Euston services. The morning train was the 10.15 (the departure time varied by minutes around 10.00) which Dalry Road crews worked through to Carlisle, returning with the equivalent morning train from London, departing Carlisle at 16.30. This was the most tightly timed train of the two, with 115 minutes southbound and 120 minutes northbound allowed for the 101.6 miles between Edinburgh and Carlisle. The afternoon train was the 14.00 ('Corridor') from Princes Street and was the heavier of the two trains, with a normal loading calculated as equal to 12½ (130/140 tons) and 121 minutes allowed for the northbound trip which had a coach from Birmingham added to the consist at Crewe. Both these trains were combined with the respective Glasgow departures, initially, as stated, at Crewe, and this method of train working was still in vogue in 1905. In true Caledonian practice, each train was allocated to one driver and one engine to and from Carlisle.

The introduction of these through southbound express services was to see the emergence of some well-known Dalry Road drivers whose exploits over what was a very demanding and hard line of route between Princes Street and Carlisle were to become public knowledge. One such Dalry Road driver was to be the aforementioned J. Dick, a man who most likely had honed his skills, and won his spurs, on these early fast workings between Edinburgh and Carlisle, and probably on the footplate of the early Sinclair and Connor locomotives. It is known that he ran the 10.00 Edinburgh to Carlisle every day for several years with his own engine. It was with this morning departure that the Caledonian Single No. 123 was to make its name during the 1888 'Races', when employed on this very same diagrammed turn, out and home to Carlisle every day, for the duration. In August 1888 it was to run the 101.6 miles between Carlisle and Princes Street in a mere 102½ minutes, with an average speed of 56.9 mph. The driver's name was not recorded during this feat, but it is not beyond the bounds of possibility that it was Dick himself. It was he who was later allocated the first, and only, 'Dunalastair I', No. 731, to come to Dalry Road, with which in April 1896 he ran the (re-timed) 10.15 ex Princes Street to Carlisle with a booked time of 120 minutes, in 115 minutes, and returned with the 16.30 from Carlisle, both legs of the journey requiring some strenuous running. This 10.15 departure from Edinburgh Princes Street was to be used as a test train on several future occasions, and indeed it was this on this very service that Drummond trialled his high pressure rebuilds of the '66' Class 4-4-0s, No's 76-79, 84 and 87 (see Chapter Five). Later, Dick, with 'Dunalastair I' No. 731, was to change diagrams and was chosen to work the new 14.00 'Corridor' express, the 14.00 ex Princes Street, which was a portion train, combining with the Glasgow departure at Crewe in the earlier days, and later at Symington.

The mid-morning departure for London and the mid-afternoon 'Corridor' from Edinburgh Princes Street represented the hardest diagrams for Dalry Road footplatemen in Caledonian Railway days, both services being worked non-stop throughout to Carlisle, with corresponding return workings, and were to see the emergence of other up-and-coming 'stars' who were serving their apprenticeship on these demanding workings as firemen. Two other Dalry Road men were later to stand out at the shed, these being William (Will) Stavert, who succeeded Dick on the 10.00 London, and another Dalry Road worthy of the time, W. Watts, who was a contemporary of Stavert and just as regularly mentioned in dispatches; the two worked the 10.00 and 14.00 express workings, with the men alternating weekly. Indeed, both men had most likely learned their

CR 4-2-2 No. 123, on well known territory, makes a smoky departure whilst heading a special train consisting of two ex-CR coaches, out of the soon to be closed Edinburgh Princes Street in April 1965. *Stuart Sellar*

trade, and learned it well, when firing on the earlier Anglo-Scottish services.

Stavert was allocated the only member of the '903' 'Cardean' Class 4-6-0, No. 905, to grace Dalry Road, before it was transferred away to Perth. The famous railway commentator of the day, Charles Rous Martin, referred to Stavert as a *'Veritable Wizard'*. He was probably best known for his truly amazing running when working the 10.05 Edinburgh Princes Street to London Euston, with his own 'Dunalastair IV' 4-4-0 No. 140. W. Watts got 'Dunalastair IV' No. 141 at that same time, a pairing that set up equally as incredible running between them. Both drivers had previously been allocated engines of the 'Dunalastair II' Class, No's 768 and 769 respectively, before taking over two newer engines of the 'Dunalastair III' Class, Nos. 896 and 899, and never failed to put up some spectacular running (see Chapter 14).

This through working of express trains from Edinburgh southwards should, logically, have been much facilitated by the original track configuration at Carstairs Junction, where a through chord line, commonly known as the 'Queen's Branch' – from the Edinburgh line (Lampits Junction) to the West Coast Main Line (Float Junction), and lying immediately to the north side of the Float Viaduct carrying the main line over the River Clyde – effectively by-passed Carstairs. This was well-engineered chord line, authorised as part of the 1845 Act, was, strangely, never intended to provide a direct line to and from Edinburgh and the south. Indeed, from the opening of the line throughout, the southbound Edinburgh trains were worked by reversing at Carstairs station over the fork from the station to the Edinburgh line. The Queen's Branch was never in regular use for other than the Royal Train workings of 1857, 1859, 1860 and 1864 (hence the name), although it has been recorded that through excursion trains from the south to Edinburgh, destined for the Exhibitions of 1851 and 1864, and nightly goods trains from the south to Edinburgh, passed over this fork. It was severed by the construction of the Dolphinton Branch in 1867 when, strangely, this easy through chord line was closed by the Caledonian Railway.

A direct running facility from the south towards Edinburgh was restored by the authorisation and construction of the Strawfrank fork in October 1872, a second, very severe and tightly curved connection, linking the new Dolphinton Junction and Strawfrank Junction. As stated, it is assumed that closure of the original Queen's Branch was undertaken to facilitate the construction of the newer Dolphinton Branch; this was an 11-mile-long branch which hardly proved to be an outstanding success, with the passenger service being withdrawn in 1945 and the branch being abandoned in its entirety in November 1950. This Strawfrank chord line has over the years proved that the ability to run express services through from Edinburgh southwards was to be severely inhibited, especially as the new through chord was subject to a most prohibitive permanent speed restriction of 15 mph because of its severe curvature, a situation which still exists to this present day. Indeed, in steam days it acted like the proverbial 'brick in the boxer's glove' for Dalry Road crews working through to Carlisle and hoping the get a top-up with water at Strawfrank troughs, since optimum speed for picking up water (generally 60 mph) was not always attainable. One may well question why one of the later companies (either the LM&SR or indeed BR) never restored this through and well-engineered chord, but the answer apparently lies in the fact that the track geometry of the junction with the main line (Float Junction) proved to be equally as difficult and restricted as the track geometry on the Strawfrank chord.

This was a situation which prevailed at the time of the 1888 'Races' to Edinburgh. Thereafter, but, with the popularisation of

CR 4-4-0 Class '900' 'Dunalastair III' Class locomotive No. 888 at Dalry Road shed, one of the class of locomotives used on the Caledonian section of the Angle-Scottish trains. CR No. 263 can be seen in the background. *CRA Archives*

the Highlands by Queen Victoria and the Royal Family, the trend of passenger traffic over the West Coast Main Line was changing, and it was the destinations of Perth, Aberdeen and the North that were gaining in popularity with the growth of the 'tourist trains'. As a result, the main thrust of the second round of the Railway Races, in 1895, between East Coast and West Coast routes, centred on these more northern destinations. The racing resulted in some examples of outstanding running between Carlisle, Perth and Aberdeen by the Caledonian Railway 4-4-0 locomotives.

Some later time, and owing to the fact that the numbers of Edinburgh passengers using the West Coast Main Line trains to access London were diminishing, full through trains could no longer be justified and portion workings with fewer coaches became the norm for through trains to and from Edinburgh and the south, the portions being combined with the Glasgow services; this continuing well into BR days, initially at Symington, lying to the south of Carstairs, and later still at Strawfrank Junction or in the platform at Carstairs proper. Now, Carstairs Junction station, is itself an awkward location, where the shunting movements involved in the combining or splitting portion trains could, and often did, block the main line and loops at critical times. Nor was Carstairs popular with passengers, since the direction of the Edinburgh portion was reversed. Symington was by far the preferred location for joining/splitting portion trains and became the normal location for this activity with Edinburgh and Glasgow portions in later LM&SR days and well into BR days.

Before Grouping, Princes Street still retained the through 10.00 London Euston service, but by then merely running with a normal formation of three 8-wheeled corridor coaches and one 12-wheeled corridor coach, as a portion train, connecting at Symington with the 10.00 Glasgow Central to Euston train departure. From July 1927 the 10.00 departures from London Euston and Glasgow Central were named 'Royal Scot' by the LM&SR and locomotive headboards displaying this name were provided. The 10.00 Edinburgh Princes Street departure, from 1927, also carried the headboard 'The Royal Scot'.

In September 1927, the mid-day 'Corridor' service, this long time Caledonian Railway working between Glasgow and London Euston, was resurrected when the LM&SR reintroduced a new early afternoon service between Glasgow and London Euston, and vice versa. In the following year the company reinstated Edinburgh Princes Street through coaches in this train, combining with the main service at Carstairs. This train, the 13.30 from London Euston and Glasgow Central, ran as a named express passenger train in its own right and was known as the 'Mid-Day Scot', although a locomotive headboard was not introduced until June 1951, by BR. This titled train was withdrawn by the LM&SR in 1939, by which time the L&NER, and its East Coast route was emerging as the undoubted principal service provider in terms of London–Edinburgh traffic, although not competitive for Manchester, Liverpool and Birmingham Anglo-Scottish traffic.

In the LM&SR summer timetables for 1936, a new Saturdays Only (SO) Anglo-Scottish service was introduced departing Euston and Glasgow Central at 13.30. Initially, this train ran in two portions in each direction throughout, and these were the 13.15 Euston to Glasgow combined with the 13.30 Euston to Edinburgh, and the 13.30 Glasgow to Euston combined with the 13.40 Edinburgh to Euston. The 13.30 SO Down train conveyed the portion for Glasgow Central which could only be joined by passengers travelling from Rugby and north thereof.

In 1937, to mark the Coronation Year of King George VI, the LM&SR introduced the much vaunted, streamlined 'Coronation Scot', a fixed formation train consisting of a BCK, FK, RFO, RK, SO, SO, RK and BSK, all specially constructed coaching stock to work the new Anglo-Scottish, Monday to Fridays Only (SX), high speed streamlined train service, the 'Coronation Scot'. This new train replaced the 'Mid-Day Scot' service; however, the 1936 Saturdays Only 13.30 service continuing to run, thus providing a full weekday through service between London and Scotland.

In the summer timetable for 1938 and 1939 'The Coronation Scot' service was replaced once more by the 'Mid-Day Scot', now running on weekdays and Sundays. As for the earlier 1936 and 1937 workings, the Saturdays Only working in these later years required some convoluted coaching stock utilisation which involved the splitting and remarshalling of individual coaches from the fixed formation special coaching stock for the weekday 'Coronation Scot' services, plus the use of additional spare coaching stock at the London end. Use of the 'Coronation Scot' coaches for Saturday and Sunday services had been strictly prohibited by Instruction in the LM&SR Marshalling Book, and it is obvious that the company's hard-pressed operators chose to adopt the 'Nelson's Eye' approach to these words of wisdom, right up until the 'Coronation Scot' coaching stock was lost to them in 1939, when it went off to the World Fair in the USA. With the coming of the nationalised railways, in September 1948 BR once more named 'The Mid-Day Scot' service, but to run between Glasgow and London only without any Edinburgh portion; a locomotive headboard for the through train was introduced for the summer of 1951.

After completion of the 1869 Cleland & Mid Calder line, regular Edinburgh to Glasgow workings were added to the daily departures from Princes Street (now some sixteen trains in each direction), adding to the sphere of influence of the of Dalry Road engines and crews, and there was a regular morning, lunch-time and evening commuter service to and from Kingsknowe to supplement the Edinburgh/Glasgow services which also stopped there. Passenger services increased in number with the opening of the Leith North Branch, the Balerno Branch, the Barnton Branch, and the transfer of the former Scottish Central Railway services from Haymarket to Princes Street via the Wester Dalry Branch. By 1919 the Edinburgh–Glasgow passenger services, although formed of non-corridor rolling stock, included a single Pullman car in the train consist; the Caledonian Railway had a total of twenty-two such cars, and four were allocated to this route. The addition of these cars was significant for the train crews, as each car was fitted with 6-wheeled bogies, was 63ft 9ins in length and weighed 42/43 tons tare, a heavy addition to any train on this difficult route. All had been withdrawn by November 1937.

The Pullman car services were:

From Glasgow Central:
08.45, 09.50, 11.00, 13.30, 14.20(SO), 16.05, 17.10, 18.45(SX) and 21.50.

From Edinburgh Princes Street:
06.25, 09.00, 10.55, 12.55(SX), 14.20(SO), 15.55(SO), 16.55(SX), 19.05 and 21.50.

The Pullman cars had been constructed for the Pullman Car Company by Cravens in 1914 and were finished in Pullman Dark Amber (Umber) and Cream (Ivory). The four cars allocated to the Edinburgh and Glasgow services, were all named after Mary, Queen of Scots' Ladies in Waiting, the famous 'Four Marys', as follows:

- No. 200 *Mary Hamilton*
- No. 201 *Mary Beaton*
- No. 202 *Mary Seaton* and
- No. 203 *Mary Carmichael.*

Parallel boilered Fowler 'Royal Scot' 4-6-0 No. 46137 *The Prince of Wales's Volunteers (South Lancashire)*, in sparkling condition, stands in Princes Street station before coupling to the coaches to work the 10.05 Princes Street to Birmingham New Street. This was a Longsight (Manchester) engine at the time. *Stuart Sellar*

All were Buffet Firsts, each with thirteen First Class seats and fourteen Third Class seats. The term 'Buffet' was not that as used today in meaning, but each car offered light refreshments plus a full meal service served at seats. The Pullman Supplement payable on the Edinburgh to Glasgow Route was 1s 0d per seat.

Edinburgh Princes Street daily departures on weekdays pre-World War Two included the following suburban destinations:

Leith North
Barnton
Balerno (Mid Calder)
Kingsknowe
Granton Gas Works.

Except for the latter, which was purely a privately-arranged workman's train service, the other suburban destinations were all, by the advent of the 20th century, coming under increasing competition from the rapidly developing and much more flexible electric tram-car systems which were appearing on the Edinburgh streets.

Main line regular departures from Princes Street included:

Ayr
Symington
Carstairs
Glasgow Central
Gourock
Beattock
Lanark
Oban
Birmingham New Street (portion train in winter but a through service in the summer timetable)
Stirling
Perth
Muirkirk
Liverpool (portion train)
Crewe (portion train)
Manchester Victoria (portion train)
Blackpool
London Euston (portion train).

Prior to World War One, in 1905, there were balanced through coach workings from the south-west of Scotland to Edinburgh Princes Street as follows:

08.55 through coach from Dumfries to Princes Street
09.30 through coach from Stranraer Town to Princes Street via Dumfries
12.35 through coach from Stranraer Harbour to Princes Street via Dumfries.

And in the opposite direction:

12.00 Princes Street to Stranraer Town via Dumfries
14.05 Princes Street to Stranraer Harbour via Dumfries.

By 1933 these through coach workings had been discontinued.

By the 1950s, Princes Street had lost its afternoon London through connection. It was to maintain through workings to industrial Lancashire and the north-west of England, however, and thus through Manchester and Liverpool services running as portion trains and connecting with the main through services from Glasgow Central at either Carstairs or Symington were still a feature of Princes Street main line departures (and arrivals) until final closure.

There were two other express passenger through workings from Princes Street which were also not to appear post-war, the first being the 'Strathearn Express' from Princes Street to St Fillans working (no headboard carried). The second was the 'Tinto Express' to Moffat, an Edinburgh portion which was attached to the 17.00 express from Glasgow Central to Moffat at Symington, and to another train which conveyed a Pullman Buffet Car in the consist. This train also slipped a coach for Lanark at Cleghorn.

Dalry Road shed crews generally ran these portion trains to and from Carstairs or Symington, but also retained some of these services as through workings to Carlisle in the heavier summer period, such as the trains to Birmingham New Street, these being the 10.15 morning service and the 22.50 overnight service, and their return workings from Carlisle.

The Balerno Branch passenger-carrying services commenced on 1st August 1874, with six trains in the Up direction from Princes Street and seven trains in the Down direction. All Up trains ran through to Midcalder station to reverse, and in the Down direction, the first morning train actually departed from West Calder station, leaving there at 07.50. The 15.05 train from Midcalder was a service which ran all the way from Glasgow and consisted of two portions, the first which left South Side station at 12.35, whilst the second departed Buchanan Street at 12.45, these two trains combining at Motherwell and running forward as a single train, via Carstairs. This working was something of an enigma, since presumably Dalry Road footplate crews worked one portion throughout, and the combined train forward from Motherwell, on the basis of route knowledge. What class of locomotive was used on this through working of 56¼ miles is unknown, but it must have been one of a class which was cleared to run over the Balerno Branch. This train took over three hours to complete the journey. Strangely, there was no corresponding west-bound through service until November 1874, when two through trains in each direction were introduced, but for an extremely short duration. In December of that same year the two through services were axed from the branch and re-routed back to the main line. Working of through main line passenger services over the Balerno Branch must have involved its own problems because of line curvature and gradients, and it would be interesting to know just what locomotives were authorised, although it is quite likely that these were one of Connor's four 0-4-4 bogie tank engines, No's 488-491 (later 167-170). Nevertheless, a through journey of 56¼ miles must have taxed their coal supply (1½ tons) and water (950 gallons) capacities.

Midcalder station (a First-Class station in Caledonian Railway station classification of importance) did offer rounding and stabling facilities which were nonexistent at Balerno at that time. There was no Sunday service over the branch when it opened. By 1896 there were twelve trains in each direction, with a further Saturday Only train in the Down direction (the 14.25 ex Princes Street). The 1918 timetable allowed for twenty-one Down trains, with one further Saturdays Only service (14.10) from Princes Street. In the Up direction there were nineteen trains. By LM&SR days, in 1936 the timetable allowed for twenty-one Down direction trains and twenty Up trains. The 22.46 Down train over the branch ran through to West Calder and Addiewell, where it terminated, on Wednesdays Only, in order to accommodate farmers returning from the weekly

Above: CR Class '104' 0-4-4T No. 169 (later LM&SR No. 15157) in Princes Street station, with crew alongside, waiting to work a Balerno Branch train.
Hamish Stevenson collection

Left: Another CR Class '104' 0-4-4T working a Balerno Branch train; here No. 167 is seen calling at Slateford station.
Hamish Stevenson collection

markets, thereafter rounding at Woodmuir Junction and returning main line to Edinburgh.

The Balerno Branch was unusual for the fact that, because of sharp curvature, it was worked with specially designed and constructed 4-wheeled coaches, and as late as 1922, thirty-nine 4-wheeled coaches of modern standards of comfort and electrically lit, designed by William Pickersgill, were ordered from R.Y. Pickering & Co. Ltd of Wishaw. These coaches were also to appear on both the Leith North Branch and the Barnton Branch after the expiry, in 1929, of the requirement that only 4-wheeled coaches could be operated over the Balerno Branch. These 4-wheelers ran with short buffers and, since the normal locomotive couplings were too long, special short coupling were provided on the 0-4-4T engines working this line. Princes Street station held two spare short couplings in the lamp room at the station.

A unique traffic over the Balerno Branch was that of the summer of

Colinton station on the Balerno Branch in 1957 with 0-6-0T No. 47163 on the branch goods working. For passengers that did not fancy exiting the station via the steps, there was also road access to the station from behind the photographer. *Stuart Sellar*

1888, when underprivileged children from the slums of Edinburgh were conveyed by train, free of charge, to be taken to Harmony House, Balerno, for a free fortnight's holiday in the fresh Pentlands air, with ten children coming and going every weekend.

The Balerno Branch closed to passenger traffic on and from Saturday 30th October 1943, with the departure of the last Up train at 20.19 from Balerno station, but freight working was to continue up until 1967.

The Leith North Branch commenced carrying passengers on 1st April 1879 with twelve trains in each direction, but by 1910 Dalry Road was faced with providing engines and crews to work some thirty-one return workings between Princes Street and Leith North, altogether an intensive suburban operation. By BR days, and immediately prior to closure, the branch was worked by DMUs, providing twenty-eight trains in each direction daily. The Leith Branch closed to passenger traffic in April 1962, as did the Granton Branch, although the northern section remained in use between Granton Breakwater Junction and Pilton West (for Granton Gas Works) until 1987.

The Barnton Branch, opened in March 1894, enjoyed some twenty-four trains each weekday, plus extra trains on Saturdays and Sundays. The branch closed on 7th May 1951, although Davidson's

ABOVE: A 1949 study in pure nostalgia. In early BR days, 0-4-4T No. 55233 pulls out of Leith North terminus with a passenger service for Edinburgh Princes Street. On the adjacent road to the right an original Edinburgh tram, No. 159, passes on a Leith-bound service.
R. Mark/Hamish Stevenson

LEFT: Ex-CR McIntosh Class '439' 0-4-4T No. 55210, in grimy condition with badly burned smokebox door, waits to leave Leith North station with the 14.30 passenger train to Edinburgh Princes Street in February 1954.
J.L. Stevenson/Hamish Stevenson

Ex-CR 0-4-4T No. 55233, heading a stopping passenger train consisting of ex-CR 4-wheeled coaching stock from Barnton, passes Dalry Middle Junction signal box in May 1949. *J.L. Stevenson/Hamish Stevenson*

Ex-CR McIntosh Class '439' 0-4-4T No. 55210 in very clean condition heads a Leith North to Princes Street stopping passenger train near Craigleith on 17th May 1955. *Stuart Sellar*

Ex-CR Pickersgill Class '72' 4-4-0 No. 54478 awaits the 'right away' from Leith North with a Princes Street local passenger service in 1957. *Stuart Sellar*

Stanier 'Black Five' No. 45022 on a train for Leith North, leaving Craigleith station is seen passing over the facing connection to the Barnton Branch (to right) at Craigleith Junction in February 1961. *Stuart Sellar*

Mains station retained a goods facility (mainly domestic coal) until 31st May 1960. Trains running to and from the Barnton Branch also served Craigleith, Murrayfield and Dalry Road stations. All in all, Dalry Road shed was required to provide engines and crews for what were very intensive, daily, suburban passenger train services numbering seventy-six trains at their peak and requiring some thirty-five drivers and thirty-five firemen when these three separate branches are considered.

In the mid-to-late 1950s, Dalry Road men worked a train of empty, non-corridor, coaching stock (06.00 ECS) from Princes Street to Shotts each weekday, coaches which then formed the 07.43 SX return Shotts to Princes Street, an early morning commuters train. Similarly, in the later DMU days an empty six-car DMU ran empty from Hamilton Central to West Calder where it terminated and reversed, forming the 07.10 from West Calder to Glasgow Central on weekdays.

Ex-CR McIntosh '812' Class, working the 13.02 Leith North to Princes Street passenger train, takes up the station stop at Craigleith in January 1958. *J.L. Stevenson/Hamish Stevenson*

The new order cometh! But not for long on this branch line. Gloucester 'Twin' DMUs have now taken over all passenger workings on Leith North Branch, heralding the withdrawal and scrapping of many of Dalry Road's ex-CR 0-4-4T engines. The date is April 1962, the station is East Pilton. *Stuart Sellar*

In the years following the Second World War, the Edinburgh and Glasgow services had been reduced to eleven trains weekdays plus one Saturdays Only (SO) turn (22.45) from Princes Street. There were no Sunday services between Edinburgh and Glasgow over the Shotts road. The late-night SO trains were notorious, just as they tended to be everywhere in the 1950s. They all comprised of non-corridor rolling stock, and the specific trains in question, were the 22.35 Princes Street to Lanark, the 22.45 Princes Street to Glasgow Central and the 22.40 train from Glasgow Central to Princes Street, and each were to feature large in the annals of Dalry Road, as will be revealed at Chapter 15. These trains, beloved of homeward bound late-night revellers, but not necessarily by the train crews involved, posed the perennial question for the latter: 'Are we going to get home to bed at a respectable hour tonight?' But, sadly, this was often not to be the case, as will be seen!

Gloucester 'Twin' DMU awaits departure from Leith North station on the last passenger service train to Edinburgh Princes Street on 28th April, 1962. The front car is No. SC53136. *Stuart Sellar*

Stanier '5MT' No. 45030 enters Kingsknowe station with the 18.10 Glasgow Central to Edinburgh Princes Street passenger service in July 1953. *J.L. Stevenson/Hamish Stevenson*

A very clean No. 44994 working the 16.40 passenger service from Princes Street to Glasgow Central nears Kingsknowe in June 1952. *S. Teasdale/Hamish Stevenson*

By 1900, Princes Street was dealing with some 180 trains per day, but this number swelled by a vast number of seasonal extras and excursions. As described at Chapter 10, Princes Street station became the preferred destination in Edinburgh for Royal Train workings to and from the capital, this even though the NBR had, many years earlier, constructed a dedicated 'Royal' station at Meadowbank, close by Holyrood House, the Royal Residence in Scotland. The fact that Princes Street was on the same level, and with direct road access to and from the main city thoroughfares, greatly facilitated the secure transfer of Royals from train to either horse-drawn coach or, later, car.

Up to 1951, balanced through coach workings operated every weekday from Edinburgh Princes Street to Ayr, via Lanark and Muirkirk, but by later BR days Dalry Road men had gained regular additional Saturday Only through services, as follows:

- 10.30 Edinburgh to Ayr and Heads of Ayr via Holytown & Gushetfaulds; return working 09.25 ex Heads of Ayr; Dalry Road men exchanged footplates en route with Ayr men.
- 15.05 Edinburgh to Ayr; return with 18.05 ex Ayr; Dalry Road men worked throughout.
- 07.55 Edinburgh to Gourock; coaches return 19.30 ex Gourock.
- 08.12 Edinburgh to Blackpool; Dalry Road men worked to Carlisle.

The 07.55 to Gourock was worked by Dalry Road men through to Paisley Gilmour Street with engine going through with a Gourock

BR Standard '6MT' Pacific No. 72004 *Clan MacDonald* of Polmadie shed is seen entering Merchiston station heading a Glasgow Central to Edinburgh stopping passenger train. *Stuart Sellar*

crew. Engine worked back on the 19.30 ex Gourock with Dalry Road men changing with a Gourock crew at Paisley Gilmour Street.

Other weekday services included the Anglo-Scottish departures:

10.10	Edinburgh to Birmingham New Street (portion in winter; through train in summer).
10.55	Edinburgh to Liverpool (portion).
11.10	Edinburgh to Manchester and Liverpool (portions).
13.45	Edinburgh to Liverpool (portion).
16.05	Edinburgh to Liverpool (portion).
17.55	Edinburgh to Crewe (portion) (WCML TPO).
23.30	Edinburgh to Birmingham New Street (through train in summer only).

The 10.10 (winter) and 11.10 departures ran through to Symington to be attached to the 10.05 Glasgow to Birmingham and the 10.40 Glasgow to Manchester trains respectively. In the summer timetable the 10.10 Princes Street to Birmingham and 15.30 ex Birmingham were both through trains, which Dalry Road men worked to and from Carlisle, as was the 23.30 Birmingham.

In the mid 1950s a normal daily workload for Princes Street station in respect of main line passenger services was as follows:

Departures 06.00–14.00		**Arrivals 06.00–14.00**	
06.27	to Glasgow Central	05.19	TPO ex London Euston
06.47	ECS to Shotts	07.43	ex Shotts
06.50	to Callander	10.15	ex Stirling
08.02	to Glasgow Central	08.30	06.55 ex Glasgow Central
08.38	to Glasgow Central	08.52	07.59 ex Carstairs
08.55	to Lanark	09.19	08.40 ex Lanark
09.25	to Perth	11.30	ex Aberdeen to Glasgow
10.10	Birmingham (to Symington)	09.53	08.40 ex Glasgow Central
10.50	Manchester (to Symington)	10.29	08.14 ex Glasgow Central
11.37	to Glasgow Central	11.07	09.57 ex Glasgow Central
12.32	to Kingsknowe	13.16	13.06 ex Kingsknowe
13.04	to Kingsknowe	13.51	13.41 ex Kingsknowe
13.35	to Glasgow Central	14.01	13.51 ex Kingsknowe

Carstairs-based ex-Midland Johnson 4-4-0 Compound No. 40904 is seen here double heading Crewe North 'Black Five' No. 45434 whilst working the 10.05 Princes Street to Birmingham New Street express passenger train. The Compound will come off at Carstairs. The train is seen here passing Slateford on 5th August 1955. *Stuart Sellar*

'Black Five' No. 44952 running tender first, awaits the 'right away' at Kingsknowe with the three-coach midday local train for Edinburgh Princes Street in July 1964. *Stuart Sellar*

A pair of Stanier Class '5MTs', No's 45011 and 45012, head a southbound express to Manchester and Liverpool out of Princes Street station in July 1964. *Stuart Sellar*

These above service departures were all, except for the 11.37 and 13.35 trains to Glasgow Central which were Polmadie shed return workings, worked by Dalry Road shed. In the summer timetable, Dalry Men worked the 10.10 Birmingham through to Carlisle, returning with the 11.15 from Birmingham.

Departures 14.00–22.00		**Arrivals 14.00–22.00**	
15.20	to Lanark	15.24	09.30 ex Manchester
15.45	to Glasgow Central	16.06	15.30 ex Carstairs
16.05	to Manchester (to Carstairs)	17.19	16.15 ex Lanark
16.40	to Glasgow Central.	17.31	15.42 ex Glasgow Central
16.48	to Muirkirk.	17.48	16.30 ex Glasgow Central
17.15	to Glasgow Central	18.00	11.15 ex Birmingham
17.55	to Lanark.	19.30	20.05 ex Glasgow Central
18.38	TPO to London Euston	20.21	18.50 ex Glasgow Central
21.28	to Glasgow Central	21.33	ex Carstairs
22.45	SO to Glasgow	(21.00	Edinburgh Connection from Down Mid-Day Scot)

Dalry Road crews worked the 15.20 to Lanark, returning with the 14.40 ex Lanark; the 17.15 to Glasgow Central, returning with the 21.33 ex Central, and the 18.38 TPO to Carstairs. They also worked the 23.20 Birmingham through to Carlisle (see below).

Departures 22.00–06.00		**Arrivals 22.00–06.00**	
22.05	to Carstairs	22.05	16.25 ex Liverpool
23.20	to Birmingham (through train)	22.57	21.55 ex-Carstairs

Dalry Road men also worked passenger trains to destinations northwards over the E&G Main line via Polmont, and these daily workings were as follows:

06.50 Princes Street to Callander to Stirling, returning with the 10.15 ex Stirling.

09.25 Princes Street to Perth; retuning double heading the 11.30 Aberdeen to Glasgow as far as Larbert where they uncoupled, picked up and worked the 15.45 Larbert to Edinburgh Princes Street.

Fairburn 2-6-4T No. 42272 on a two-coach train for Carstairs/ Lanark, runs into Merchiston station.
J.L. Stevenson/Hamish Stevenson

BR Standard '7MT' Pacific No. 70003 *John Bunyan* heads a WCML portion for Edinburgh Waverley past Morningside Road station in August 1964.
Stuart Sellar

9 Dalry Road and the Welsh Rugby Specials

From Caledonian Railway days, there was another regular special passenger working for rugby enthusiasts domiciled in the west of Scotland. Each year, dining car special trains for rugby enthusiasts from Glasgow and the West of Scotland were run on the match Saturdays in January and February when Scotland were playing at home in the Four Nations Championship. These trains were usually of ten to twelve coach formation and had, in earlier days, included Pullman stock. Proving very popular, with meals being served at all seats, several trains were run on the match Saturdays, from Glasgow and the West of Scotland, direct to the platforms at Murrayfield station on the North Leith Branch, with the empty coaches being taken forward to Crew Junction, Newhaven, or the sidings at Leith North, for stabling and servicing for the return journey. In latter BR days, Polmadie generally turned out two BR Standard Class '5MT' 4-6-0 locomotives to double-head each of these heavy workings which normally were routed over the 1869 Glasgow to Edinburgh via Shotts line. Engines allocated to work the dining cars specials, as recorded in these latter years of this service were:

February 1959:	Standard Class '5':	No's 73058 & 73072.
March 1960:	ditto	No's 73062 & 73063 and No's 73060 & 73076.
January 1962:	ditto	No's 73055 & 73057 and No's 73098 & 73099.

However, there was another side to the story regarding Rugby Specials, involving even more trains, and that was when special through trains from Wales were run, carrying up to 15,000 Welsh rugby supporters to Murrayfield for the original Home Nations Rugby Championship (1888-1909 and 1932-1939).

It was only when the Welsh team came north to Edinburgh to play that rail traffic increased dramatically, because special trains from various Welsh starting points were being run through to Edinburgh and, in the main, destined for Edinburgh Princes Street station. This was a biennial traffic, involving much co-operation and coordination between the GWR and LM&SR pre-nationalisation, the Midland, Scottish and Western Regions of British Railways post-nationalisation, with Edinburgh Princes Street station being the primary destination – though a lesser number of specials worked into Edinburgh Waverley, mainly running over the Border Union Railway from Carlisle. This traffic had gained a significant hold pre-war, and indeed in 1938 a total of no less than thirty-eight specials were run by the GWR and LM&SR; this number was never to be exceeded. Coaches on these trains were always a mix of GWR and LM&SR coaching stock. The West Coast Main Line, between Crewe Junction and Edinburgh Princes Street, was specially cleared by Instruction, contained within the LM&SR General Appendix to the Working Timetable dated March 1937 (page 22), for the running of the GWR Company's wider coaching stock which was 60 feet in length, 9 feet 3 inches wide over body and 9 feet 4½ inches over handles.

A number of the Welsh supporters traditionally made a holiday of the event, and were ever-popular visitors in the city, with their recognisable red scarves and good humour So, these specials started

Murrayfield station, with its extra-long platforms for Rugby Specials, on the Dalry to Leith North branch.
David Dickson collection

to arrive from the Wednesday of match week onwards, with arrivals continuing until the Saturday of the actual match. Return workings commenced late on match evening and continued through the following Sunday. With so many foreign locomotives requiring servicing and coaling, Dalry Road shed was put under severe pressure and the stabling of so many engines was a biennial problem. Year upon year, throughout the 1950s, the number of specials increased, with the late 1950s proving to be the peak post-war years. This peak of the mid to late 1950s is examined in more detail hereunder.

Dalry Road had also to provide engines and crews to steam heat the ECS from the West of Scotland, when they were stabled at Crew Junction or Newhaven. The Rugby Specials overall posed a philosophical logistics problem in the working of Princes Street station, Dalry Road shed and, indeed, the whole Edinburgh District. For example, since Edinburgh did not have any 'barracks' accommodation for crews requiring to lodge, it became the norm for a rake of sleeping cars to be stabled in Lothian Road Goods Sidings, to act as a hostel for foreign train crews and dining car staff who had worked in to Edinburgh with the specials, and a further engine had to be booked out from Dalry Road shed to steam heat these cars.

In the early 1960s the cold gaze of Doctor Beeching relentlessly highlighted rolling stock which was kept in reserve for occasional events, such as these Rugby Specials. Spare capacity in any form, be it coaching stock or motive power, was now being viewed as inefficient, wasteful and no longer acceptable. The Welsh Rugby Specials obviously came under this scrutiny and their death knell began to toll. Even the more regular and very popular 'Starlight Special' holiday excursion trains to and from London were victims of the new regime. The non-availability of rolling stock and other resources, at a time of growing car ownership and the ever-increasing popularity of coach travel, combined to bring to an end a long-standing and immensely popular tradition, in which the men of Dalry Road, and its associated stations and depots, had taken so much pride.

A tendency during the great years of the Rugby Specials was for increasing numbers of Welsh supporters to arrive earlier and make the event a holiday in Edinburgh. The activities spread to neighbouring towns and suburbs, as accommodation in the city centre became more difficult. Noisy, yet hugely popular, these good-natured fans enjoyed Scottish hospitality and, of course, Scottish 'refreshments' to the extreme. There is the famous apocryphal tale of a group of Welsh supporters who, after a week's carousing in the city and while making their way to Princes Street station to join one of the last trains home to Wales, helped a particularly inebriated compatriot to the train by putting him on convenient parcel trolley, wheeling him to the side of the coach and ensuring that he was boarded safely. It turned out that the individual was an ex-patriate Welshman, who had relocated to work and live in Edinburgh several years before, and who was most surprised to wake up in Pontllanfraith High Level (or wherever).

To illustrate the magnitude of the achievements of the Scottish Railway team during the heyday of Rugby Specials, it is useful to examine the arrangements for some individual years.

February 1955

Post World War Two, it had become the norm for special trains to be run direct to Edinburgh (Princes Street) from Wales, for the International matches when Scotland were playing the Welsh team at Murrayfield. In 1955, over the four days prior to the actual match, some twenty Welsh Rugby Specials arrived in Princes Street, hauled by a variety of ex LM&SR 4-6-0s, such as 'Jubilees', 'Royal Scots' and the ubiquitous 'Black Fives', all from southern depots. All these locomotives required servicing, coaling and stabling until required for return workings, and caused severe logistical problems for the small Dalry Road shed and its small manual coaling stage with its single coal drop. For the many Welsh supporters who travelled north to support their home team, that particular year proved to be a long weary trip for nothing, since Scotland won the day by 15 points to 11, though an interesting day for railway enthusiasts.

Indeed, rumour (unconfirmed) has it that an ex-'Claughton' rebuild, No. 45500 *Patriot* of Willesden shed (1A) also turned up on a Rugby Special. Allegedly the joiner at Dalry shed was called out specially to saw bits off the shed door to accommodate this engine – but that must, in the author's view, be taken with a pinch of salt, particularly since the shed doors had long since disappeared in early LM&SR days.

Ex LM&SR Stanier Class '5X' No. 45564 *New South Wales*, a Leeds Holbeck locomotive, stands on the ashpits at Dalry Road on 5th February 1955, having worked a special train in connection with the Five Nations Rugby International at Murrayfield. At this time of the year there were numerous specials run from the south for this event. *Stuart Sellar*

Date	Worked by	Shed
Wednesday, 2nd February 1955		
W663	5MT No. 45151	Motherwell (66B)
Thursday, 3rd February 1955		
W	7P No. 46138 *London Irish Regiment*	Crewe North (5A)
W631	7P No. 46163 *Civil Service Rifleman*	Crewe North (5A)
W632	5X No. 45703 *Thunderer*	Crewe North (5A)
W634	5MT No. 45316	Patricroft (10C)
W642	5X No. 45599 *Bechuanaland*	Carlisle Upperby (12A)
Friday, 4th February 1955		
W636	5X No. 45643 *Rodney*	Crewe North (5A)
W641	7P No. 46115 *Scots Guardsman*	Longsight (9A)
W637	7P No. 46106 *Gordon Highlander*	Crewe North (5A)
W638	5X No. 45604 *Ceylon*	Crewe North (5A)
Saturday, 5th February 1955		
W644 20.10 ex Newport and 20.00 ex Blaenavon	7P No. 46148 *The Manchester Regiment*	Crewe North (5A)
W645 20.00 ex Carmarthen	7P No. 46118 *Royal Welch Regiment*	Crewe North (5A)
W646 19.40 ex Swansea Victoria	5X No. 45606 *Falkland Islands*	Camden (1B)
W647 20.50 ex Pontllanfraith High Level	5X No. 45601 *British Guiana*	Camden (1B)
W648 22.00 ex Pantyffynnon	??	
W649 21.19 ex Treherbert	7P No. 46127 *Old Contemptibles*	Crewe North (5A)
W651 21.20 ex Kidwelly	5X No. 45680 *Camperdown*	Longsight (9A)
W653 23.00 ex Swansea Victoria	5X No. 45692 *Cyclops*	Longsight (9A)
M993 17.30 ex Cymmer Afan	5X No. 45565 *Victoria*	Leeds Holbeck (20A)
M994 18.35 ex Neath	5X No. 45564 *New South Wales*	Leeds Holbeck (20A)
W652 23.00 ex Aberdare High Level	??	

These Welsh specials in 1955, were as shown above. Whilst two locomotives are unaccounted for in the above list, by chance records show two 'foreign' engines spotted in Dalry Road shed on the same 5th February, these being Class '5X' No's 45640 *Frobisher* of Carlisle Kingmoor shed (68A) and No. 45674 *Duncan* of Crewe North shed (5A). Thus, that particular shortcoming might well be resolved.

As further five Rugby Specials ran into Edinburgh Waverley, but at least Dalry Road were spared the problems of dealing with these engines and they would have gone to either Haymarket or St. Margaret's in the normal course of events. Whatever, Dalry Road coped with this mammoth task until the back sidings behind the north side of the shed were full and, thereafter, Carstairs shed helped with locomotive stabling. For the return workings, many of the returning special trains were piloted over Cobbinshaw Summit by Fairburn 2-6-4T engines from both Dalry Road or Carstairs sheds.

Stanier '5X' 4-6-0 No. 45680 *Camperdown* of Manchester Longsight shed (9A) takes coal at Dalry Road shed coaling stage on Saturday 5th February 1955, after working a Welsh Rugby Special train (No. W651) from Kidwelly to Edinburgh Princes Street for the Wales/ Scotland international rugby match. It is seen here in the normal poor weather applying on these occasions, still carrying the headboard with the train reporting number.
M.J. Robertson/Hamish Stevenson

Stanier Class '5X' No. 45700 *Amethyst* of Newton Heath shed and '5MT' No. 44827 of Longsight shed working a returning Welsh Rugby Special, passing Slateford Junction on 5th February 1955. *Stuart Sellar*

Fairburn 2-6-4T No. 42268 of Dalry Road shed double heads Stanier '5MT' No. 44953, a Carstairs engine, on a returning Welsh Rugby Special train, passing Slateford Junction on 5th February 1955. The leading coach behind the 'Black Five' is an ex-GWR bow-ended Brake Third. *Stuart Sellar*

FEBRUARY 1957

This year the Welsh Rugby Specials peaked with thirty being run from Wales – twenty-five to Edinburgh Princes Street and five to Edinburgh Waverley. Classed in railway jargon as Parspec's (Party Specials), each consisted of eleven coaches, with two of this number, W648 and M994, conveying Second Class Sleeping Cars (see below). The special trains booked to run to Edinburgh Princes Street were:

Wednesday 30th January 1957	
W655 ex Cardiff	W630 ex Llanelli
Thursday 31st January	
W656 ex Newport	W634 ex Treherbert
W632 ex Llanelly	W625 ex Cardiff
W631 ex Swansea Victoria	W636 ex Neath
W633 ex Swansea High Street	
Friday 1st February 1957	
W637 ex Cardiff	W640 ex Swansea Victoria
W638 ex Merthyr	W641 ex Newport
W639 ex Treherbert	W642 ex Bargoed
W657 ex Treherbert	
Saturday 2nd February 1957	
W643 ex Newport	M992 ex Newport
W644 ex Swansea Victoria	M996 ex Cardiff
M995 ex Blaina	W649 ex Kidwelly
W645 ex Carmarthen	W650 ex Aberdare
W647 ex Pontllanfraith	

The other five specials were routed via Hawick to Edinburgh Waverley, including the two conveying sleeping cars.

The two regular dining car special trains from Glasgow Central on Saturday 2nd February were double-headed as usual. The first was worked by Stanier '5MT' No. 45099 of Motherwell shed and BR Standard '5MT' No. 73058 of Polmadie, with the second hauled by Stanier '5MT' No. 45008, again a Motherwell engine, and Standard '5MT' No. 73078 of Glasgow Eastfield shed. In addition, a special train starting from Barrhead was worked through to Murrayfield by BR Standard '6MT' No. 72000 *Clan Buchanan*, and a further five Rugby Specials were worked from the West of Scotland by the following engines:

- Stanier '5MT' No. 44845 (Leeds Holbeck shed)
- Stanier '5MT' No. 44850 (Motherwell shed)
- Stanier '5MT' No. 45049 (Stirling shed)
- BR Standard '6MT' No. 72003 *Clan Fraser* (Polmadie shed)
- BR Standard '5MT' No. 73121 (Glasgow Corkerhill shed).

In this same year, and on the very same Saturday, Edinburgh was also hosting, not one, but two football matches, in the 5th round of the Scottish Cup: Heart of Midlothian playing Glasgow Rangers at Tynecastle, and Hibernian playing Aberdeen at Easter Road; BR (Scottish Region) managed to provide locomotives, train crews and coaches for a total of fifteen special train workings from Glasgow and the West of Scotland, and a further six Football Specials, from Aberdeen, Dundee and Perth, for these two football matches, and this over and above the Welsh rugby commitments.

Such was the pressure on Dalry Road shed, with its modest allocation of engines, that on this particular Saturday afternoon every vacuum-fitted engine allocated there, with the exception of ex-Caledonian McIntosh 4-4-0 'Dunalastair IV' No. 54452, was actually out on train running duties.

This time round, coaches were worked to Slateford, Saughton Junction, Portobello Yard, Law Junction and Stepps, for servicing and stabling. Lessons had been learned from previous years, and

Ex-CR 0-4-4T, No. 55229 provides steam heating for the ECS of a Rugby Special amongst the mineral wagons in Crew Junction yard. *J.L. Stevenson/ Hamish Stevenson*

Dalry Road locomotives No's 55210, 42271 and 55229 provide steam heating for coaches stabled at Crew Junction, coaches which will make up the return workings of Rugby Special trains from Murrayfield to Glasgow and the west of Scotland.
J.L. Stevenson/Hamish.Stevenson

many of the incoming English locomotives were quickly dispersed to the Glasgow Area and Carstairs, but foreign locomotives which remained 'on shed' at Dalry Road included:

- Stanier '5MT' No. 45000 (5B)
- Stanier '5MT' No. 45041 (6A)
- Stanier '5MT' No. 45060 (5B)
- Stanier '5MT' No. 45294 (26F)
- Stanier '5MT' No. 45065 (3D)
- Stanier '5X' No. 45569 *Tasmania* (55A)
- Stanier '5X' No. 45600 *Bermuda* (26F)
- Stanier '5X' No. 45625 *Sarawak* (5A)
- Stanier '5X' No. 45672 *Anson* (12B)
- Stanier '5X' No. 45689 *Ajax* (5A).

The engines which had been dispersed elsewhere were worked back to Dalry Road in sufficient time to take up the booked return workings, and the first fourteen returning specials departed Princes Street station between 23.00 (Saturday evening) and 01.50 (Sunday), running virtually 'Block for Block' to Carstairs. The remaining eleven specials left Princes Street between 08.45 and 13.20 on Sunday. Each of the twenty-five trains needed pilot assistance to Dolphinton Junction (Carstairs).

FEBRUARY 1959

In this year a total of twenty-five Rugby Specials left Wales for Edinburgh and, as in previous years, some twenty were destined for Edinburgh Princes Street with remaining five running into Edinburgh Waverley over the Border Union Railway. The following engines worked the specials into Edinburgh.

Thursday 5th February:

- Stanier '5MT' No. 44935 (6G)
- Stanier '5MT' No. 45079 (25G)
- Stanier '5MT' No. 44938 (2A)
- Stanier '5MT' No. 45216 (27A)
- Stanier '5MT' No. 45227 (14B)
- Stanier '5MT' No. 45307 (1E).

Friday 6th February:

- Stanier '5MT' No. 44946 (56F)
- Stanier '5MT' No. 45181 (8A)
- Stanier '5MT' No. 45375 (1A)
- Stanier '5X' No. 45556 *Bombay* (5A).

Saturday 7th February:

- Stanier '5MT' No. 45238 (14A)
- Stanier '5MT' No. 45261 (26B)
- Stanier '5X' No. 45569 *Tasmania* (55A)
- Stanier '5X' No. 45582 *Central Provinces* (24K)
- Stanier '5X' No. 45635 *Tobago* (26B)
- Stanier '5X' No. 45639 *Raleigh* (55A)
- Stanier '5X' No. 45671 *Prince Rupert* (9A)
- Stanier '5X' No. 45689 *Ajax* (5A).

Empty coaching stock from the Glasgow specials was stabled at Leith North Sidings and Crew Yard and, as in former years, a suitable engine was provided to steam heat the sleeping cars at Lothian Road Goods. On this occasion ex-Caledonian Class '72' 4-4-0 No. 54478 was taken out long-term storage at Dalry Road shed to provide this service.

There was one unfortunate incident with returning special trains this particular year, when the 00.41 (Sunday) departure from Princes Street, with Nos. 45022 as train engine and pilot No. 45639 *Raleigh* collided with a bus which had run through the level crossing gates at Camps Junction. Fortunately, no one was injured but No. 45639 suffered damage which required that it be detached; No. 45022, with a Leeds (Holbeck) crew in charge, worked the train forward unassisted after incurring a 90-minute delay.

The Great Days Remembered

With the inclusion of France in 1910, the event became the 'The Five Nations Rugby Union International Competition' (1910-31 and 1947-99). From 1999, with the inclusion of Italy, the event became 'The Six Nations', and so it is today. Sponsored by the Royal Bank of Scotland, the event was known as the 'RBS Six Nations', but

Above: BR Standard Class '5' 4-6-0s No's 73060 and 73062 have coupled onto a train of empty coaches stabled at Newhaven Junction, ready to form a westbound Rugby Special train in March 1960, whilst Class J39/3 0-6-0 No. 64986 heads a Leith North to Princes Street extra passenger service, laid on for the rugby international, away from Newhaven station in March 1960. *Stuart Sellar*

Below: Shortly afterwards, No's 73060 and 73062 head the empty coaches to Murrayfield station where homeward-bound fans will enjoy the pleasures of the on-board dining facilities on the Rugby Special, which will be worked over the Shotts line to Glasgow. *Stuart Sellar*

in 2018 sponsorship was assumed by the NatWest Banking Group and so the event is now the 'NatWest Six Nations'. The matches were, and still are, played over a series of Saturdays in January and February every year, at the home venue of the respective teams, on a rotating biennial basis, as follows:

- Scotland: Murrayfield (Edinburgh)
- France: Stade de France, Paris
- Wales: Cardiff Arms Park, St. Helen's, Swansea (pre-1954) and Rodney Parade, Newport (pre-1913)
- England: Twickenham
- Ireland: Lansdowne Road (now Aviva Stadium), Dublin
- Italy: Stadio Olimpica, Rome.

Sadly, in 2018, the Rugby Specials of yore are no longer a feature of Edinburgh life, and the 1938 pre-war and 1957 post-war events will be remembered as being the joint zeniths of the Welsh Rugby Specials, so much a part of the railway scene in Edinburgh's history. Who can ever forget, if a rugby enthusiast like the author, the great days of the Five Nations, and in particular the Welsh Internationals at Murrayfield, when the glorious voices of the massive Welsh support, singing the Welsh National Anthem 'Hen Wlad Fy Nhadau' (Land of My Fathers) to inspire their team. Truly a special moment for everyone, when the hairs on the back of one's neck stood up to attention, moved by the sheer volume of several thousand Welsh voices, united in harmony, in the singing of a most beautiful and poignant song, and the sound of same reverberating around the stadium. However, even though the truly great days of Welsh Rugby Specials were long gone, BR continued to run Rugby Specials from Glasgow and the West of Scotland direct to Murrayfield station until the early 1960s.

Edinburgh, being Edinburgh – now a World Heritage Site and, from 1947, truly 'The Festival City', with an annual International Arts Festival, the ever-expanding Fringe Festival, Book Festival, Film Festival and Jazz Festival, and the world famous and spectacular Edinburgh Military Tattoo held on the esplanade of that most famous city landmark, Edinburgh Castle – became a magnet for tourists and visitors. It was also to be the destination for many more excursion trains and, just as for the rugby traffic, Dalry Road had to step up to the mark each time. In the 1950s and 1960s, before foreign holiday destinations took over, it was the destination for home visitors, and this meant many extra trains were to arrive, and Dalry Road was ever to prove a rail enthusiasts Mecca. During these great times, Edinburgh was to prove a wonderful place to be when in railway employment, and the author will forever be unashamedly grateful for, and remember fondly, the opportunity afforded him to participate in full.

Unusual motive power on the Leith North Branch. Here ex-L&NER Class J39/3 0-6-0 No. 64986 heads an extra service train in connection with the Rugby International from Leith North past Newhaven Junction in March 1960. *Stuart Sellar*

Stanier '5X' 4-6-0 No. 45643 *Rodney* of Crewe North shed, being prepared for duty at Dalry Road, before working the return Welsh Rugby Special train, reporting number W636, back home, on Saturday 6th February 1960. This locomotive had worked the same Up Rugby Special into Edinburgh two days previously, on the 4th of the month. *John Robertson/Hamish Stevenson*

The Glasgow-bound Rugby Special worked by locomotives No's 73076 and 73075 passes Granton Junction in February 1963.
Stuart Sellar

BR Standard 5 locomotives No's 73063 and 76075, double heading a Rugby Special train for Glasgow at Murrayfield station, awaiting the 'right away', February 1963.
Stuart Sellar

BR Standard 5s No's 73076 and 73075 take the Slateford line at Coltbridge Junction with a 10-coach Rugby Special return working to Glasgow. The train will work over the heavily graded Shotts line with this big train which also includes restaurant car facilities, hence the double heading. *Stuart Sellar*

BR Standard 5s No's 73060 and 73076 in March 1960, working a Rugby Dining Special from Glasgow and destined for Murrayfield station in Edinburgh, has just cleared Fauldhouse North and the viaduct over the Breich Water (the County March between West Lothian and Midlothian) to rear, and is passing the site of former Muldron (Mouldron) Junction Signal Box and the solum of the former Muldron (Mouldron) Branch (running off to the left). *Roy Crombie/SRPS*

10 DALRY ROAD AND ROYAL TRAIN WORKINGS

The first ever Royal Train workings over Caledonian Railway lines, which took place at the time of the Slateford to Haymarket Branch Line debacle, have been discussed in some detail at Chapter 3, these being the workings from Meadowbank station – The Queen's Platform (NBR) – to Bangor on 15th October 1859 and again from Meadowbank station to Gosport on 17th September 1860.

It is assumed that initially HM Queen Victoria, the first monarch to use rail, used the Royal Saloon built by the London & Birmingham Railway Company in 1838 for Queen Adelaide (Queen Consort of William IV). This was a 4-wheeled coach, with sumptuous accommodation based on three stage-coach passenger compartments. This saloon was scrapped in 1850 but in 1869 Queen Victoria commissioned the construction of a pair of coaches which would form *her* Royal Train. The cost was £1,800, to which she contributed £800. The coaches were built by the L&NWR at the then new Wolverton Works to the design of Richard Bore, and consisted of two 6-wheeled coaches containing a day saloon, lavatory and bedroom, and inter-connected by a flexible gangway which, incidentally, the Queen refused to use when the train was in motion. She also had a system of external signals provided on the roof, with which she could communicate with the footplate and have the train slowed down or stopped at her command. Bore was obliged to redesign the train at the Queen's insistence and combined both coach bodies on a 12-wheeled underframe forming a lavish self-contained 'palace on wheels', finished to the highest standards with opulent Royal blue silk furnishings and 23 carat gold paint, using the finest birds-eye maple wood sculpted by the top craftsmen of the day. This Saloon, later numbered 802 by the LM&SR, was withdrawn in 1902 and preserved, and can be seen today in the NRM at York.

From the details (supplied by Mr G.P. Neele, in his reminiscences of his railway career) it can also be gathered that the overall organisation and management of Royal Train journeys over the WCML and in Scotland were very much in the hands of the L&NWR, with their Superintendent of the Line, the same Mr Neele, accompanying just over 100 royal journeys system wide during his long career. The L&NWR Company had a set of detailed Internal Working Instructions pertaining to this important operation. However, these same Internal Instructions were to form the basis of the Instructions issued by every other railway company in the event

Royal Train engine 'Dunalastair IV' No. 923, seen here in resplendent condition resting between royal duties at its home shed of Dalry Road. Note the masonic device worked into the smokebox door. *James Murie/CRA Archives*

The royal visit to Scotland in 1914. Here, the royal party, King George V, Queen Mary and the Princess Royal are seen at Edinburgh Princes Street, embarking on to the Royal Train for a trip to Glasgow Central. The benefits offered to such workings at Edinburgh Princes Street are obvious, with the royal horse-drawn landaus being able to draw alongside the train. The date is Tuesday 7th July and this trip is the first of several due to take place in the week following. The train engine on this day was Dalry Road 'Dunalastair IV' No. 923, piloted by 'Dunalastair III' No. 899 of the same shed. *CRA Archives*

of having to convey HM Queen Victoria over their metals. The Caledonian Railway was no different, and it is assumed that in the two workings described above, and all workings to follow, they also provided, in consideration of the Queen's external system of signals, the mandatory third man as 'look out' on the footplate of the Royal Train locomotive. This man was so provided to maintain a close watch *rearward*, for any signal which might be given from the train itself, thus ensuring that the driver and fireman could concentrate on the road ahead. Without doubt, a sinecure of a task!

One interesting fact, and a bonus indeed for Dalry Road shed, was that, with the opening of the final Edinburgh Princes Street station in 1894, this station was to become the preferred arrival and departure point for the 'Royals' travelling to and from Edinburgh, because the station lay at street level, and enjoyed free and unrestricted road access, with maximum security, right into platform level and train-side. This meant that the open, horse-drawn landaus, and later the motor saloon cars, could be driven right up to the side of the Royal Train, thus facilitating the transfer of the royal personages. This gave rise to Dalry Road footplate crews being involved in many Royal Train workings, including the empty royal coaching stock workings. Ravelrig Junction on the WCML was a very convenient and secure location, frequently used for stabling the Royals overnight when a mid-morning arrival in the city was required.

It became the tradition from the earliest times to run a pilot engine, carrying a Royal Train Pilot headboard to identify itself, some 15 minutes ahead of every Royal Train as a security measure, thus ensuring that the track over which the Royal Train would run had in no way been obstructed or otherwise damaged; in the annals of the Caledonian Railway, this was a task which was entrusted for many years to the famous 'Caley Single' No. 123, which was always turned out in sparkling condition. The actual Royal Train locomotive, or locomotives, were also turned out cleaned to perfection and fitted with the special three white discs (one at the chimney and two at either side of the upper cab facing forward) signifying its role to all concerned. However, there is photographic evidence to show that the practice of running the pilot engine in advance of the actual Royal Train was a practice which was falling into decline by that most momentous year of 1914. In that year, the Royals – King George V, Queen Mary and the 18-year-old Mary, The Princess Royal, all destined to be the last members of the Royal

House of Saxe-Coburg-Gotha lineage and first of the New House of Windsor (1917) – came north on a seven day visit to Scotland, residing at Holyrood House in Edinburgh and making several trips by Royal Train during that period.

Arriving on Monday 6th July by train, the royal party travelled to the following destinations to carry out various official duties:

Tuesday 7th July	10.00 departure Princes Street to Glasgow Central via Holytown
Wednesday 8th July	10.00 departure from Princes Street to Eglinton Street.
Thursday 9th July	10.00 departure from Princes Street to Parkhead (Glasgow)
Friday 10th July	10.00 departure from Princes Street to Dundee Tay Bridge (via NBR)
Saturday 11th July	10.00 departure from Princes Street to Dunblane
Monday 13th July	10.20 departure from Princes Street for return to London

For these workings Dalry Road shed provided two of its own allocated locomotives: the first a McIntosh 'Dunalastair IV', No. 923 and one of the later 1908 builds, as the train engine; with 'Dunalastair III' No. 889 as pilot engine. However, on the final journey, the return to London, the Royal Train pilot engine, a Carlisle-based 'Dunalastair IV', No. 925, carrying headboard, was attached as pilot to the train engine No. 889 on that day, working the 10.05 service departure to London Euston, thereby still running the mandatory 15 minutes in advance of the Royal Train, but also piloting the heavy, preceding London departure, proving a far more sensible use of motive power.

It was whilst the author was working as a clerk at Dalry Road, in June and July 1961 that a very interesting, and slightly bizarre, incident arose. Mention has already been made about HM The Queen, coming north to open the new, permanent site for the Royal Highland Show, Scotland's premier and most prestigious Agricultural Show, at Ingliston, on the western outskirts of Edinburgh.

The working arrangements had been circulated weeks before, and the train was to be worked north from Carlisle by Kingmoor crews, with two Black Fives being employed. Relieved by Dalry Road crews, the Royal Train was to be stabled, with the Royals aboard, up the Balerno Branch at Ravelrig Junction, and with the engines left coupled to provide steam heating overnight. On the following morning, Dalry Road men (Sandy Walker and unknown fireman) with a Class '8P' engine would proceed to Ravelrig Junction, tender-leading, and head the Royal Train into Princes Street station. That was the plan and in due course, Dalry Road shed asked for the loan of a suitable Class '8' engine from Haymarket MPD for this working. The Shed Master and Mechanical Foreman at the latter, selected Class 'A1' Pacific No. 60159 *Bonnie Dundee*, this being the latest engine out of General Repair at Doncaster Works, and nicely run in, a quite proper and correct selection, and off, in due course, went '159' to Dalry Road, via the Wester Dalry Branch. There it was placed alongside the outside wall on the south side of the shed... and there it was to lie, unused, on the Big Day. It is thought by the author that the authorities at Dalry Road had confidently expected

The 10.05 Edinburgh Princes Street to London Euston is seen here drawing out of former station on Monday 11th July. This is an interesting photograph, since it shows the Royal Train Pilot locomotive – which normally preceded the Royal Working, running light engine some 15 minutes ahead of the Royal Train – attached as a pilot to the 10.05 express. The pilot locomotive, 'Dunalastair IV' No. 925, allocated to Carlisle shed, carries the Royal Train Pilot headboard and three white discs signifying a Royal Working. Since the Royal Train was not scheduled to leave until 10.20, it could be argued that the pilot is quite properly running ahead at the prescribed time interval, but it is more likely that this wasteful nature of the preceding pilot exercise has at last been recognised. *CRA Archives*

a Class 'A4' Pacific but, for reasons stated, this was not to be. This led to an extraordinary big fit of pique at 64C, and Polmadie shed was, at the 11th hour, asked for the loan of a Class '8P' Pacific. No. 46224 *Princes Alexandra*, in rather bedraggled condition, duly appeared on shed at Dalry Road on the day before the special working. It is known that Charlie Rowan, Shed Master, and Jimmy Fyfe, the Loco Inspector, spent the late evening and night alongside the shed labourers, cleaning No .46224 from stem to stern, and come the morning she presented a magnificent sight, before going off shed to Ravelrig Junction, and working the Royal Train into Princes Street. No. 159 was returned to Haymarket, much unloved by Dalry Road shed. A strange episode all round!

However, there was to be an interesting, but later, Royal Working on 16th October 1962 involving Dalry Road men, when King Olav V of Norway made a state visit to Edinburgh to meet with HM The Queen. He sailed into Leith Docks where he disembarked

A Carstairs Fairburn 2-6-4T, No. 42173, with incorrect headlamps set, seen on a less than normal working as it heads the empty coaches for the Royal Train past Dalry Road shed and likely destined for overnight storage at Ravelrig Junction on 3rd July 1956.
David Anderson

LEFT: A 'proper' Royal Train working (occasion unknown) has just passed Dalry Road shed (located behind the overbridge to rear) and is generating some excitement amongst junior 'spotters' in Dundee Street. The Type 4 heading the train, number not obtained, is well turned out for this special duty. This street had gained the notorious reputation of being a convenient open air car workshop for amateur DIY, where engine oil was just drained from sumps into the Corporation drains. This picture appears to support this reputation. *Ian Musgrave*

and was taken to Leith North station where he boarded a special short-formed Royal Train consisting of a 12-wheeled Royal Saloon (either No. 798 or 799), two Pullman Firsts and a BR BCK bringing up the rear. Hauled by an English Electric, Type 4 Diesel-Electric 1-Co-Co-1 locomotive, No. D368 of Haymarket shed with an ex-Dalry Road crew in charge, it worked this short train from Leith North over the Leith and Granton Branch (by then closed to passenger traffic) to Edinburgh Princes Street station, all of 5½ miles, where King Olav on de-training was met by HM The Queen and Duke of Edinburgh, before the Royal Party were conveyed by road to Holyrood House. A lot of trouble for little benefit and it is likely that the King could have been conveyed by road from Leith to Holyrood in much less time, nevertheless the train provided a wonderful spectacle for those who lived alongside the rail route, and King Olav was thus probably to be the very last passenger ever to travel over the Granton and Leith Branch.

A sparklingly clean Stanier 'Princess Coronation' 4-6-2, No. 46224 *Princess Alexandra* of Polmadie shed, stands in Dalry Road shed yard in June 1961. The engine is fresh from working a Royal Train from Ravelrig Junction into Edinburgh Princes Street, conveying HM The Queen on the occasion she opened the new, permanent home of the Royal Scottish Highland Show at Ingliston, west of the city. The engine, too big for the turntable at Princes Street station, has turned on the Dalry Junction, Coltbridge Junction, Slateford Junction triangle and has come on shed for fire cleaning, coaling and preparation, prior to working home to Glasgow on the 17.16 stopping passenger train from Princes Street. The author rode home to West Calder on the footplate on this occasion, and even took the shovel from the Polmadie passed cleaner, who was somewhat overawed by his large steed. This was the occasion of the big fit of pique at 64C (described herein), after 64B had loaned Peppercorn Class A1 No. 60159 *Bonnie Dundee* for this working – which was not to be used and is in fact stabled behind the Black Five seen standing alongside the shed wall in the background. *Author*

Black Five No. 45085, coupled to an unidentified sister engine leading, head what appears to be a Royal Train or Royal Train ECS, whilst locomotive Inspector J. Fyfe passes on words of wisdom to the crew members.
J.L. Stevenson/Hamish Stevenson

Two Carlisle Kingmoor Black Fives, No's 44676 and 44993 in appropriately clean condition, reverse out of Dalry Road en route to Princes Street to work a Royal Train southward, on 22nd June 1961. *David Anderson*

Stanier Black Fives No's 45236 and 45161 head the empty coaches of the Royal Train at Curriehill, en route to Ravelrig Junction for stabling, in June 1961. HM The Queen had arrived in Edinburgh by train that same morning to carry out official duties. *Stuart Sellar*

This is a series of views of an unusual Royal Train working in October 1962. The train, consisting of a single Royal Saloon, two Pullman coaches and a Brake, is headed by Haymarket Type 4 No. 368, conveying King Olav V of Norway who had arrived by sea at Leith and is being taken by train from Leith North to Edinburgh Princes Street, from where he will finish his journey to Holyrood Palace and a meeting with Queen Elizabeth, by road.

Right: The train is seen here passing over the Slateford to Haymarket line built in 1853. To the left, the connecting line from Coltbridge Junction (to the rear) to Granton Junction can also be seen. *Rae Montgomery*

Another view of the Royal working for the King of Norway, showing the Royal Saloon and train engine approaching Dalry Middle Junction. The signals on the right apply to the Wester Dalry Branch on the approach to the same junction. *Rae Montgomery*

No. D368 being prepared at Haymarket shed prior to working the Royal Train from Leith to Edinburgh Princes Street in October 1962, whilst Haymarket stalwart ex-NBR Class 'J36' No. 65243 *Maude* looks on. *Rae Montgomery*

11 Dalry Road Shed: Freight Workings

Freight trains were not to feature large in the early days of the Caledonian Railway in Edinburgh – yet, as has been discussed, it was the potential for freight revenue which brought about many of the expansionist policies being pursued by the company. Envious eyes had been focussed on the sheer volume of coal traffic already passing through Leith, even in those formative days of the company in Edinburgh. With the early expansion of branches in and around Edinburgh, the Caledonian Railway was soon generating its own lucrative freight and mineral business, and this can be seen by examination of the early Caledonian Railway Working Timetables. The 1869 Mid Calder to Cleland line was to feature large in this traffic development.

In 1888 the Caledonian Railway had established a small Train Control Centre in the HQ of the District Traffic Superintendent's Office in Glasgow Central station; but by 1900 this was proving inadequate for needs, with the burgeoning Scottish iron, steel and coal industries, much of it served by the Caledonian, and with an annual production of around 8 million tons passing to rail, demanding a rethink. By 1900 a new Central Mineral Train Control Office had been established at Motherwell, an office in telephonic communication with district traffic offices, yards and ports in the area bounded by Carstairs in the south to Stirling in the north, Greenock in the west and Edinburgh in the east. The centralised control had a dramatic effect on the improvement of locomotive (and crews) utilisation, traffic movement and empty wagon supply to customers. Edinburgh had a district traffic office.

Amongst the earliest (post 1869) records of freight workings involving Dalry Road engines, is the following list of diagrams:

No. 1 Train (Gartsherrie)

New Goods engine. Off shed at 00.45. To leave Edinburgh at 01.00 with empty bogies; supply Westfield Pit (Newpark) and lift Limestone there, taking it forward to Gartsherrie; return light to Mossend; uplift train of goods traffic for Edinburgh, calling at intermediate stations, arriving at Edinburgh about 11.24.

Note: traffic for Hartwood, Shotts, Shotts Iron Works to be left at Omoa and taken forward by Motherwell No. 49 Train.

This limestone was mined on behalf of Baird Brothers, steel masters in Coatbridge, and to whose iron works at Gartsherrie and the largest such facility in the town the limestone was destined. William Baird was a significant shareholder in the Caledonian Railway Company.

No. 2 Train (West Calder)

First Class engine. Off shed at 05.35. To leave Gorgie at 05.50 with Caledonian empty wagons and goods for Camps, Newpark and West Calder, and the Cleland and Midcalder Road Van to West Calder, which will be worked forward by 13.35 goods train from Leith; deliver goods and empty wagons at Camps, lifting limestone traffic for the west, pick up train left at Camps Junction; call at Midcalder and Midcalder Junction, lifting traffic for Newpark and West Calder; shunt Newpark; call at Limefield Junction to leave Hermand traffic; shunt West Calder station, take forward empty wagons from West Calder and Addiewell to Woodmuir Junction; work Loganlea Colliery and lift traffic at Woodmuir Junction to make up train, calling at Addiewell and Limefield Junction; work Hermand Oil Works and Brick Works; thence to West Calder for east-going goods traffic; return to Limefield Junction and make up train, calling at Newpark; thence to Edinburgh, arriving about 16.20.

Note: Reference to Addiewell is Addiewell Oil Works, accessed from Addiewell Oil Works Sidings signal box.

No. 3 Train (Cultrigg)

First Class engine. Off shed at 06.50. To leave Edinburgh at 07.05 with a train of Caledonian empties and important goods traffic for West Calder; place the West Calder traffic in position; call at Woodmuir Junction to work Loganlea and to leave or lift empty wagons for Levenseat, calling at Fauldhouse Goods. If necessary take the traffic to Benhar; life empty wagons at Benhar for Benhar and Cultrigg pits; work pits and Braehead Quarry, bringing the traffic to Benhar; then lift train for Edinburgh or Crew Junction as required, calling at Woodmuir and Limefield Junctions to load up and working Loganlea Colliery: arriving in Edinburgh about 17.45.

No. 4 Train (Benhar)

New Goods engine. Off shed at 08.30. Leave Edinburgh at 08.50 and call at Gorgie; shunt Slateford, Kingsknowe, Balerno Junction, Curriehill and Ravelrig Junction; work Kaimes Siding; call at Newpark, if required, to leave off empties or lift Limestone; work to Woodmuir Junction and take forward West traffic to Benhar; return from Benhar with local traffic; call at Woodmuir and Limefield Junctions; go to Camps station, lift the West and South traffic, leaving it off at Gorgie; make up with stone traffic at Ravelrig Junction and reach Edinburgh about 18.50.

No. 5 Train (Leith New Lines No. 1)

Special Class Tank engine. (Double shift of No. 6.) Off shed at 06.00. To make three trips between Crew Junction and Seafield Yard. Leave Crew Junction at 09.00. Arrive North Leith at 17.50.

Note: This engine will do all the necessary shunting at stations and sidings on the Leith New Lines and will make an extra run from Crew Junction to Seafield Sidings with shipment traffic when required. Men change at North Leith at 06.00.

No. 6 Train (Leith New Lines No. 2)

Special Class Tank engine. (Double shift of No. 5.) Off shed at 18.00. To make three trips between Crew Junction, Seafield Yard and Gorgie. Leave North Leith at 18.15 and arrive Seafield Yard at 05.30.

Note: This engine will do all the necessary shunting at stations and sidings on the Leith New Lines and will make an extra run from Crew Junction to Seafield Sidings with shipment traffic when required. Men change at North Leith at 18.00.

No. 7 Trip (Craigleith)

Tank engine. Off shed at 05.45. Work 06.00 Goods Train, Edinburgh to Leith and empty wagons.

Leith to Crew Junction; thence to Edinburgh and relieve No's 1 and 2 shunting engines from 08.00 till 10.00 during meal hours; work traffic between Crew Junction and Bruce Peebles Co. Siding, Pilton East Junction about 11.00; work Craigleith Quarry, leaving there for Leith with Stone traffic about 13.50, calling Crew Junction at 14.00, arriving at Leith at 14.15. Leave Leith at 14.50, calling at Pilton East Junction, Crew Junction and Craigleith, and arriving at Edinburgh at 16.30.

No. 8 Train (Shieldmuir)

New Goods engine. Off shed at 20.45. To work train of Goods Gorgie to Carstairs at 21.15; then a train of empty and loaded wagons Carstairs to Law Junction, Garriongill and Back of Motherwell Shop; returning from Motherwell and Shieldmuir with traffic for Carstairs, Edinburgh, Leith and Granton, making up load at Garriongill. Law Junction, Carstairs and Cobbinshaw.

On Saturdays leave Edinburgh at 07.20 with a train of empty mineral wagons, and calls at Camps Junction to load up with Mineral traffic.

No. 9 Train (Ross Junction)

New Goods Engine. Off shed at 12.15 to leave Edinburgh at 12.55 with a train of empty wagons, calling at Gorgie, Midcalder Junction, Woodmuir, Benhar Junction thence to Ross Junction; lift train for Edinburgh or Crew junction, calling at Benhar; arriving Edinburgh about 22.00.

Dalry Road shed had also to provide shunting pilot engines, as follows:

Edinburgh Princes Street station. Two pilots, 06.00 until 16.15.

Edinburgh Goods (Lothian Road). Three pilots (two 06.00 until 18.00 and one 18.00 until 06.00 daily).

McEwan's Brewery Siding. Single shifted pilot 09.00 until 20.00. Shunted McEwan's complex (five sidings), Robertson's Oil Mills, West End Engine Works and Manure Siding and attending to all transfer of traffic between depot, goods yard and cattle sidings.

Morrison Street Mineral Yard

No. 1 pilot. 06.00 till 18.00.

No. 2 pilot. 18.00 till 06.00 and both covering shunting of all outlying sidings.

Both. Shunt mineral traffic in Morrison Street and all outlying sidings in connection therewith. Night shift pilot suspended from May to October.

Gorgie. Two pilots 05.00 until 17.00.

Leith

No. 1 pilot. 05.00 to 17.00.

No. 2 pilot. 18.00 until 06.00.

Both. Shunting goods yard and assists trains as required to Crew Junction or Coltbridge Junction.

No. 3 pilot. 06.00 until 18.00 } Shunting Albert and
No. 4 pilot. 18.00 until 06.00 } Edinburgh Docks Sidings.

Both. Shunt Leith High Depot and Mineral Yard. Work Goods and mineral traffic between Yard and Docks.

Ex-CR Class '439' 0-4-4T No. 55233, acting as station pilot at Edinburgh Princes Street, moves out the empty coaches from an earlier inbound service, bound for the carriage sidings. *J.L. Stevenson/Hamish Stevenson*

CR Drummond 0-4-0ST of 1885, built for dock working, at Dalry Road shed. *CRA Archives*

No. 5 pilot. 06.00 till 18.00. Shunts Leith Depot and Mineral Yard High. After docks work is finished assists in shunting trains.
No. 6 pilot. 18.00 till 06.00. Shunts Leith Depot and Mineral Yard High. On Saturdays, finishes at 12.00 midnight or when traffic is over.

Both. After docks work is finished, shunt Mineral Depot bringing coal from Crew Junction and working empty wagons there. Assist Goods trains to Crew Junction and Coltbridge Junction as required.

No's 7 & 8 Pilots. Both trip engines.

Granton

No. 1 pilot. 05.30 till 17.30. Shunting Granton Breakwater Sidings. Also works fish from Mineral Wharf to Crew Junction, and also to Edinburgh when necessary. Supplies two Steam Cranes and Shoot on Mineral Wharf with coal for shipment. Assists to work coal to Caroline Park Sidings, also empties to Crew Junction. Works traffic in to and out of the different works, and 21.40 goods train to Gorgie.

No. 2 pilot. As above.

No. 3 pilot. 08.05 until 19.05. Shunts Goods Yard and Exchange sidings. Also exchanges all traffic to NBR Coy. Works traffic to and from Middle Pier. Shunts Goods Warehouse and Yard. Works traffic to and from Mineral Wharf and works the 18.30 Train to Edinburgh.

From the foregoing it is obvious that the Caledonian Railway handled large quantities of fish traffic; this was conveyed in either 6-ton, 8-ton or 10-ton, 4-wheeled open fish trucks, all with 4-plank, drop-sides and fitted with passenger-rated brake gear. It is thought that they also may have used the 12-ton, 6-wheeled drop-sided open trucks known as carriage trucks for this fish traffic. The fish was conveyed to the Glasgow Fish Market by special trains from Crew Junction, or attached to passenger train services from Princes Street as necessary, dependent on quantities. There was, however, an early dedicated through fish train working which ran from Granton, departing 05.40, to Glasgow Gushetfaulds Yard in the immediate pre-World War One period, which was a train worked by Dalry Road men and engine.

A somewhat later indication (early 1900s) of goods workings for Edinburgh (Dalry Road) engines is as follows:

Engine No. 1 (South Leith)

18 × 26ins Tank Engine. Off shed at 12.35. Proceed to Morrison Street (12.45), and shunt. Make two trips between Crew Junction and Seafield Yard, shunting all intermediate stations and sidings on the Leith New lines, and make a third trip from Crew Junction to Seafield sidings with shipment traffic, when required.

Engine No. 3 (Camps)

18 × 26ins Goods engine. Off shed (10.50). Work train from Gorgie to Cobbinshaw, calling at Ravelrig Junction, Kaimes Quarry, Camps Goods station, and Oakbank. Work train Oakbank to Westwood shale pit, making two runs to Limefield

Originally CR No. 469, this McIntosh Class '439' 0-4-4T was renumbered as No. 15202 by the LM&SR and then No. 55202 by BR. For some unknown reason, the LM&SR number has reappeared on top of the BR number, with the letters LMS on the side tank. It is seen here shunting in Morrison Street mineral yard. *Stuart Sellar*

Junction, then work train to Gorgie, calling at Oakbank, Camps Junction and Ravelrig Junction.

Engine No. 4

The local shunting working.

Engine No. 5 (Westwood)

18 × 26ins Goods Engine. Off shed **M&WX** at 06.20, **M&WO** at 05.00. Train Gorgie to Camps and Oakbank. Make up train at Camps Junction for Breich Sidings (on West Calder Loop Line), and Westwood Pit, and return with train from Oakbank to Gorgie. On Mondays and Wednesdays, leave Gorgie at 05.25 and run to Camps. Work train to Oakbank. Lift empty wagons there for Westwood shale mines, work train of shale, Westwood to Oakbank, then empty wagons, Oakbank to Westwood shale mines. (Take forward traffic from Limefield Junction to West Calder.)

Engine No. 6 (Benhar)

18 × 26ins Goods Engine. Off shed at 10.05. Leave Gorgie with train for Kingsknowe, Curriehill, Ravelrig Junction, Newpark, Woodmuir Junction and Benhar Junction. Return with train for Gorgie calling at Midcalder Junction, Midcalder station, Camps Junction, Camps station and Ravelrig Junction. Deliver traffic from Camps at Curriehill and Kingsknowe. Work empty oil tanks Midcalder Junction to Camps. Make second run Camps to Camps Junction when necessary.

Engine No. 7 (Loganlea)

18 × 26ins Goods Engine. Off shed at 07.55. Leave Edinburgh with train, empty wagons, for Woodmuir Junction, work traffic to and from Loganlea No's 2 and 3 collieries. Leave Woodmuir Junction with train for Crew Junction, calling at Ravelrig Junction, and returning with train of any residual traffic, for Granton or Crew Junction, to Edinburgh, when required.

Engine No. 8 (Fauldhouse)

18 × 26ins Goods Engine. Off shed at 08.55. Leave Gorgie with train for Benhar Junction, calling at West Calder and Woodmuir Junction. Return with train from Benhar Junction to Edinburgh, calling at Fauldhouse Goods and Colliery, Woodmuir Junction, Loganlea No. 2 Colliery and Oakbank. On Mondays, Wednesdays and Fridays, work Levenseat Quarries.

From the foregoing freight engine diagrams it is clear just what an influence the developing Scottish shale oil industry had on the Caledonian Railway, and vice versa, after the opening of the Mid Calder to Cleland line in 1869, a line which bisected the Lothian shale fields – and also just what efforts the Caledonian Railway made to serve the new industry by rail. Not all the oil works had their own refining capacity; thus there was considerable movement of crude oil, conveyed in (registered) private owner tank wagons, with much of the oil traffic generated on the Caledonian Railway territory being destined for Pumpherston Oil Works, the biggest oil refinery in the shale fields. This meant transfer and exchange of oil tanks with the NBR at Camps Goods.

Ex-CR McIntosh Class '782' No. 56253 0-6-0 goods locomotive heads a short freight train on the Leith to Dalry Junction line, between Craigleith and Murrayfield stations in April 1956. *David Anderson*

Perusal of these Caledonian Railway engine workings described above, plus the later LM&SR and BR trip workings detailed below, tends to justify the author's view that the West Calder Loop was not worked as a through facility (which physically it was), but that sidings on the Loop were served from either end, from Woodmuir Junction at the westerly access point and at Limefield Junction at the easterly connection.

Tarbrax Oil Works, and the train workings serving same, was, as previously stated, the domain of Carstairs shed, but Edinburgh main line freight workings uplifted oil traffic left off at Cobbinshaw and took it forward to Camps Junction. Carstairs trip workings transferred crude oil produced at Tarbrax (by 1883 in the ownership of the North British Oil & Candle Company) to that company's Lanark Oil Refinery. At a later time, when Tarbrax Oil Works passed into the Pumpherston Oil Company's ownership, all the crude oil produced was conveyed to the NBR exchange facility on the Camps Branch. The thriving coal mining and iron and steel industries around Wilsontown, although theoretically lying on the Edinburgh/Carstairs main line, remained very much the domain of Carstairs engines.

All the oil companies had a number of their own wagons registered to run on the main line railway. The Oakbank Oil Company – with its original oil works close by Midcalder Junction, and their later and more modern oil works at Niddrie Castle (Winchburgh) (served by the NBR) – had the largest number of oil tank wagons and open wagons of any oil company registered to be allowed to run over Caledonian Railway metals, amounting to some 101 in 1910. These including some 40-ton bogie oil tanks which were unique to the Oakbank Oil Company. All the oil works had a number of similarly registered wagons.

Carstairs had two very convoluted engine workings at the turn of the 20th century, involving shale working, the first of which (No. 5) was diagrammed, as follows:

Carstairs Engine No. 5 (Limestone Engine)

First Class engine. Off shed at 06.50. To leave Carstairs at 06.10 with a train of mineral wagons for Oakbank Oil Works and Camps; call at Oakbank; deliver all traffic and bring out all empty wagons and goods from there; leave the empty wagons at Midcalder Junction and the goods at Midcalder station; shunt that station; then proceed to Camps and deliver all traffic for NB line; shunt the station (Camps Goods), take forward the South traffic and lift all limestone traffic, leaving it at Midcalder station; return to Oakbank and work oil traffic from there, leaving west bound traffic at Midcalder Junction and east going traffic at Midcalder station; return and lift empty wagons and south going traffic from Midcalder Junction and Harburn; leave empty wagons at Wilsontown Junction; make up train and proceed to Carstairs.

The second of the relevant Carstairs engines was:

Carstairs Engine No. 8 (The Tarbrax Engine)

First Class Goods engine. Off shed at 06.30. To leave Carstairs at 06.40 with a train of Goods and Mineral traffic for Carnwath, Cobbinshaw and the Tarbrax Branch. Shunt all sidings on the Branch, working outwards to Cobbinshaw: and leaving same at

ABOVE: Ex-LM&SR Fowler Class '2F' 0-6-0T Docks tank No. 47163, one of two allocated to Dalry shed, is seen here on what was also an regular alternative working on the Balerno Branch. Here the freight follows the winding course of the Water of Leith between Colinton and Juniper Green with the Balerno Branch goods in the spring of 1956. The branch was more of a loop line than a branch and at one time through trains worked over it for destinations west of Mid Calder. Rail connected from the branch were a number of paper mills, grain mills, a tannery and a stone quarry.
David Anderson

RIGHT: A view of No. 55210, looking back from the footplate on 31st October 1954.
Stuart Sellar

Cobbinshaw for onward working next morning by the 05.00 Goods train from Carstairs, a return main line goods working, worked by Dalry Road shed: Work train of empty wagons, Cobbinshaw to Haywood No's 4 and 14 Pits, work train of loaded traffic from there to Cobbinshaw: lift traffic for, and work Tarbrax taking all traffic to Carstairs and Lanark Oil Works, and return to Carstairs with empty Oil Tanks.

Note: Carnwath to wire Inspector, Carstairs at 18.00 the previous evening what traffic is to uplift.

Thus was the remote Tarbrax Branch most efficiently serviced by the Caledonian Railway.

The foregoing also indicates the extent of the influence of the Scottish shale oil industry on Caledonian Railway revenue, but the fragility of oil revenues at the time. For example, when the Caledonian Railway increased the rate per ton of shale carried to Oakbank Oil Works by a mere fraction of a penny per ton, this was enough to bring about closure of the Oakbank works, so precarious were the finances of that company.

Coal traffic originating from the Benhar Branch, from the Loganlea pits and Foulshiels Colliery, all owned by United Collieries, passed to the Caledonian Railway at Woodmuir Junction, although Foulshiels Colliery was also served by the NBR from their Bathgate to Addiewell Branch. Greenrigg pit, served by both railway companies, produced a very high-quality splint steam coal, much in demand by all railway companies for motive power use, but most of the coal from the Benhar Branch went westwards to the steel works of industrial Lanarkshire. The coal emanating from the West Calder Loop was destined for the domestic market in the main. Much of the coal and other goods traffic was worked into Slateford Yard for remarshalling, before being worked westwards to Mossend Yard for further marshalling and working to destinations; Dalry Road was soon providing engine power for working these trains via Shotts and returning with Edinburgh-bound traffic from Mossend.

And so the goods traffic, much of it mineral in content, grew and grew within the Central Belt of Scotland; but also emerging was a significant cross-Border flow of freight from the other railway companies serving the West Coast Main Line, and who were also to be constituent companies in the new London, Midland & Scottish Railway Company. Back in Victorian days an example of this developing cross-flow of freight traffic was demonstrated in and around the Birmingham area: the growth of perishable fruit and vegetable traffic from places like the very fertile and productive Vale of Evesham led to the introduction of loose-coupled, express goods trains from that area running north to the rapidly expanding conurbations of the industrial Midlands, and on into Edinburgh and Glasgow to serve the Central Belt of Scotland. In 1887, one such train (the 16.30 from Birmingham) was extended by the Midland Railway to run through to Leeds from Birmingham Lawley Street, conveying, in the main, 'Scotch Traffic'. Indeed, what was being referred to as 'Scotch Traffic' was growing so quickly that by 1931 the LM&SR had extended this same train yet again, to run as a Class 'D' express goods through to Carlisle, often loaded

No. 57654, ex-CR Class '300' No. 298, heads the local Barnton Branch freight working past the site of House O' Hill Halt on 22nd March 1960. *Stuart Sellar*

up to 60 vehicles. This led to a later daily booked through working from Evesham to Glasgow Buchanan Street and Edinburgh Lothian Road Goods during the main fruit season. The Dalry Road element in this working was the 05.45 Class 'D' express goods from Carlisle Viaduct to Lothian Road Goods, which was a return leg of an outwards freight working for Dalry Road crews.

In order to improve connecting freight services, in 1936 the LM&SR introduced a more intensive marshalling programme centred on Water Orton sidings in Birmingham, from whence two express freight trains left for the north each day, the 16.40 Carlisle and the 16.50 Leeds. By the end of World War Two the demand for fast freights was growing yet again and a new 03.50 Water Orton to Carlisle was introduced. By 1952 there was a through 16.45 Water Orton to Glasgow introduced by BR, which conveyed not only Glasgow traffic but also took traffic for Edinburgh Lothian Road and perishable traffic for Dumfries. As a result, the introduction of the much-vaunted Birmingham Saltley shed (21A) through lodging turns to Carlisle came about. This traffic was largely seasonal and essentially a one-way flow, with traffic in the opposite direction generally confined to wagon load traffic only and forwarded by an express freight working departing each evening from Glasgow Buchanan Street Goods to Wolverhampton (Oxley). Connecting traffic destined for the Midlands from Edinburgh was worked through to Buchanan Street each evening by a Dalry Road engine and crew.

In the late 1950s and early 1960s there arose a new demand, somewhat akin to the 21st-century phenomenon of on-line (internet) shopping and the growth of Amazon etc. – this was home shopping by catalogue (mail order shopping); a new express parcels service was introduced by using the 23.20 Manchester Exchange to Edinburgh Lothian Road express parcels and newspaper train. This train had its origins in the immediate post-World War Two years, when the then very popular repertory theatre companies recommenced their regular tours, playing at theatre venues country-wide. This train was used extensively to convey items of stage scenery and other stage furniture for use by the theatre company in question. Later, as the popularity of such touring theatre companies waned, this train continued in use but now conveyed, in addition to newspaper traffic, vulnerable and high value mail order items, loaded from Oldham (Mumps) and Manchester Victoria. This train regularly conveyed, or wholly consisted of, long wheel-based CCTs (BR-built 4-wheeled, long wheel-based, fully fitted general parcels and revenue traffic vans), and on one particular winter early morning, this service was involved in a very destructive mishap at Harburn, lying on the Edinburgh–Carstairs line of route, as described in Chapter 15).

Also, in the late 1950s, a new, daily, fully-fitted express freight service was introduced, running between Deanside Transit Terminal at Hillington on the west side of Glasgow, where a 'break bulk' facility had been developed by Scottish road haulage contractor J.G.

No. 47163 heads the Balerno Branch goods (Edinburgh District Target E17) between Juniper Green and Currie. The fireman is checking the water level in the side tanks. *Stuart Sellar*

Russell Ltd, and Lothian Road Goods. This train was commonly known as the 'Dog Meat' – after one of the principal commodity conveyed, which was canned pet food from Wisbech (East Anglia) to Scotland – and was regularly to see an ex-LM&SR 'Princess Coronation' Pacific locomotive employed, worked by Polmadie men. Due to its size, the Pacific always turned on the Slateford/Coltbridge/Dalry Junction triangle. Deanside Transit is still active but, whilst it was at a later time the centre for parcel traffic (Parcel Force) going to and from London Willesden by rail, the Deanside facility currently sees no use by rail traffic.

By the 1960s most local freight working was still in the hands of Dalry Road goods engines carrying Edinburgh Control District target numbers; in 1961 these were as follows:

TARGET NO. E16

Class '5F' engine. Off shed at 22.10. Work to Control orders.

TARGET NO. E17

Class '3F' engine. Off shed at 06.20. Shed to Slateford, Newhaven Junction, Leith East, Seafield Yard, Newhaven Junction, Slateford Yard, Dalry shed. Work all Leith lines.

TARGET NO. E18

Class '3F' engine. SX. Off shed at 07.00. LE to Slateford Yard, Midcalder station, West Calder, Woodmuir Junction, Benhar Junction, Fauldhouse North, Woodmuir Junction, West Calder, Limefield Junction, Hermand shale mine, Limefield Junction, Westwood Oil Works, Limefield Junction, Hermand shale mine, Limefield Junction, Newpark, Midcalder station, Camps Junction, Dalry Road shed. (Uplifts from Midcalder station both traffic and empties detached by S.16, the latter a Carstairs engine & trip diagram.)

SO. Off shed at 07.15. LE to Slateford Yard, Midcalder station, West Calder, Woodmuir Junction, Benhar Junction, Fauldhouse North, Woodmuir Junction, West Calder, Limefield Junction, Hermand shale mine, Limefield Junction, Westwood Oil Works, Hermand shale mine, Limefield Junction, Newpark, Midcalder Junction, Camps Junction, Slateford Yard, Dalry Road shed.

TARGET NO. E19

Class '3F' engine. Off shed at 07.55. LE to Slateford Yard, Work Murrayfield, Jeffrey's Brewery, Duff Street, Lorimer & Clarks etc.

SO. Works as required by Control after return from Murrayfield, Duff Street, etc. When working at Lorimer & Clarks, coal, and other wagons, to be placed above vans for outward loading.

TARGET NO. E20

Class '5MT' engine. Off shed at 08.45. LE to Slateford Yard; Work to Control Instructions.

One of Dalry Road's ubiquitous Class '812' engines, No. 57564 (CR No. 826), hard at work on Edinburgh trip working E18 as it transfers a train of oil shale from Hermand Mine to Westwood Oil Works; it has crossed the main line at Limefield Junction and is now about to cross the Breich Water viaduct on the West Calder Loop Line between Limefield Junction and Westwood. *Roy Crombie/SRPS*

Target No. E21

350 HP Diesel locomotive. SX. Off shed at 09.25. LE to Slateford Yard, Colinton, Currie, Kinleith Mill, Juniper Green, West Mill, Colinton, Currie, Balerno, Ravelrig Junction, Midcalder station, Camps Junction, Ravelrig Junction, Balerno, Currie, Kinleith Mill, Juniper Green, West Mills, Slateford Yard, Dalry Road shed.
SO. Off shed at 07.20. LE to Slateford Yard, Colinton, Currie, Kinleith Mill, Balerno, Ravelrig Junction, Midcalder station, Camps Junction, Ravelrig Junction, Balerno, Currie, Kinleith Mill, Juniper Green, West Mill, Slateford Yard, Dalry Road shed. Works to Camps Goods if required.

Target No. E22

Class '5F' engine. Off shed at 13.00. Morrison Street, Crew Junction, Seafield, Lothian Road, Slateford Yard, Lothian Road, Slateford Yard, Lothian Road, Slateford Yard, Dalry Road shed. Conveys any north traffic off E24 to Lothian Road.

Target No. E23

350 HP Diesel locomotive. SX. Enginemen travel by 13.05 from Princes Street to Craigleith to join diesel locomotive at Crew Junction, thereafter proceed to Granton. Work coal to Gas Works via Pilton West along with E114. Also works Shell Mex between 15.30 and 16.30 and makes trip to Lothian Road or Morrison Street at end of shift.

Target No. E24

350 HP Diesel locomotive. Off shed at 13.00. LE to Slateford Yard, Lothian Road, Slateford Yard, Bruce Peebles, Leith North, Slateford Yard, Leith North, Slateford Yard, Dalry Road. (On arrival at Slateford from Leith North, Shunt as required.)

Target No. E25

Class '5F' engine. Off shed at 10.05. LE to Slateford Yard. Works to Control Orders.

Target No. E26

Class '3F' engine. SX. Off shed at 14.05. LE to Slateford Yard, Leith East (attaches biscuit traffic), Seafield. (Works as requested at Leith Walk West, Rosebank and Chancelot Mills.) Thereafter Control Instructions.
SO. Off shed at 09.25, LE to Slateford Yard, Leith North, Lothian Road, Slateford Yard, Morrison Street, Slateford Yard, Niddrie West, Slateford Yard, Morrison Street, Dalry Road.

Target No. E27

Class '3F' engine. SX. Off shed at 15.35. LE to Lothian Road, Gorgie East, Haymarket West Junction, Lothian Road, Gorgie East, Lothian Road, Dalry Road shed.

Target No. E28

350 HP Diesel Locomotive. Off shed at 19.50. LE to Lothian Road, with brake vans front and rear to Slateford Junction, Niddrie West, Leith Walk East, Portobello, Niddrie West, Craiglockhart, Slateford Yard, Dalry Road shed. (Shunts at Slateford Yard and trips to Morrison Street and Lothian Road as necessary.)

By 1961, as can be seen by scrutiny of the listed workings, it is obvious that the Scottish shale oil industry was in terminal decline and in fact it disappeared in the following year.

Over the years, both in LM&SR days and into BR times, goods traffic changed and developed. The very speedy growth of the iron and steel industry in and around Motherwell, Rutherglen and

The daily goods service over the closed to passenger Barnton Branch, headed by ex-CR Class '300' No. 57654, pauses at Davidson's Mains on 22nd March 1960 prior to shunting the goods yard here. There are clear signs of trespass and vandalism. *Stuart Sellar*

Freight trains to and from Slateford pass on the double junction at Craiglockhart Junction in November 1960. The new and very basic wooden hut which is the signal box can clearly be seen standing in what can only be described as particularly untidy surroundings. The train engine in the foreground is ex-L&NER Class 'J37' 0-6-0 No. 64586 of St. Margarets shed. *Stuart Sellar*

Coatbridge presented never-ending demands for raw materials such as coal, home produced ironstone, fireclay and imported iron ore, matched by an equally important demand for the carriage of finished steel products. These included steel plate (for the Clyde shipbuilding industry) and, in later days, strip coil. The steel coil, ingots and girders all required specially constructed rolling stock capable of carrying exceptionally heavy loads – long loads, loads requiring special handling in loading and unloading – and thus an intensive goods and freight train service was to grow up around this industry. In the 1880s, on the former Wishaw & Coltness Railway W&CR), this was to see the development of what was probably the most important marshalling, trip and transfer yard facility in Scotland, and this was Mossend Yard.

Located at the intersection of two main lines and with full triangular connections to and from each main route, this yard has been described elsewhere, with some justification, as being located within a veritable maelstrom of railway lines. Dalry Road shed had several freight workings to and from Mossend, spread over 24 hours, generally with traffic for remarshalling; it also had several through freight turns for other destinations, which detached or attached at Mossend Yard. Motherwell trip engines worked the coal, uplifted from the West Lothian coalfields, to Mossend Yard for remarshalling, except for the bulk of the coal produced by Polkemmet Colliery, which was conveyed in block trains of 24-ton steel mineral wagons, in circuit working, directly to the Ravenscraig Steel Complex at Motherwell, again worked by Motherwell shed locos and men.

Mossend Yard lay immediately to the north of Mossend passenger station (formerly Holytown [1844-82], closed 1962) and south of Coatbridge (Carnbroe); it was formed by a series of separate yards, these being:

- **Up Side.** No's 1, 2 & 3 Yards. No's 1 & 2 yards contained a total of twelve sidings and were used for empty wagons. Up Side No. 3 Yard had ten sidings and was used for loaded goods vehicles.
- **Down Side.** Consisted of a Down Mineral Yard, Down Goods Yard and a Down Steel Yard. Also on the Down side there were three Down Loops capable of holding 206 wagons, but as they also served as running loops they seldom lay occupied for long.

All in all, Mossend Yard could accommodate just over 2,000 wagons. The yard was the hub for many local, regional and Anglo-Scottish express freight workings.

In the 1950s, Wm. McEwan Ltd of Fountain Brewery had six custom built, conventional rail tank wagons constructed to convey beer in bulk from Edinburgh by rail to Glasgow for bottling, these being filled in a specially adapted rail tanker loading facility on site at Fountainbridge, and BR laid on a special freight turn

No. 47163 comes off the Balerno Branch with the daily branch freight working and heads for Slateford Yard, at Balerno Junction in April 1960. *Stuart Sellar*

for this purpose. This fully-fitted freight train was the 20.15 Slateford–Buchanan Street working, conveying mainly beer traffic from the McEwan Brewery at Fountainbridge, which ran via Holytown, Coatbridge Whifflet and the old Garnkirk & Glasgow Railway into Buchanan Street Goods.

In the mid to late 1950s, there was a procession of freight trains in the Edinburgh area, both inwards and outwards, for destinations to the south and west. These included the following services:

22.00–06.00: Outwards from Edinburgh

00.01 Class 'E' Slateford to Carlisle Kingmoor.
Return 05.45 Carlisle Viaduct to Lothian Road.

00.50 Class 'H' Slateford to Mossend.
Return 03.30 Mossend to Slateford.

01.40 Class 'J' Crew Junction to Clyde Iron Works.
Return 06.40 Strathclyde Junction to Crew Junction.

02.23 Class 'J' Crew Junction to Newton Junction.
Return 07.15 Newton to Crew Junction.

04.35 Class 'J' Crew Junction to Rutherglen.
Return 10.00 Clyde Iron Works to Crew Junction.

06.00–18.00: Outwards

07.15 Class 'K' Slateford to Woodmuir.

08.40 Class 'J' Crew Junction to Shettleston.

09.05 Class 'K' Slateford Yard to Benhar Junction.

10.00 Class 'J' Crew Junction to Dalzell.
Return 15.00 Dalzell to Crew Junction.

13.35 Class 'J' Crew Junction to Shettleston.
Return with 19.10 Shettleston to Crew Junction.

17.05 Class 'C' Lothian Road to Dumfries milk.
Return with the 21.35 milk from Dumfries.

Inwards to Edinburgh:

01.29 Class 'C' (Milk)	21.35 Dumfries to Princes Street via G&SW.
04.30 Class 'E'	21.55 Buchanan Street to Lothian Road.
04.30 Class 'F'	02.55 Dalzell to Crew Junction.
05.38 Class 'H'	03.30 Mossend to Slateford.
06.00 Class 'D'	02.25 Kingmoor to Slateford.
06.30 Class 'D'	02.25 Kingmoor to Lothian Road.
07.10 Class 'H'	04.20 Mossend to Slateford.
07.25 Class 'F'	05.10 Bridgeton to Slateford.
09.02 Class 'E'	05.45 Carlisle (Viaduct) to Slateford Yard (detach).
09.40 Class 'E'	05.45 Carlisle Viaduct to Lothian Road (main portion of the above train).
09.43 Class 'F'	06.40 Strathclyde Jn. to Crew Junction.
09.55 Class 'F'	07.15 Newton to Crew Junction.
12.55 Class 'F'	10.00 Clydesmill to Caledonian Crew Junction.
16.20 Class 'F'	15.00 Dalzell to Crew Junction.
16.35 Class 'K'	11.30 Benhar junction to Slateford via Camps.
16.47 Class 'F'	14.08 Shettleston to Crew Junction.
20.55 Class 'H'	19.33 Carstairs to Slateford Yard.
21.48 Class 'F'	19.10 Shettleston to Crew Junction.

Dalry Road shed crews worked the Class 'C' fast freight, the 17.05 'Dumfries Milk', right through to Dumfries, going out via Carstairs, the WCML and Lockerbie and returning via the G&SW and the GPK&A. All the outward freight workings listed above, between the hours of 00.01 and 11.59 formed early shift turns for Dalry Road crews, the remainder being late shift turns.

The Class 'J' freight workings (later to be Class '9') to the Lanarkshire steel works from Crew Junction were especially arduous, since the trains conveyed imported Norwegian Iron Ore, in block train formation of 16-ton mineral wagons with as much as 600-800 tons behind the tender. Speed on these workings was sacrificed for sheer tonnage, hence the trains were run as lowly Class 'J' freights. One night in 1958, the author, as a young cleaner/fireman at Haymarket, and whilst on cleaning duties on the night shift at his home depot, was dispatched to Dalry Road shed, post haste, in the early hours of the morning, when that latter shed found itself short of a fireman for the 01.40 Crew Junction to Clyde Iron Works, as described at Chapter 14.

In the early 1950s, Dalry Road men also worked an unusual freight turn, paired with a Dalry Road 'Black Five'; this was the 20.25 Lothian Road to Saltney, via Carlisle, but with a strange routing. The train worked over the Wester Dalry Branch to take the E&G main line to Bo'ness Junction, where it was booked to uplift traffic (refractory bricks from J.&G. Stein Ltd., loaded in specially constructed Palbrick wagons, no doubt) before proceeding to Falkirk Grahamston; here it also picked up traffic, before rejoining the ex-Scottish Central line to Greenhill Lower and the Caledonian main line south, picking up further traffic at both Coatbridge (Whifflet) and Law Junction before arriving at Carstairs. The Dalry Road men may have been relieved at Carstairs, and indeed, it was most likely that they were, returning home with the first available train working northbound for Edinburgh from Carlisle. There was no corresponding return working from Saltney to Edinburgh – which regularly saw, no doubt, a Dalry Road engine 'on shed' at Mold Junction (6B), left to work its weary way home as a common user locomotive, on a variety of freight workings. Now Saltney, hardly the centre of the universe, nor indeed a major railway centre of any note, was an unusual destination, lying as it does on the England/Wales border, and it all adds to the mystery of this particular working. It is, however, most likely that the primary traffic conveyed on this service were the quality refractory bricks from J.&G. Stein's works at both Manuel and Greenhill, always in great demand for lining blast furnaces, bound for the giant Shotton Steel Works in Flintshire belonging to J. Summers & Sons (1896 to 1967), thereafter British Steel and now Tata.

There was yet another strange Dalry Road turn of duty involving a freight turn to the west side of Glasgow (but otherwise still yet unidentified), where the Dalry Road engine (usually a 'Black Five') was stabled in Dawsholm shed (65D) for the best part of an early shift.

In the late 1950s, BR introduced several fully fitted express goods services in the Scottish Region. These were formed by a total of seven freight trains, all of which were introduced around the same time. These trains were all named, 'fully fitted' or 'through piped' services, with the continuous vacuum brake operative throughout the complete train. Three of these services cleverly contained the word 'Piper', a reference with both Scottish connotations and to the fact that they were through-piped. Two Edinburgh services were worked by Dalry Road engines (normally Stanier Class '5MT' 4-6-0s) and men, to and from Johnstone High on the GPK&A line, where they changed footplates with the Stranraer men; these were the 18.55 Edinburgh Lothian Road to Stranraer ('The Galloway Piper') and returning with the 18.00 Stranraer to Edinburgh Lothian Road ('The Lothian Piper'). No headboards were carried on any of these services. The other trains were:

- 'The Hielan Piper' 19.15 Glasgow Bell's Yard to Inverness
- 'The Killie' 21.12 Aberdeen to Kilmarnock
- 'The Kitty' 17.25 Dumfries to Aberdeen (Kittybrewster)
- 'The Fifer' 20.20 Irvine to Thornton
- 'The Humber Fife' 20.50 Hull to Glasgow.

Ex-CR No. 501 Class '782' 0-6-0T No. 56313 shunts at Lothian Road Goods station. *J.L. Stevenson/Hamish Stevenson*

RIGHT: The new order on the Balerno Branch. E.E. 350 hp. 0-6-0 diesel shunting locomotive No. 3891 has displaced the Fowler 0-6-0T on the daily branch freight working and is seen here at Currie on 17th December 1960. *Stuart Sellar*

BELOW: Having arrived at Ravelrig Junction, D3891 prepares to run round its train prior to retuning to Slateford via the Balerno Branch. *Stuart Sellar*

D3891, having run round its train, will now work back to Edinburgh via the Balerno Branch. *Stuart Sellar*

12 INDUSTRIAL RELATIONS

As with the other railway companies in Edinburgh, early footplate life on the Caledonian Railway was no sinecure, and was typified by long working days of 12-hour shifts, or even longer, being the norm. In addition, drivers and firemen were required to undertake other duties, often involving signing on at least two hours before setting off on what might be a 12 to 15-hour trip away from the shed. The fireman might be required to examine the firebars to ensure that they were properly set in place before lighting up, and be held responsible for any delay occurring as a result of the firebars being misplaced, unless he had specially advised the foreman of the circumstances. The driver had normal preparation duties to carry out but was often required to carry out other small repairs. Out on the road, footplate conditions could not have been worse. The early engines had no cabs to speak of and the crews were totally exposed to all the elements. On the West Coast Main Line out of Edinburgh, and working though to Carlisle, as many of the early crews were required to do, trains passed over two significant summits, Cobbinshaw at 950 feet and Beattock at 1,016 feet above sea level. In the winter months the weather conditions at these altitudes could be, and generally were, as described in Chapter 4, severe. Footplate life was anything but easy.

The engine driver of the day was in fact nothing more than a self-taught artisan, who, if he was particularly fortunate, might have had some previous encounter with steam boilers (colliery engineman for example), but elsewhere engine driving has been described as follows:

> *'Engine driving is a job which almost any man may learn in a few days. The class of men generally employed to drive engines would not earn above 1/6d or 2/0d per day. Engine drivers are a parcel of weavers, waiters, barbers or bakers who know as much about the construction of the machine, as a carter knows about the anatomy of a horse.'*

Indeed, that doyen of the Great Western Railway, the much-vaunted Isambard Kingdom Brunel was to say of drivers:

> *'I am not one to sneer at education, but I would not give 6d* [2½ pence] *in hiring an engineman because of his knowing how to read or write. I believe that of the two, the non-reading man is best. If you are going 5 or 6 miles without anything to attract your attention, depend upon it you will begin thinking of something else. It is impossible that a man that indulges in reading should make a good engine driver; it requires a species of machine, an intelligent man, a sober man, a steady man, but I would much rather not have a thinking man.'*

These are both extremely harsh points of view and the driver of these early days had, for the sake of his own job security, to very quickly become a competent engineer who could, and did, confidently tackle running repairs, both large and small. He was expected as a matter of course to carry out gland packing, renewal of trimmings, packing injector keys and even attend to big ends and small ends short of dismantling them. He also was required to be a man who *could* read and, preferably, write – despite Brunel's words of (doubtful) wisdom – since the Rules and Regulations governing the safe running of trains were indeed *written* Rules and Regulations, which *had* to be clearly understood by all. Before too many years were to pass, through long hours of hard travail for modest rewards, drivers were ready to prove that, not only could they read and write, but that they had also become *thinking* men!

The driving task was rendered all the more difficult by the fact that drivers were expected to run to time whilst maintaining full control of the movement being undertaken, often at quite significant speeds, but without any semblance of an adequate braking system, and this would occur on lines where other movements were taking place at the same time, and where train separation was down to an estimated period of time. In Chapter 15, the consequences of inattention to any of these factors will be discussed. Of course, as time passed, firemen were learning their trade from working with these early drivers and, if lucky, were encouraged to 'take hold' under supervision. Thus was the skill of engine driving passed on. In the early days, and in keeping with the policies of other railway companies, the Caledonian operated a system of 'same engine daily', where the same engine, with same crew, would work the same train, perhaps for several years, and thus, drivers, having their 'own' engine, would ensure that it was always in first class order, both in terms of mechanical condition, and cleanliness. The latter was typified by the extreme measures crews took to adorn smokebox doors etc, with decorations such as Masonic symbols, while buffers, couplings, and wingplate edgings were scoured and kept polished down to the bare metal, and with paintwork which always gleamed.

The railway industry offered a reasonably secure tenure of employment, despite the inevitably long and arduous turns of duty, but the companies were run on similar lines to the military – indeed many early railway officers had been serving Army Officers themselves, and old habits die hard. Thus, daily working life was enforced by a rigid hierarchy and iron discipline. Instant dismissal followed any infraction of the Rules and Regulations. Railway companies in general, the Caledonian Railway amongst them, were autocratic institutions, run by martinets, who ruled with a rod of iron.

In the late 1800s, however, all was not well in railway circles. Traffic levels were booming across the board, but footplate life was still Spartan in the extreme. Men were working 144-hour fortnights with a minimum 12-hour working day being the norm – although fifteen to sixteen-hour shifts were not unknown, there being no hard definition of just exactly what a 'normal' day's work might be. On the NBR, one driver was recorded as working 100 hours and 30 minutes in a mere six days. On the Highland Railway there was cited the case of one driver named Johnson who was required to work a single, continuous duty of 72 hours and 20 minutes. As unrest spread, these situations saw the creation and rapid development of organised trade unions, the earliest being the Amalgamated Society of Railway Servants (ASRS) in 1871. This proved to be little more than a friendly society, rather than a credible trade union, and was unwilling to confront railway management. By the late 1800s, drivers were speaking to drivers of other companies, and one particular ill-considered decision on the part of the management of the GWR to abrogate on an 1867 agreement on rates of pay was to lead to the development of a new, and certainly more powerful and better organised, trade union. The Associated Society of Locomotive Engineers & Firemen (ASLEF) came into being in 1880. The union's first confrontation with railway management was to be known as the *'Midland Strike'*, when the management of the Midland Railway

A view of the cab interior of ex-CR 0-4-4T No. 55202, taken at Dalry Road shed in May 1955. *Stuart Sellar*

started imposing financial penalties on their drivers for what, with the best will in the world, could only be described as 'petty offences', such as actually suspending a driver for twelve days, for incurring a 3-minute delay to a train at Trent. The ensuing strike, with the majority of Midland drivers being entirely disorganised in terms of union membership, threw the Midland Railway into chaos. ASLEF had never sanctioned the strike, and the MR, who broke the strike with imported labour, won the day.

The next confrontation between ASLEF and a railway company was to come in 1887, following the fatal railway collision which occurred at Hexthorpe, near Doncaster, in September of that year. A train belonging to the Manchester, Sheffield & Lincoln Railway Company collided with the rear of a standing special passenger train, killing twenty-five people. The management of the MS&LR held that their own engine crew were to blame, and both men were arrested, arraigned and appeared in due course, at the York Assizes, charged with manslaughter. ASLEF obtained the services of two eminent counsels to defend the men, provided specialist support, and both men were, quite properly, acquitted. The judge had some very harsh things to say to the MS&LR managers about the signalling practices and inadequate train braking systems in use at that time. ASLEF proved itself to be a union with *teeth*, and drivers and firemen had, for the first time, a champion for their cause. This case, and its outcome, sent tremors of concern throughout railway managements everywhere. Indeed, the homogeneity and culture of ASLEF, confined as it was to representing footplate grades, the locomotive men who had acquired their hard-won status through lengthy training and service, was to prove its strength. Such were the concerns of railway management, that in Scotland the management of the North British Railway, the Caledonian Railway and the Glasgow & South Western Railway issued a joint document warning their staff of the perils of joining a trade union, in an attempt to defer the inevitable.

Meanwhile, long hours and inadequate rest were taking their toll, and in Scotland dissatisfaction was to spill over on Sunday 21st December 1890. On that day, employees (drivers, firemen, guards and signalmen) of the NBR, the CR and the G&SWR withdrew their labour and so commenced a strike six weeks long. The respective managements portrayed the strike as simply being driven by a demand for a pay increase, totally ignoring the other elements – elements which they certainly did not want exposed, and discussed, in the public domain. The newspapers, to their eternal shame (and no doubt being leaned upon by central government and lobbied by the respective company managements) followed this line of much biased reporting. The Caledonian Railway management were to prove especially vindictive and stooped to evicting whole railway families from their company homes in the Motherwell area, by serving the eviction notices over the Christmas period, on the 27th December 1890. This action resulted in much civil unrest amongst the neighbouring, and supportive, steel workers and miners, in what became known as the 'Motherwell Riots', during which Motherwell station became the target for the strikers' anger and suffered much damage to infrastructure in consequence. The strikers, on returning to work, had won very little at that time. Some striking men were never to be re-employed, but the strike had pricked the political conscience and in 1891 a select committee was set up by the government of the day with the remit to *'inquire whether, and if so, in what way, the hours worked by railway servants, should be restricted by Law'.* In 1892, the committee was damning in its report to Parliament, which included the statement that *'overwork on the railways of the United Kingdom is widespread, and in general, systematic, and not accidental or exceptional'.*

In 1913, the National Union of Railwaymen (NUR) was formed, comprised of the ASRS, and two other minor unions, and were to represent all grades of Railway Employees (except white collar workers), although the footplatemen were largely to remain with ASLEF. To represent the 'white collar' brigade, in 1899 the Railway Clerk's Association (RCA) was formed in Sheffield, and in 1951 this union adopted the name Transport Salaried Staff Association (TSSA) – but it was to be 1919 before the railway companies jointly recognised any trade union.

By the turn of the 20th century it was becoming clear to every railway company director and manager that there was to be no going back to the working conditions which they had imposed in the latter half of the 19th century, and with by now very well organised trade union representation, things must, and were, inevitably going to change. The 1890 strike in Scotland was to be the first shot fired across the proverbial bows of the railway managements, and was followed by another, but shorter, national strike in 1911.

In May 1904, the Caledonian Railway introduced a new system of payment for drivers, firemen and brakesmen working mineral trains which was a form of incentive bonus. The payment kicked in where a crew were requested to make an extra run, whereupon this extra work would be paid for at fixed rates. This was (as always) conditional on certain requirements being made and in this case the whole of the extra work, plus the whole of the ordinary diagrammed work, being completed. In the Edinburgh area, the Special Runs and Rates were as follows:

Class 'a' working denotes a train working in both directions.
Class 'b' working denotes running out light and returning with a train.
Class 'c' working denotes going out with a train and returning light engine.

Edinburgh District payment:

Granton or Leith to Gorgie or Edinburgh:
Class 'a' – drivers 9d, firemen 6d, brakesman 8d, additional brakesman 6d,
Class 'b' – drivers 6d, firemen,4d, brakesman 5d, additional brakesman 4d.
Class 'c' – drivers 6d, firemen 4d, brakesman 5d, additional brakesman 4d.

Camps Junction to Camps:
Class 'b' – drivers 6d, firemen 4d, brakesman 5d, additional brakesman 4d.
Class 'c' – drivers 6d, firemen,4d, brakesman 5d, additional brakesman 4d.

Oakbank or Midcalder Junction to Camps:
Class 'b' – drivers 9d, firemen 6d, brakesman 8d, additional brakesman 6d.
Class 'c' – drivers 9d, firemen 6d, brakesmen 8d, additional brakesman 6d.

These rates were somewhat derisory.

By 1910, the working day for drivers on the Caledonian Railway had been reduced to eleven hours, but the NBR men had had their working day reduced to ten hours and the 10-hour day was soon to become the norm across the board. By post World War One times, the big railway trade unions – the NUR and ASLEF, and to a lesser extent the Railway Clerk's Association (RCA) – had become well established. With a powerful voice they were now to be instrumental, following the general election in 1918, in achieving National Agreements on pay, working hours and paid holidays for their members. In 1919, with the establishment of Whitley Councils, the Secretary General of the ASLEF Union, one Jack Bromley, was to negotiate a National Agreement within the railway industry, ensuring that from August 1919 the working week would become forty-eight hours, with a maximum daily turn of duty being set at eight hours, and with enhanced payment for overtime, night duty and Sunday duty. Also established was one full week's paid holiday, granted to every member of staff with twelve years or more service, and pay was standardised across the industry at, for drivers, 15s (75 pence) per day, firemen 7s to 9s 6d (35 pence to 47½ pence) per day and 4s (20 pence) for cleaners. In following years, further improvements were won, such as the issue of uniform (protective clothing in the form of overalls, jackets, waterproof coats and headwear), the 44-hour week, mileage payment and one 'rest day' every fortnight, about which later'. All this meant that suddenly, because of the shorter working week and with holidays now to cover, increased staffing levels were required, especially amongst drivers, and many firemen were quickly elevated to become drivers at a very young age.

Also, because of the 1919 National Agreements, footplate staff won the right to payment for what amounted to working beyond the agreed national limit of distance. This was awarded in the form of 'Mileage Payments' after railway management conceded that a *normal* day's work in terms of miles run, for both driver and fireman, would be 140 miles. Beyond that limit, a mileage payment was made on the basis of one-hour extra payment for every fifteen additional miles run. At Dalry Road, a shed with few mileage turns, this was to mean little other than for the through turns to Carlisle. These were, based on running shed to shed, a total of 206.4 miles daily, thus earning an extra 4 hours 30 minutes extra payment. Over a six-day week, this amounted to 27 hours extra in the pay packet. But to put this into proper perspective and what it could mean: at a mere one mile distant from Dalry Road shed was Haymarket shed, a shed where there were numerous (thirteen at least) daily diagrammed express passenger workings to Newcastle and return, representing 256 miles daily in total. Thus, on the same six-day week at Haymarket, a footplate crew would earn an extra 46.5 hours mileage payment in the week, equivalent to or just slightly over, an additional week's wages. Mileage payments at Haymarket assumed such an importance that daily roster sheets were avidly scanned by the men at the shed, just in case they were losing out. For the roster clerk this could be a nightmare, especially if he had slipped up and given a mileage turn to other than the correct man. If this occurred, a claim would then be submitted and, if the claim was proved to be valid, inevitably paid, so that the turn was paid for twice, once to the man who had actually worked it, and again to the claimant. Result, roster clerk in the doghouse!

At Dalry Road shed, whilst mileage payments were seen as nice little earners, they never generated the same level of scrutiny, and avarice, as they did at the sister shed. Incidentally, the rostering procedures at Dalry Road and other ex-LM&SR sheds, as described at Chapter 13, went a long way to ensuring that the right crew always got the right turn of duty, whether mileage payments were involved or not, since rest-day coverage was confined within the actual link. Lodging away from home, whilst thought to be required at one time, and a regular event at many former Caledonian Railway and LM&SR sheds, had quickly died out. By BR days, all Dalry Road footplate crews worked out and home daily.

From the earliest days the footplate manning structure was based on boys joining as engine cleaners, and in time, being 'passed' to act as firemen as necessary, and later being appointed as regular firemen as and when vacancies arose. However, a lot depended on the physical nature of the new applicant (there was no formal medical examination in the earlier times) and a big, strong-looking lad could, and often did, find himself on firing duties very quickly. The others had to prove themselves in what was a very hard school indeed. Firemen were subject to the whims of the drivers they worked to, and a driver's word, and a foreman's opinion, could often shape the future of that individual – promotion on the long ladder to becoming a driver being in no way automatic.

Up until the onset of the First World War, this unregulated method of promotion was the norm, with cleaners being elevated to firemen, and firemen to drivers in a most haphazard manner, the personal opinions and preferences of foremen meaning everything. After 1919 and the introduction of the very first National Agreements, and the reduction in the hours of a working day, there suddenly was the need for more drivers and firemen, and some very young firemen were being elevated to drivers, merely on seniority. Thereafter, from 1919, the promotion process was to become much more structured, with seniority now playing a major role. Medicals and eyesight tests were introduced, and for boys starting out on the long ladder of footplate promotion this was to prove a very fair process, and this, along with a formalised system of structured examination in the theory and practical elements of footplate work, ensured that suitability was checked at proper intervals. Indeed, this leaning towards formalised training was taken one massive step forward by the great John F. McIntosh himself, who, in the closing years of the 19th century established, at St. Rollox Works, what was to become the Mutual Improvement concept, whereby proper, structured and practical mechanical training and theoretical training classes were established, involving acknowledged experts in their own respective fields. Attendance was purely voluntary, but McIntosh himself had placed great store on this initiative and conducted many of the classes himself. The experts, in areas such as valve setting, were roped in, and the courses involved a series of shed visits and hands-on problem solving. Live locomotives became the classroom models, and such was the success that very soon up to ninety footplatemen from the Caledonian Railway sheds in and around Glasgow were attending every course. Inevitably, the word got out in Springburn, and NBR locomotive men were soon lobbying Matthew Holmes, Locomotive Superintendent of the NBR at Cowlairs, for the establishment of similar classes.

Thus commenced what was to become known as the Mutual Improvement Movement, which was carried on, system-wide, through all the post-grouping companies, and well into the days of BR, until steam traction was finally eliminated in the 1960s. It was all down to the foresight of one man, one very enlightened and great man, John Farquharson McIntosh of the Caledonian Railway.

13 Shed Administration, Supervision and Characters

As stated in the Introduction, Dalry Road shed did not have an incumbent who recorded shed life for posterity – people such as Norman McKillop (Toram Beg) of 64B, or Willie Hennigan Senior and Junior, and Charlie Meacher at 64A. This is a great shame, because Dalry Road in the early days of the Caledonian Railway had footplatemen of a calibre to equal the well-known exploits of the later renowned Curries, Gibsons, or Ranochans of Polmadie, the Armstrongs, Crooks or Robinsons of Carlisle and the Mitchells and Soutars of Perth.

It is known that one of the earliest drivers on the books at Dalry Road was one John Nicoll, who had been allocated the flagship 09.00 ex Euston working from Carstairs to Edinburgh as his regular booked working because he was recognised to be 'of good conduct'. Regrettably, Nicoll was to one of the earliest Caledonian Railway casualties when, along with his fireman, he was killed in the accident at Auchengray (see Chapter 15). Both men entered railway service at Dalry Road on its opening in 1848, and both were dead in the same year.

At Dalry Road, it fell to men such as J. Dick, Will Stavert and W. Watts to fly the flag for the Caledonian Railway, and this they all did with great success. As an aside, there was, when the author was cleaner/fireman at Haymarket in the late 1950s, also a passed fireman, John (Jackie) Stavert working there. Given the name Stavert gaining mention at Dalry Road, was he a just another footplateman or, perhaps, another coincidence? However, scrutiny of the BT Lothian Area Telephone Directory revealed that there are now no Staverts' in residence in the Edinburgh and Lothians vicinity.

A one-time driver at Dalry Road, one Jimmy Blake, who had decided to come off main line driving duties early, was accommodated as a Shift Foreman Cleaner at Haymarket shed in the early 1950s. Jimmy was succeeded at Dalry Road by his two sons, Eddie and James, and the author became friendly with the former during his short time at Dalry Road and travelled with him on the footplate many times. Eddie was a driver there and James Junior (also Jimmy) a passed fireman. Jimmy (Senior) was a valuable source of both immediately pre and post World War Two information about Dalry Road and was to suffer endless queries from one of his cleaning squad, the author.

Whilst the author was 'on loan' to Dalry Road shed in a clerical capacity, in June and July 1961, some of the top link men also became known to him, since the 17.16 Class 'B' stopping passenger train from Princes Street to Glasgow Central was a turn in that link and was the train used by the author when travelling home after work. Since the engine went off shed anyway, it became the norm for him to join the engine there and travel down to Princes Street, but the top link men, genial older drivers in the main, were happy to let him remain on the footplate for the duration of the journey until his stop at West Calder. Drivers G. Elder and J. Findlay were two such, as was Driver Alexander (Sandy) Walker. Sandy Walker was one of the regular Royal Train drivers at Dalry Road and conveyed

A group of CR employees at Dalry Road taken in front of the running shed. The photograph is undated, but the running shed is still only a two-road wooden shed and may well be the original of 1843.
CRA Archives

Here top link Dalry Road driver, A. (Sandy) Walker gives a cheery wave to the camera from the cab of Carlisle Upperby Black Five No. 452356 as he hustles an express from the south towards Princes Street. He will have worked this train from Carlisle. The photograph was taken by a family member from Dundee Terrace and was obviously pre-arranged. *Harry Archibald*

the present Royal Family on numerous occasions when Royal Trains were more in vogue. It was he who had control of Stanier Princess Coronation Pacific No. 46224 *Princes Alexandra* when it worked the train conveying HM The Queen into Edinburgh in June 1961. She had come north to open the new, permanent Royal Highland Show Ground at Ingliston, to the west of Edinburgh (see Chapter 10).

The reason for the author being at Dalry Road in the first instance was, as stated earlier, a shortage of clerical staff, and as was the norm, where a smaller number of bodies were covering *all* the normal clerical work, official overtime working was sanctioned by the DMPS Edinburgh, and this generally took the form of three hours on Tuesdays and three hours on Thursdays. Whilst very welcome to those involved, it did interfere with travel arrangements, but fortunately for the author the engine (normally a Black Five) for the 20.15 Slateford to Glasgow Buchanan Street Goods, went 'off shed' at 20.00 and a rush to complete work enabled him to join the engine at the shed points and travel home on the footplate. Often in the hands of young drivers, it was on this working that he encountered the aforementioned Eddie Blake and Magnus Clark (see below), and was re-united with the man who had been his driver on the Clyde Iron Works working (see Chapter 14), R. (Bob) Ellis.

Magnus Clarke was a young driver at Dalry Road who had transferred, on promotion, from Haymarket, where he had been a passed fireman. Now the author had fired to Magnus at 64B, so it was friendship renewed when he turned up at Dalry Road, and Magnus was always happy to have the author on the footplate with him. He was a young man and a fine driver who regrettably passed away far too soon. W. (Bill) Brown was a fireman at Dalry Road who had married a West Calder lass and now resided in the village; he and the author struck up a friendship and were frequently travelling companions.

The Shed Master at Dalry Road at that time was Charlie Rowan, another character, who knew exactly where to find missing members of the staff when necessary. Dalry Road, like the other two sheds in Edinburgh, had regular 'watering holes' for the staff and the nearest and most popular was the Athletic Arms, a pub that stood, and still does, on the corner of Angle Park Terrace and Ardmillan Terrace. Despite its 'Sunday' name, that pub is still known as the 'Grave Diggers', or even just the 'Diggers', so-called because the grave diggers from Dalry Cemetery (almost opposite) used it as a regular refreshment haunt. It was a hop, skip and step away from Dalry Road shed by escaping over the wall into the delightfully named Coffin Lane which formed the western boundary of the shed. This pub is where the shed labourers were generally to be found. Younger hands, if missing on a Wednesday or Saturday afternoon, could generally be found at Tynecastle Park, home of Heart of Midlothian, Edinburgh's other famous football club. Charlie merely arranged for a suitable tannoy message to be broadcast, advising all miscreants that their presence was required elsewhere, and quickly! It seldom failed!

One of the Running Foremen was James (Jimmy) Fyfe, a man who was to become an Edinburgh District Motive Power Inspector in the early 1950s. He was followed at Dalry Road shed by John Buchanan, another Running Foreman who was also to become a Locomotive Inspector. Jimmy Fyfe, a dyed in the wool Caledonian man, but now working in the wider horizons of the Edinburgh District sheds, became the self-appointed tormentor of the drivers and passed firemen at Haymarket shed. In the Inspectors' room at Waverley one day, he was idly glancing through some accident reports when a name caught his eye. This was in regard to an incident at Carlowrie accommodation level crossing, a name which meant nothing to him, but a name that he decided to identify further. In the fullness of time he found out that it was a private, user-operated (field-to-field) level crossing located between Turnhouse and

Dalmeny on the Edinburgh to Dundee and Aberdeen main line. Armed with this knowledge, he then accosted Haymarket drivers and passed firemen at the shed, asking each if they had signed for the Dundee road, and on receiving a response in the affirmative, he asked the whereabouts of Carlowrie level crossing. Now all the men knew the crossing, often by another name but not necessarily by its Sunday name, and on receiving a blank look or a shake of the head, he would castigate the individual about appending his name on his Route Card, for a route which he obviously did not know in sufficient detail. In time, this jape lost its impact as the word got around and everyone at the shed, cleaners included, knew of, and could identify to the nearest inch, Carlowrie level crossing.

On the Admin side at Dalry Road, the then Chief Clerk was Norman Thorburn, who with his wife had become a pioneer of continental holidays using rail passes. He regaled and enthralled the younger members of staff (author included) with stories of the delights (and horrors – generally toilet) to be found in Spain, or Italy, or wherever, and awakened the desire to travel and widen this author's horizons. Gordon Laing was for some time a junior clerk there, as were Alastair Scott and another well-known Edinburgh face, and author, A.A. (Sandy) MacLean, who also worked in the clerical grades at the shed. Sandy MacLean played a significant, but understated role in getting ex-Caledonian McIntosh Class '439' 0-4-4T No. 55189, which had earlier been withdrawn and placed into store at Carstairs MPD, brought back to Dalry Road. The journey to return No. 55189 from Carstairs took place almost in secret, and ex-CR McIntosh Class '652' 0-6-0 goods engine No. 57630 arrived, unannounced, one day with No. 55189 in tow. There, at Dalry Road, No. 55189 was re-acquainted with a proper Caledonian lipped chimney in place of the stovepipe 'lum'. All this was achieved under the 'old pals' act, for No. 55189 was, of course, bought by the SRPS and eventually restored to full running order in Caley Blue livery and carrying the original Caledonian Railway number, 419.

The staff clerk at Dalry Road was a gentleman named Harrison (first name now forgotten), who had been a one-time station master at Leadburn and later a Controller in Edinburgh District Control.

As already mentioned, ex-Caledonian Railway sheds had a completely different system of rostering footplate staff from that pertaining at the ex-NBR sheds in Edinburgh, with which the author had been trained. At Dalry Road, the top link contained most of the express, and also some local, passenger work. Top link men worked to Carlisle, Ayr, Gourock, Carstairs, Stirling, Perth and Glasgow Central. There was a second passenger link covering the

Ex-CR McIntosh Class '439' 0-4-4T No. 55189 taking water at Currie station whilst working an Officers' Special Inspection Saloon on the Balerno Branch in July 1961. This locomotive was later to be preserved as CR No. 419 and can be seen today, still at work, on the SRPS Bo'ness to Manuel Railway. *Stuart Sellar*

local branch line passenger work with, at its peak, at least thirty-five crews involved; No. 3 link had the express goods work, again with wide route knowledge; No. 4 link had the heavy mineral work, with a further link for all the freight trip workings and shunting pilots. Whilst Haymarket and St. Margarets depended on large links of spare drivers and firemen to cover holidays, rest days, sickness and special workings, at Dalry Road the allocation of rest days, and coverage of same, was built into each link, an eminently sensible practice as it turned out. The shed did not then carry large spare links – although some spare capacity was carried to provide for sickness and annual leave purposes. This Rest Day allocation system worked very well, as follows.

Each link contained twelve turns of duty, arranged, as required by National Agreements, into rotating early and late turns of duty – an early turn being a shift which required taking duty between 00.01 and 11.59 and a late shift taking duty between 12 noon and 23.59.

The top link was configured thus:

Week 1. Early. Rest Day Monday.
Week 2. Late.
Week 3. Early. Rest day Tuesday.
Week 4. Late.
Week 5. Early. Rest Day Wednesday.
Week 6. Late.
Week 7. Early. Rest Day Thursday.
Week 8. Late.
Week 9. Early. Rest Day Friday.
Week 10. Late.
Week 11. Early. Cover above rest days Monday to Friday (five) and own Rest Day Saturday.
Week 12. Late.

In No. 2 link, rest days were built into the late turns but on the same basis, and the 12th turn in the link (Saturday) was the rest day coverage turn of duty, giving every member of staff a long weekend every twelve week. It worked well and ensured a fair system, each crew in the link having a rest day once every fortnight and taking their turn as rest day relief in weeks No. 11 or 12 once every twelve weeks, and enjoying their own rostered rest day on the Saturday of that same week.

The mineral, pilot and branch passenger links were similarly arranged, although not all rest days were allocated to early turns of duty, but the system worked equally well on late turn weeks. Special Train working was covered by stepping up 'passed' staff to act as driver or fireman as required. It was a much more economical system which avoided large numbers of spare crews hanging around. It will also be noted that in the Edinburgh District Workings, there were two Class '5F' engines, along with crews booked 'Work to Control Orders', and of course Class '5F' engines ('Black Fives' in the main) were equally at home on passenger and freight turns of duty, thus the Control Office could fall back on these diagrams for any eventuality which might arise. As a last resort, as the author found out to his advantage, the Running Foremen at Dalry Road would, and quite frequently did, request assistance from the cleaning squads at Haymarket under the aforementioned 'old pals act', and generally on night turns (see Chapter 14).

LM&SR Fowler 'Patriot' Class 4-6-0 No. 45503 *The Royal Leicestershire Regiment* of Crewe North shed stands on the ashpits at Dalry Road having worked the northbound through passenger service from Birmingham New Street to Edinburgh Princes Street. This locomotive will return with the 10.05 Edinburgh Princes Street to Birmingham New Street the next morning, with Dalry Road men working the train as far as Carlisle Citadel station. The Running Foreman is climbing into the cab to check fire cleaning is underway. *David Anderson*

14 Footplate Work at Dalry Road

The Dalry Road footplate crews were faced with the need for some spectacular running, particularly in the earlier days when many of the summer passenger train workings ran non-stop through to Carlisle. It is known that J. Dick (mentioned previously) was an early top link driver who did sterling work with No. 123 during the 1888 'Races' to Edinburgh. He was later given the first 'Dunalastair I' (No. 731) when it came new to the shed. Since the Caledonian Railway operated a 'one engine, one train' policy, where the same engine and driver worked the same train, day in and day out, and often for some years, Dick's regular booked turn of duty for a number of years was the 10.00 mid-morning departure for London Euston (actual departure times could vary by a few minutes) from Princes Street, and the forerunner of the LM&SR 'Royal Scot'. Dick was followed by the great Will Stavert and W. Watts, the former probably being the foremost of all the Dalry Road men of the day, albeit that Driver Watts was never far behind when it came to hard running.

Dalry Road drivers were, like their counterparts elsewhere on the Caledonian system, totally impervious to blandishments from their respective Locomotive Engineers' preaching full regulator, short cut-off methods of driving. Having been provided with locomotives with large boilers that steamed well under all driving methods, they continued to thrash their steeds along using longer cut-off and with no concerns about shortage of steam. This is clear from the following account of two timed runs on what were very heavy workings indeed.

Will Stavert it was, who was to set up an exceptional run with his regular booked train, the 10.05 departure for London Euston from Princes Street, which was then the fastest train on the Caledonian Railway and was booked to run the 101.6 miles to Carlisle, in the even two hours, non-stop. On the day in question (regrettably unspecified by Rous Marten, but a day in the summer of 1905), Stavert had his own unsuperheated 'Dunalastair IV', No. 140, with the train behind the tender weighing no less than 404 tons tare, 435 tons gross. He was given a pilot from Dalry Road shed, a Connor 7ft Class '30' 2-4-0, No. 33, but only as far as Cobbinshaw Summit. Stavert ran the train over the 18.4 miles to Cobbinshaw in 28 minutes, 57 seconds; then, after a brief stop to detach No. 33, he took the train down to Strawfrank Junction (9 miles) cautiously, passing there in 10 minutes 32 seconds. From there he accelerated away along Upper Clydesdale, averaging 46½ mph and, with the engine working full-out for the final 2.5 miles of the ascent of the 1 in 99 rising gradient, the train passed Elvanfoot at 36 mph. From Elvanfoot to Beattock Summit (2.9 miles), Stavert took only 4 minutes 13 seconds, maintaining the minimum speed of 36 mph, which required that No. 140 was working flat-out, and demanding an incredible equivalent drawbar horsepower of 1,400, representing a drawbar pull of 6 tons. With the hard work done, he then ran the 49.7 miles down to Carlisle in 46 minutes 7 seconds, arriving in Carlisle 2¼ minutes early, having taken 117 minutes 50 seconds overall from departure in Edinburgh, and a mere 87 minutes, 21 seconds for the 82.2 miles from Cobbinshaw to Carlisle, start to stop, attaining speeds of 76½ mph at Wamphray and 80½ mph between Kirtlebridge and Gretna. Fortunately, the great Charles Rous-Marten was a passenger on the train on the day in question, and carefully recorded the trip, as was his wont, although he was not to publish details of this run recorded for *The Engineer* magazine until the December 1905 issue. McIntosh had indeed given his drivers quite remarkable engines.

Driver Watts, in that same year of 1905, was also making some extraordinary runs with his 'Dunalastair IV', No. 141, and was achieving equally inspired timings on his week on his regular booked workings – also the 10.00 from Edinburgh to Euston, and the 14.00 'Corridor' on which he and Stavert rotated weekly. On yet another unspecified day, on the Up leg of the earlier part of the diagram, and over the same portion of line, he was recorded as running the 66.9 miles from Symington to Carlisle in 72 minutes and 5 seconds. On the return leg of the same diagrammed working northbound (10.00 ex Euston and conveying a through coach from Birmingham for Edinburgh), despite bad weather and slippery rails, Watts attained a speed of 75 mph before the Solway crossing, and maintained nothing less than 60 mph until passing Lockerbie. He then averaged 67.2 mph over the next 13.9 miles to Beattock and, despite being brought to a complete stand at Auchencastle for 2 minutes 43 seconds, on getting underway he cleared Beattock Summit in 56 minutes 57 seconds from the start at Carlisle, climbing Beattock Bank in 19 minutes 38 seconds, despite the enforced stop. The overall journey from Carlisle to Edinburgh took only 110 minutes and 12 seconds. Again, Charles Rous Marten was fortunately to have been on hand to record both these rather incredible runs. Dalry Road certainly was to have its fair share of 'firebrands'!

Whilst passenger work was perhaps the more glamorous activity in train working, freight was the 'bread and butter' of nearly all railway companies. The Caledonian Railway and Dalry Road shed were to be no different, and several of these freight diagrams were demanding in the extreme.

The booked freight workings and their variety at Dalry Road have been discussed in Chapter 11, where particular mention was made to the large number of Class 'J' freight diagrams that the depot worked in the late 1950s. Class '9' freight trains were generally timed to reflect an average speed of 45 mph or lower, and both the working and the speed required to be specially authorised. The head-code carried by the locomotive was a single lamp over the left-hand buffer (in direction of travel). The Class 'J' trains were all trains of iron ore, imported from Norway via Leith Docks and loaded in BR standard, 16-ton, steel mineral wagons; these were made up into block train loads at Crew Junction for onward conveyance to the blast furnaces of North Lanarkshire and were subject to a lower maximum speed of 25 mph. These trains, by the very nature of the commodity, were very heavy trains indeed, and being described as Class 'J' freights, they sacrificed speed for sheer tonnage. Trains

McIntosh 'Dunalastair IV' Class 4-4-0 'No. 145 heads an express train for the Up West Coast Main Line, in Princes Street station. Dalry Road shed had an initial allocation of two of these extremely capable engines. *CRA Archives*

Dears

consisting of forty to forty-five wagons weighing 640 to 720 tons were not unusual, and trains of 800 tons have been known. These trains generally worked over the 1869 Mid Calder to Cleland line, a route well known for its long, hard climbs (see Chapter 4).

What follows is a description of footplate work involved in working just one of those heavy trains and undertaken in the relative comfort in the cab of a 'Black Five', but it makes one wonder just what footplate work was like in the Spartan, cab-less days of the Sinclair 2-2-2s, over what was a very bleak line of route, even in the best of weathers. These early crews were truly men of iron!

As a reminder, the author's experience of these trains had been, by and large, confined to his (quite irregular) travelling home from very late shifts at Haymarket MPD, by making his way up to Coltbridge Signal Box which lay close by Haymarket shed and cadging (begging) a lift home on the first available service coming up from Crew Junction and going west. Inevitably it was one of the three heavy iron ore trains, and the Dalry Road drivers were generally amenable to giving him a lift, since the station nearest the author's home lay on a 1 in 105 rising gradient, and detraining did not require any steadying of speed at that location. Indeed, he was never to be refused access to the train engine. The author was not averse to taking the shovel to work his passage home and became known for giving the Dalry Road fireman a break for the first 17 miles of the long drag. However, there came the one momentous night when it all became for real, as described below.

* * *

I was, as an 18-year-old passed cleaner, booked nightshift cleaning at Haymarket shed (22.00 to 06.00) in the early spring of 1958, and was senior cleaner in the squad. Around midnight one evening, I was called into the Running Foreman's Office and asked if I knew how to find my way round to Dalry Road shed. In replying in the affirmative, I was instructed to make my way over to that shed and report to the Running Foreman there. Now, to explain, this was not an entirely unusual situation in the summer months, and quite often a passed cleaner would be loaned from Haymarket, generally on the night shift, to cover a firing turn at Dalry Road shed.

I duly collected my satchel containing food, tea can and jacket, and, on what was a fine, dry, but overcast night, walked round the lonely and deserted streets to Dalry Road proper, then going south up Coffin Lane. I knew, from my illicit night lifts on same, it was possible that I was about to experience an example of train working which was totally unknown and alien to the 'Glamour Boys', as the predominantly express passenger train crews were known at Haymarket shed. I entered Dalry Road shed via the wooden stairway leading down from Dundee Street and reported as instructed.

The running foreman at Dalry Road shed that evening was one John Buchanan, who was later to become a district locomotive inspector, and he instructed me as to my night's duty. It appeared, as I had thought, that the shed was short of a fireman for the 01.40 Crew Junction to the long-established Clyde Iron Works (1786-1978) iron ore working, and I was advised to seek out passed fireman R. (Bob) Ellis, who was to be my driver, and prepare a 'Black Five', No. 45360, which, incidentally, was not one of Dalry's own engines. The engine was found standing out in the stabling sidings on the south side of the shed and appeared to be in good condition, and I made myself known to my driver for the evening. I was a bit puzzled by the fact that the engine was fitted with tablet exchange mechanism, but on sweeping up the front footplate, I noticed that the shed code plate indicated that this was a steed allocated to 60A (Inverness) and was obviously being appropriated for this night's working.

My new mate asked me if I knew just what the Caledonian Mid Calder to Cleland line was like and was highly amused when I said that I lived in West Calder and had frequently used this very train as transport home in the wee sma' hours. I was totally familiar with the cab layout and firebox of a 'Black Five' – thanks to my Hamilton mentors on Motherwell trip diagram, target No. M23, which shunted Shotts daily, where I had been a junior clerk – and so had no difficulty with the preparation duties, although I was given some assistance with filling the sands, owing to my not being familiar with the sand kiln at the shed. My mate reappeared in the cab, stowed away his oil cans, had a good look round and declared himself satisfied. I had no particular concerns at this strange working, having seen, and experienced for myself at first hand, just what a fireman had to do to keep those big heavy freights on the move.

Having filled our respective tea cans from a freshly-made pot in the bothy, we rejoined the engine and I wound off the handbrake. We moved slowly forward, out to the shed exit signal, where I phoned out to Dalry Junction signal box. When the signal cleared we moved slowly out on to the main line, chimney leading, until the tender had cleared the Granton Branch points, where we were signalled on to the branch, now running tender-first. We clanked past Dalry Middle Junction and then over Granton Junction, and I was delighted to have a bird's eye view of my own home shed at Haymarket as we passed over the ex NBR main lines by the 'Caley Brig' at Coltbridge Junction.

Soon after passing through the dark, deserted Murrayfield and Craigleith stations, we arrived at Crew Junction, lying to the south of Granton, where we were met by our guard. He signalled us on to our train for the night, and he coupled up and advised the driver of the load, forty plus a brake van, equal to 660 tons, and then walked back the length of the train, to rejoin his van. I set the single headlamp over the left bracket on the buffer beam to signify that we were running as a Class '9' freight and, on rejoining the footplate, I stowed the second, unused, headlamp and set about attending to my fire. I started by filling up the rear of the box right up to the bottom ring of the firedoor, not neglecting both sides of the box, as I had seen the Dalry Road firemen do on my many nocturnal trips home, I also tested both the exhaust and live-steam injectors, since I was always deeply suspicious of the injectors provided on 'Black Fives', as they sometimes did not pick up as quickly and cleanly as those provided on my home-grown Pacifics, but in the event they both picked up immediately and appeared to be in good order.

With the blower on and pressure rising, as we waited for the 'right away', Bob quizzed me about what took me to Haymarket, and how I managed to travel to and from West Calder for the different shifts. He was highly amused at the fact that I often used this very train, amongst others, for this purpose.

The engine began to blow off, and I was somewhat concerned since the yard was surrounded by houses, but before I could get the injector on, the yard exit signal cleared, right time at 01.40. Looking back, I saw a green handsignal from the guard in his van. I confirmed this to Bob, and immediately, with the reverser well out, he swung the regulator up into first valve, and with cylinder cocks roaring, 45360 got this heavy train on the move and out on to the main line. At a nod from Bob, I shut the cylinder cocks and the engine settled down, with a very distinctive bark at the chimney,

Stanier '5MT' 4-6-0 No. 45360 of Inverness shed, fitted with tablet exchange apparatus, stands in Dalry Road shed yard. Despite the fact that this was not a Dalry Road engine, the Running Foreman had commandeered it to work the 01.40 Crew Junction to Clyde Iron Works Class 'J' freight on the evening when the author was loaned as a fireman for this turn of duty. *J.L. Stevenson/Hamish Stevenson*

to slowly accelerate this big, heavy train towards Craigleith and on to Murrayfield, through what was a very salubrious residential area, and I wondered just what the denizens of same made of this nightly explosion of noise and vibration. At Coltbridge Junction we had the signal for the right-hand divergence at the junction, which would take us up to Slateford. Picking up the shovel, I began to spear coal down each side of the box and topped up the hump below the door. Lifting the flap, and setting the exhaust injector, with steam pressure sitting on the red mark, I sat down on my seat. For some reason, and I think it was because of the Belpaire firebox, ex-LM&S (and Caley) crews tended to run with the water level very high in the gauge glasses, indeed almost out of sight, and so I decided to follow suit.

We had clear signals approaching Slateford Junction, so up into the roof went the regulator and the reverser came out to about 40/45% cut off, and the roar at the chimney was incredible, but a noise with which I was wholly familiar, since as a boy, and for as long as I could remember, I lay in my bed of an evening, listening to the same 'Black Fives' as they hit the start of the gradient from West Calder up to Benhar Junction, and I would hear the sharp, staccato bark at the chimney, as they, with their heavy loads, got to grips with the gradient, on this long haul. I could hear them approach our home, oh so slowly, to pass close by, crawling up the long weary climb over the moorlands, and the noise becoming fainter and fainter till it faded away completely. And now, here was I, very much in the hot seat as it were, and actually living the memories of childhood.

At the end of Slateford Platform we proceeded noisily, smokily and slowly across the viaduct over the Water of Leith and Balerno Junction, and hit the 1 in 102 rising gradient which marked the long, unremitting, uphill climb which would take us to Midcalder Junction. Up past the signal box we slogged, speed dropping to a little more than walking pace. Bob let out the reverser and 45360 began throwing fire out just as quickly as I was feeding it in to the box, by now a blindingly white, searing hot furnace, and the chimney appearing as a veritable volcano against the night sky, along with the vicious crack of the exhaust. The trailing boxes were knocking quite badly, belying the first impressions on the condition of the engine, and every revolution of the driving wheels was accompanied by a bone-shaking, crashing thump, which was felt from the soles of my boots to the top of my head. The tender fall-plate rose and fell, and shimmied from side to side, as the engine rolled and lurched, which made firing all the more difficult. The reflected heat, with flap lowered and fire-doors open for firing, was incredible, making me realise just how much better the arrangement of the L&NER half-trap fire-door really was for the fireman.

Through Kingsknowe and up the 1 in 142 gradient past Curriehill we blasted, and then, inch by inch, and painfully slowly, the lights of lonely Ravelrig Junction signal box came into view. I was firing continuously now and was conscious of the fact that I was shovelling a lot more coal into that hungry maw than I ever would have, on a home-grown steed, but a case of different horses for different courses! It must be said that the steam pressure sat unwaveringly, rock steady, on the red line, but I had to use the live steam injector to supplement the exhaust injector which had been on continuously, to put back what was being taken out of the boiler. Taking time to put my head over the side and breathe in some fresh, cold night air, and with Ravelrig now behind us, the signals at Camps Junction were showing all clear, and the street lights of Kirknewton village twinkled away to the left, in the darkness. Bob crossed the cab and checking the tender water gauge, he shouted in my ear *'we'll stop for water at Midcalder station'*, and gave two crows on the whistle to let the Signalman at Camps Junction know of our intention, the loud, deep tone of the Caley type hooter echoing around the district. I pondered this turn of events since, here we were, a mere 23½ miles, and one hour time-wise, from our starting point, and it was now thought necessary to fill the tender up. Although, on the minus side, it was all of another 23 miles to Holytown, and the next location where water could be taken, and given the amount of uphill work which was still before us, it was probably a prudent decision, made on the basis, I suspected, of bitter experience, and given the amount of water already used up. The coal was still falling freely on to the shovel plate, although I had made inroads into what had been a very well filled tender. We clanked our way to a stand at the water column at Midcalder station, the level crossing gates remaining closed over the line ahead.

We spent seven or eight minutes taking water whilst I filled the boiler, made up the fire in readiness for the slog still to come and took advantage of the break to grab a quick lid-full of tea from my tea-can sitting, and warming nicely, on the shelf above the firedoors. With a full tank and a fire in apple-pie order, and refreshments taken, Bob gave a blast on the whistle to let the signalman in Midcalder Station signal box know we were ready. The level crossing gates were swung across the road, off came the Platform Starting (Home) signal and the Up Starting signal and we moved off. Faced with a 1 in 120 climb for the next mile until Midcalder Junction was reached, Bob had the regulator out into big valve, the reverser well down and 45360 responded accordingly, with the sharp blast of exhaust at the chimney and a following train which was accelerating nicely. Passing over the lonely 'Ma Broon's level crossing' (Greenloan Public Level Crossing to be entirely accurate), so named by locomotive men after the resident female crossing keeper, Mrs Brown, and with all signals displaying a beckoning green we reached the very small signal box which was Midcalder Junction and, taking the right-hand diverging line, we were on to the 1869 Midcalder to Cleland line, described at Chapter 4. On passing over the junction, we dropped our nose down the 1 in 130 falling gradient, and my mate snapped the regulator shut and wound back the reverser. The ensuing silence was sheer bliss as the weight of the train now accelerated us forward. 45360 was blowing off fiercely as we picked up speed. Downhill we raced with nothing but the engine brake to control our speed, but approaching Newpark station there was short section of absolutely level track at Nether Williamston, which, with the weight behind us, steadied our speed. With speed now falling away, we hit a small rising gradient which would take us back on to level track at Limefield Junction. I was very much on home territory now and vastly enjoying the whole experience. Still drifting with steam off, we were back on the level stretch of track approaching West Calder. I picked up the shovel and began to fire down the sides of the box and filling up the rear half of the grate. Lifting the flap, I set the exhaust injector. Bob, who had been watching this performance, looked across and gave me a nod of approval.

At the end of West Calder platform, a platform upon which I had spent much of my spare time in boyhood days, we ran on to the 1 in 105 uphill gradient which would remain constant for the next seven miles, except for a short stretch of level track at Breich station. Again the regulator went up to the roof and the reverser let out several turns, and once more came that glorious explosion of sound from the chimney as 45360 dug her heels in, a sound which brought back many happy childhood memories. Back to the shovel and firing almost constantly, we moved this heavy train almost at walking speed up past the great bing (heap) of red, spent oil shale lying alongside the right-hand side of the track, one of many (twenty-nine in all) distinctive, red bings, remnants and reminders of the great Scottish shale oil industry, now defacing both Midlothian and West Lothian, as we passed through the area which saw the development of Scotland's first oil boom. This particular bing (Addiewell South) had been created with spent oil shale which had been burned in the retorts of Addiewell Oil Works, latterly only a producer of crude oil from the shale which had been mined literally from under our feet. Through Addiewell station we blasted and up on to the bleak moorlands on which lay Woodmuir Junction, a very lonely signal box indeed.

Across the moors we struggled onwards, with me firing almost continuously, but with steam and water levels holding up. Crossing the wide valley of Breich Water (the County March) by a stone viaduct, we thundered our way through Fauldhouse North station and up onto the summit at Behar Junction, another lonely outpost. This signal box I knew well since, when a junior clerk at Shotts, I had been taught to work it under the eagle eye of a Shotts relief signalman, one Wallace Dougall. Indeed, the brother of one of the regular signalmen here, one Neil Gemmell, was a top link driver at Haymarket MPD (R. (Bert) Gemmell). Over the top and the hard work was done for a while, and with the heavy train now propelling us forward it was merely a matter of keeping the speed in check by use of the engine brake, assisted by the guard's brake in rear, as we wound our way down through Shotts, Hartwood and on to Cleland (Omoa). The glow and glare in the sky ahead heralded the presence of the many blast furnaces and steel works in the Lower Clyde Valley, one of which was our intended destination. Through Holytown, speed was steadied to allow us to take the right-hand diverging line at Fullwood Junction, to take us on through Mossend Yard on the WCML to Perth and the north. There were a series of options of routes available to reach Clyde Iron Works, but on this night the signalman at Fullwood Junction, probably under the (very thoughtful) direction of District Control, routed us via Mossend Yard, in order to avoid the descent into the Clyde Valley with a very heavy, un-braked train, and involving the 3-mile long 1 in 70 falling gradient, which was the Bellshill Bank, lying between Bellshill and the junction with the WCML at Uddingston Junction, beyond which the River Clyde was crossed. This was all new territory to me and I looked out with great interest. Beyond Carnbroe, we swung to the left at Whifflet South Junction to take the easier R&C (Rutherglen & Coatbridge) line, passing through Mount Vernon and Carmyle, to eventually enter the sidings at Clyde Iron Works at around 04.15, where we left our train.

On uncoupling from our train, and being joined by our guard, a short trip through Rutherglen took us to Polmadie locomotive shed where we turned the engine, took on some coal and had our break. Fed and watered, we virtually just went around the corner from the loco to Strathclyde Junction, where we uplifted a train of empty 16-ton mineral wagons for our return working, the 06.40 Strathclyde Junction to Crew Junction. The guard advised my driver that we had fifty empty wagons, plus brake van, in the train, an easier load of 395 tons. We ran back the main line via Shotts and had a far easier time in the process, and arriving at Crew Junction at 09.50, almost on time. I coupled off quickly and the signalman had the road set for us back to Dalry Road where, at Dalry Middle Junction, we were signalled into the shed coaling road, where we were relieved. I had booked on duty at Haymarket at 22.00 the previous evening and was permitted to sign off by phone, from the Running Foreman's Office at Dalry Road, at 10.15 after a most interesting, but strenuous 12¼ hour firing turn which, happily for me, was without incident.

Harry Knox. (Based on an extract from his *Steam Days at Haymarket*, Irwell Press, 2007. Courtesy of Irwell Press.)

15 INCIDENTS, ACCIDENTS AND UNUSUAL HAPPENINGS

INCIDENTS

In 1948, Dalry Road shed was confronted with a new problem. In the August of the year, both the East Coast Main Line and the Waverley Routes, had to be closed owing to catastrophic flooding, which washed away bridges and caused numerous landslips. A series of diversionary arrangements had to be set in place to allow passenger train services to be run with some degree of normality. One of the immediate alternative routes was to divert the East Coast Anglo-Scottish express trains to run via Carstairs and Carlisle. The means by which this was achieved has been described in detail at Chapter 3. Dalry Road shed had to step up to the mark by providing pilot power over the Wester Dalry Branch, and Dalry passed firemen were also utilised as conductors in this important role. For the six days until the Waverley route was again available, a total of fifty-three Up trains and eighty-one Down trains were passed over this diversionary route.

Mention was made at Chapter 8 of the late-night Saturday trains and the problems trainmen encountered. In this regard, there was one particular Saturdays Only train, the 22.40 from Glasgow Central to Edinburgh Princes Street, which fell to the lot of Dalry Road crews. Here is the tale:

The 22.40 from Glasgow Central was the last evening train from Glasgow, serving, in the main, the mining towns of North Lanarkshire and West Lothian. Interference with the communication cord was a regular source of entertainment with the youthful male (and female) passengers. The Dalry Road crews worked this train, normally with one of their own Fairburn 2-6-4Ts. However, the train seldom ran to time and on one evening in 1955 the crew had suffered a number of instances of the communication cord being pulled between Holytown and Glasgow Central. At Holytown station, a most unfortunately misnamed town, the guard had given the 'right away' but before the train could move the cord was pulled yet again. The fireman, one Benny Chisholm of Dalry Road, was, not unreasonably, wanting to get home to bed, and after the cord had been pulled for a second time, he walked back the train, firing shovel in hand. The guard, equally desirous of seeing his bed that evening, identified the miscreants and Benny set to work with his shovel handle. The cord was never again pulled on that evening, nor on any subsequent Saturdays, the word having got around that the consequences of such an idle pursuit could be physically painful. Management took a pragmatic view of the whole matter.

Of the Dalry Road characters, we have already just met Benny Chisholm and his firing shovel, but there were two other passed firemen at the shed who shared an evening of, what was not exactly, glory. They were J. McDougall and J. McDougall, both totally unrelated, other than by clan, but who found themselves together as the footplate crew on Fairburn 2-6-4T No. 42273 on a late shift Lanark turn in January 1958. This involved returning from Carstairs with the Edinburgh portion (three coaches) off the 16.25 Liverpool to Edinburgh Princes Street and Glasgow Central. This departed Carstairs at 21.30. They made light work of this lightweight train but, on the approach to Princes Street, two Carstairs locomotive men, travelling passenger on the train, became alarmed at the failure to reduce speed after passing through Merchiston station. They warned the relatively few passengers aboard to brace for impact. Sure enough, poor old 42273, still running hard, entered Platform 2 in Princes Street station, struck the buffer stops very hard indeed and reared up over the concourse, spewing steam and water everywhere. Two coaches were derailed, and the unfortunate No. 42273 suffered heavy damage to the front end and bogie. Two passengers complained of minor injuries, but thanks to the quick thinking of the Carstairs crew the outcome was far less serious than it might have been. And what was the reason and who was to blame? Well, management knew that J. McDougall was the driver, but which one? The Messrs McDougalls together, bless them, managed to muddy the waters at the subsequent Inquiry to the point where no one could say with any certainty who had been doing what, and when, or indeed if either had actually been there at the time, and with neither able to remember who was actually driving. The outcome was that no one was identified as being the culprit and the findings were left open, with no blame being apportioned to any one individual. A degree of justice was, however, served with both men being charged, and disciplined, for mismanagement of the engine when in charge of same, and both shared a well-deserved black mark on their respective service history cards.

The 23.20 express parcels train from Manchester Victoria to Edinburgh, which was worked by ex-Dalry Road men, but who by the time of this particular incident were based at Edinburgh Haymarket's Diesel Depot. This train was worked by these men through from Carlisle. The author, as Assistant Area Manager at Bathgate, was called in the wee sma' hours one January morning, a cold snowy, frosty morning, to be advised that the Manchester Parcels had been derailed in his area, *'One mile on the Harburn side of Cobbinshaw'*. Edinburgh Control had also alerted the Area Manager, despite the fact the he was not on call that week. It was agreed that the author would pick him up en route to site. Cobbinshaw, lying around 950 feet above sea level on bleak moorland, was reached in double quick time but no signs of any derailed train could be seen. The Area Manager decided to take the car to Harburn and walk back, whilst the author walked the line forward towards Harburn. At Torphin level-crossing the author discovered signs of derailment and the derailed train was immediately found, lying to the west of what had been Harburn station, and *one mile on the Cobbinshaw side of Harburn!* It was observed the guard had properly laid down the protecting detonators. The author, on his long, cold walk, found evidence that one axlebox had come adrift and disintegrated (a sheared tower bolt and other debris was found, telling their own story) and marks on the rail heads and sleepers revealed that the CCT vehicle involved, located in the centre of the train, had derailed to the cess side on the approach to an overbridge at Harburn

Fairburn 2-6-4T No. 42273 of Dalry Road depot in less than happy circumstances after running into Princes Street station too quickly and demolishing the train indicator board and buffer stops. Two coaches were derailed, but happily no one was seriously hurt. *Author's collection*

Golf Course. The derailed CCT had caught the abutment of the bridge, then had been pulled transversely across the Down Main line by the impact. The other CCTs following behind smashed their way through, totally destroying this derailed vehicle, before running into derailment themselves. Damage and destruction was absolute, with mail order items strewing the track. Much of the glass and china ware was rendered unusable, but there was also lot of clothing, footwear and other items, which had a salvage value. Thus, to safeguard site security and minimise the risk of pilferage, a rubber-tyred Chase-side mechanical shovel, working at that time on the Bathgate shale contract at Livingston, was commandeered from the contractor and, running backwards and forwards on the actual track, soon had all salvageable mail order items loaded into the shovel, and taken to a secure area which had been set up in the former goods yard at Harburn station – but not before one enterprising P. Way man who was 'assisting' in clearing up was observed to be secreting recovered golf clubs into the signalling cable channelling. The BT Police waited until he had collected a full set of irons before swooping and recovering his haul. The derailment was a breakdown crane job, and the St. Margarets crane was soon in attendance, but it was to be thirty-eight hours before the author saw home, and bed, again.

Two further incidents describe Saturday night fun and games on the Glasgow via Shotts route, but *not* involving Dalry Road men, although occurring in regular Dalry Road territory.

The first was the 22.45 from Princes Street, worked by Polmadie men, generally had an easier time, except for a number of Saturday nights at West Calder, where there was regular Saturday night dancing which attracted youngsters from Addiewell, Breich, Fauldhouse and Shotts. This train generally managed to run to time, except for this one evening when one of the young men from the west, on the platform, and who had just been jilted in his love life, decided that he had had enough and jumped in front of the incoming train. He escaped totally unscathed, but on stating that he was determined to do it again, the local police were involved and a close eye was kept on him by station staff. On the following Saturday, whilst in the crowd thronging the platform, he escaped supervision and jumped once more. He lost a foot which was not what he expected, or intended, but his dancing days were surely over.

Carstairs men worked the last Lanark (22.35) out of Princes Street on a Saturday. One evening, having turned his engine on arrival at Princes Street station from Carstairs, the infamous Driver Lennie Nichol of Carstairs shed fell into conversation with Polmadie Driver Dalgleish, who had followed him to the turntable with his engine. With their engines turned and stabled in the engine siding at Princes Street, both drivers with their respective firemen repaired to the Rutland Bar, located just outside the station, for 'refreshments'. Refreshments having been taken, they rejoined their engines and, coupled to their respective trains, waited the 'right away'. Off went the Lanark on time, followed 10 minutes later by the Glasgow Central. For Dalgleish, on the latter train, all went well to Fauldhouse (North) – but there the Down platform was under repair and foreshortened. This required trains to make a double stop. Having got the handsignal to draw forward, Dalgleish, having forgotten the platform works (which had been published in his Weekly Operating Notice) took this as a 'right away', set off, hell for leather for the next station stop at Shotts, but was very quickly brought to stand just off the platform, when the guard operated the emergency brake valve in the van. The station master was called out, and was inundated with numerous passenger complaints, the matter escalating into something of significant proportions for poor Dalgleish. Driver Nichol on the Lanark had an uneventful journey until, on the approach to Lanark station, he went about two or three feet too far into the station, striking the buffer stops with some force.

Accidents

Apart from the buffer stop collision at Edinburgh Princes Street, described above, Dalry Road led a somewhat charmed life when it came to serious accidents, avoiding the catastrophic accidents which were a part of the sister sheds in Edinburgh. Possibly the most serious accidents are as described hereafter.

23rd May 1848: Auchengray

Whilst details are now difficult to obtain, this accident was caused in part by poor track formation, a degree of over-speeding and with probable axle loading problems on the locomotive. As mentioned in Chapter 6, the Class '4' 2-2-2s were notorious difficulty to balance and, unless the weight distribution over the three axles was correct, known to be prone to pitching when running. The passenger train involved has been identified as the Edinburgh portion of the 09.00 express from London, which had been detached at either Symington or Carstairs and consisted of two coaches. It was hauled by Sinclair Class '4' 2-2-2 No. 45, being worked by a very early Dalry Road shed crew. The driver was John Nicoll, who was allocated this new 'flagship' train as his regular working because of his recognised good conduct up to that time, but his fireman was, unfortunately, not mentioned by name.

The track-bed 'floated' over the unstable moss conditions and tended to flex when a train passed over. This, coupled with an engine prone to pitching when running, plus an element of over-speeding, were considered by the BoT Inspecting Officer, to have been enough to throw the train into derailment. In the hours of darkness, the train had just passed through Auchengray station when the locomotive and tender left the rails and plunged into a bog, leaving the two coaches derailed but still on the line. The engine and tender, along with the crew, were completely immersed in the bog and, on recovery, the driver and fireman were both later found to be dead. The guard also received injuries from which he later died.

The engine weighed upwards of 18 tons, but with the weight being distributed marginally unequally over the three axles. The leading axle carried a weight of upwards of 6 tons, with the remainder of the weight being distributed over the driving axle and trailing axle. As stated, the slight imbalance was thought to be one of the causal factors. The station master at Carstairs had, however, noted that Driver Nicoll had been involved in an altercation with his fireman before leaving the station; on starting he had done so in a very aggressive manner and it may have been that he was still driving somewhat faster than was prudent given the newness of the trackbed.

This accident occurred in the same month that passenger trains commenced running to and from Edinburgh, and must have been one of the earliest accidents on record for the Caledonian Railway.

24th May 1853: Slateford Station

The method of train control on the Edinburgh Branch was Time Interval Working, with very basic visual signals given by coloured discs (lamps at night). Three discs were employed by the Caledonian Railway, a red meaning 'Danger! Stop!', white for 'Line Clear', and a green caution signal enjoining 'Proceed with Care'! At Currie (now Curriehill), King's Knowe and Slateford there were no green discs provided and, therefore, the respective station masters were instructed to give a horizontal wave of the hand to indicate this signal. Talk about a recipe for disaster!

On the morning in question, the 08.00 passenger train from Carstairs to Edinburgh had arrived at Slateford station at the booked time of 09.19, where half a dozen intending passengers were ready to join. At that same moment, the train was struck in the rear with some violence by a mineral train, running at some speed and consisting of eighteen fully laden wagons. Eleven passengers were injured, some seriously, and the police who had been summoned, arrested Thomas Smith of Dalry Road shed, the mineral train driver, and, strangely, also arrested the driver and fireman of the passenger train. The circumstances were as follows.

It was a company rule that no mineral train should leave any station within ten minutes of a preceding stopping passenger train. This rule was broken at King's Knowe station that morning, when the station master authorised the driver of the mineral train to proceed towards Slateford, by giving the aforementioned caution hand signal. Driver Smith had already received this same handsignal from the station master at Currie and, anticipating receiving a red disc to stop, he reduced speed in order to take his train slowly down the long 1 in 100 falling gradient to King's Knowe. For brake power on his train he was totally reliant upon two brakesmen, each riding on a different wagon, and each operating a very primitive manual brake lever. At King's Knowe, the station master had, quite properly, raised the red disc for the approaching mineral train, but on hearing the engine whistle of this train, he thought that he may have overestimated the ten minutes. Cancelling the red signal, he then gave the driver a caution hand signal – but only some eight minutes after the departure of the passenger train. The mineral train ran on, down the falling gradient. At Slateford the only person on duty was a 15-year-old clerk, the son of the station master at King's Knowe, who had quite properly hoisted the red danger disc on the arrival of the passenger train. Driver (Smith) observed the red disc, but with the wholly inadequate braking power available, the momentum of his train on the falling gradient took over, causing the violent collision as described. The young clerk had attempted, in vain, to indicate to the driver of the passenger train to proceed before the crash occurred. And who were the culprits? Well, there was only one, and that was the Caledonian Railway, and its Officers, who were undoubtedly culpable. No clock or watch with which to measure the ten-minute interval, had been provided at King's Knowe, leaving the station master there to estimate same.

The driver of the mineral train, having spent two months on remand, was totally absolved.

It was without doubt a consequence of this mishap that the Caledonian Railway, on the 19th of July that same year, decided to *'get clocks put up at all stations and give time pieces to all Guards'.*

The Time Interval System of train control, forever inherently dangerous, was later to be superseded by Absolute Block Working, facilitate by introduction of the electric telegraph.

The inadequacies of the Caledonian Railway operating procedures were to be highlighted yet again on the Balerno Branch in 1880 (see below).

1877: Balerno Branch

On 4th April, the 06.20 Edinburgh Princes Street to Midcalder via the Balerno Branch became derailed when negotiating a sharp right-hand curve (6¼ chains radius) on the approach side of a river bridge between Currie and Balerno on a climbing gradient, with speed being no more than 12 mph. The track below the leading right-hand wheels of the locomotive (unidentified) spread under the weight, and immediately all wheels on the right-hand side of the train also dropped off inside the low (R) rail. No one was injured. The cause was found to be the loosening of the spikes holding the rail into the chairs in the vicinity of the site of derailment. Provision of a check rail was recommended.

1880: Balerno Branch (Ravelrig Junction)

By coincidence, the 06.20 Edinburgh Princes Street to Midcalder via the Balerno Branch was to be once more involved in what was a significantly more serious incident. The train consisted of eight carriages (the first of which was a brake carriage) plus a brake van, hauled by an unidentified 0-4-4T driven by Alexander Stavert of Dalry Road shed (see Chapter 10); it was running on the downgrade between Balerno station and Ravelrig Junction.

At that time at Ravelrig Junction, the 03.00 Paisley to Leith Goods train had just arrived to detach three wagons. The signalling interlocking at the time, as recommended by the BoT Inspecting Officer, required the signalman to set the road as if the goods train was proceeding over the Balerno Branch, and this was duly done, but with both the Down direction distant and home signals set at Danger, and locked, as required by Special Signal Box Instructions. This, as it turned out, was not an unusual set of circumstances.

Meanwhile the passenger had arrived on time at Balerno station at 06.49 and was due to depart for Midcalder at 06.52. Driver Stavert had checked and set his watch with the station clock at Currie. He was very surprised, therefore, when the Guard signalled his train off at 06.50, two minutes early by his (Stavert's) watch. Having left Balerno two minutes ahead of time, and believing that the Currie station clock was slow and that his guard had the right time, Stavert set off down the slope. It is at this point where Stavert's evidence and that given by the guard conflicted. Stavert maintained that he controlled the speed of the train and shut the regulator when he observed the Ravelrig distant signal showing caution. The guard contradicted this by saying that he felt the speed had been too high all the way down from Balerno. On sighting the distant at caution, Stavert instructed his fireman to apply the engine hand brake (there was no continuous automatic brake on the train) ready to stop at the home signal. He estimated that as he shut off steam, his speed was 15/16 mph. Observing that the handbrake was not having any effect, he threw the engine into reverse, opened the regulator and applied sand. The engine wheels picked up and the train, by now out of control despite the guard applying the brake in the van, was approaching Ravelrig; at the divergence of the branch line the train was diverted onto the same track as the goods train, owing to the interlocking requirements described above, and thus, inevitably the two trains collided.

On 1st May 1954, Fairburn 2-6-4T No. 44271, showing collision damage, awaits repair at Dalry Road. Repairs will most likely involve a trip to Main Works. *Stuart Sellar*

Two passengers and the guard of the 06.50 were injured, both locomotives were damaged, and two coaches and two wagons damaged; a signal post was demolished. At the subsequent Inquiry, both the fireman and guard sought to incriminate Stavert. The Inspecting Officer blamed the driver's excessive speed, and only dwelt briefly in passing on the fact that the complete passenger train was totally un-braked, the fact that guard has set the train off early, and the shortcomings in the interlocking at Ravelrig Junction (which had been *demanded* by an earlier Inspecting Officer), but did manage to place some of the blame on the station porter at Balerno for allowing the train to depart before time. It was Dugald Drummond, the Caledonian Railway Locomotive Superintendent, who instituted a programme of fitting passenger coaches on the branch trains with automatic, continuous brakes thereafter. The rules concerning train operation over the branch were also altered to require additional brake vans and provision of brakesmen on branch trains. There was no mention of the van handbrake being found to be defective after the collision, which it was!

Stavert, who had been arrested, was lucky not to stand arraigned in Court, and although there are now no records, it must be assumed that he was dismissed the service.

This accident reveals just how harshly drivers could be dealt with in the early days of railways, and before the men enjoyed the protection of a trade union. This is yet another case where the Caledonian Railway as a company was clearly culpable. Indeed, there are so many similarities between this and the accident at Hexthorpe, described at Chapter 12, that one must assume that Stavert was not a member of ASLEF or any other trade union.

25th July 1898: Edinburgh Princes Street

At around 16.05 on the above afternoon, a train of nine coaches was being loose shunted in the station throat, but the move was inadvertently, and wrongly, routed into No. 4 platform by a signalman's error, where the coaches struck the locomotive working the 16.02 Princes Street to Glasgow Central causing considerable damage, but without serious injury. Neither of the locomotives involved were identified by number.

Perth-based Stanier 'Black Five' No. 44975 is seen in a spot of bother just west of Dalry Road station in this undated picture. The St. Margaret's crane is already on the job and re-railing will be swift. *David Dickson collection*

November 1956: Shotts Iron Works/Benhar Junction

At this time, the author had just recently started his railway career as a junior clerk at Shotts Central station in Lanarkshire and had made his way to Addiewell station to catch his normal train to work – the 08.00 ex Princes Street (08.39 ex Addiewell), Shotts arrive 09.01 – to be advised that the train was cancelled because of a derailment between Shotts Iron Works and Benhar Junction which was blocking the main line. Alternative transport was quickly arranged and involved being pillion passenger on the Chief Clerk's motor cycle. After a freezing cold journey, they reached Shotts safely and the cause of the upset was discovered. It transpired that the return of an early morning Slateford to Mossend freight working, with Dalry Road men on Stanier '5MT' 4-6-0 No. 45030 and a Slateford guard in charge, were returning, LE and Brake Van, to Edinburgh, the latter being propelled (quite properly) as was often the norm in these days. The guard was out in the leading veranda enjoying the crisp morning air, when on approaching the commencement of the 1 in 99 rising gradient to Benhar Junction, he observed to his consternation an empty 24½ ton steel mineral wagon, derailed and lying sideways across both lines immediately in front of his van. By the time this had registered in his mind, it was all far too late, and the van struck the mineral wagon and derailed, followed by the engine.

The mineral wagon, one from a train of similar empty wagons in circuit between Ravenscraig No. 4 Yard and Polkemmet Colliery, had been the last wagon on the train, and had broken away during shunting in the Benhar Junction sidings. As the signalman at Benhar Junction, the aforementioned Neil Gemmell, had omitted to normalise the points on the main line after arrival of the train of empties, the wagon in question had run out onto the Up-Main line and continued westwards down the falling gradient, until it derailed on the catch points located at the foot of same.

5th February 1962: Polmont East

At approximately 07.20 on the morning of the above date, on the Edinburgh/Glasgow main line, the 06.50 Edinburgh Princes Street to Callander express passenger train, consisting of five coaches hauled by a Fairburn 2-6-4T (unidentified), was irregularly permitted to enter the block section between Bo'ness Junction and Polmont East Junction where, at the latter location, it collided heavily with rear of the 05.25 Class 'C' goods from Niddrie West to Glasgow. The driver was G. Elder, a top link driver of Dalry Road shed who, with Passed Fireman W. Allan, was in charge of the locomotive. Another Dalry Road driver, J. Donaldson, was on the footplate in the course of route learning. There was considerable damage to the rear wagons in the freight train, and the locomotive of the passenger train received front end damage and was derailed all wheels. The leading coach was damaged and also derailed all wheels, the second coach received some damage to the bodywork but was not derailed. The remaining three coaches also remained on the rails and there was, thankfully, no telescoping. The cause was irregular access by the signalman to the relay cabinet in Polmont East Signal Box, so as to improperly manipulate the track circuit relays. No blame was apportioned to the Dalry Road crew.

16 Caledonian Railway Lines Planned but Never Constructed

Slateford to Granton: 1846

In that year, the Caledonian Railway submitted a Bill to Parliament for authority to construct a line of railway from Slateford to Granton which failed.

Carstairs to Edinburgh: 1848

The first line falling into this category has been mentioned briefly at Chapter 1; this was, of course, Locke's proposed connecting route from the WCML into Edinburgh, which he suggested should leave the main line at or near Symington. Running via Biggar, it was to pass south and east of the Pentland Hills to Penicuik, a village lying south-east of Edinburgh. Now, Penicuik was an early Caledonian Railway goal, not least because of the rich coal workings and the oil shale industry in the shape of the Clippens Oil Company's Pentland Oil Works at Straiton. The railway company also recognised the great number of paper mills in operation along the valley of the River North Esk. From Penicuik, it was intended that the line should run north through Liberton and terminate in the Meadows on Edinburgh's south side. This terminal lay some way to the south of the main city centre at that time and certainly would not have been quite so convenient as the later Lothian Road terminus.

The sheer costs of the engineering of this line, £250,000 if a single line, and £356,000 if double line, resulting in a route which would have been 31¾ miles in overall length, caused Locke to think again, and to give further consideration to the route running to the north of the Pentlands, as proposed by Mr McCallum. This latter option was to win the approval of the Board.

Corstorphine & Bangholm Branch: 1860

Mentioned in Caledonian Minutes, at the time when the company was seeking running powers from Haymarket and Corstorphine (Haymarket West) to Larbert, this most strange proposal was never to be pursued. Just what the Company envisaged is not known, and since the Bangholm district of Edinburgh is in the Trinity/Goldenacre area of the city and not anywhere near Corstorphine, or indeed near any Caledonian line of railway, this proposed branch must remain an unexplained mystery.

Slateford to Penicuik: 1865

At this time, the Caledonian Railway, still with an eye to the rich pickings in and around Penicuik in the form of coal, and harbouring desires to create their own branch line to that town, sought approval to construct a 12¾ mile long branch line from Slateford to the desired location. It was planned as a double-line passenger branch, and the Caledonian Railway proposed to provide stations at Morningside, Liberton, Burdiehouse, Loanhead, Roslin and Auchendinny. The estimated cost was £197,000; the proposal was reviewed, and approved, by the Caledonian Railway Board at the same time as they were considering the proposed Balerno Branch (16th September 1864). Objections were submitted by the NBR and the new Esk Valley Railway Company (then under construction at Polton) and this Caledonian initiative failed. The NBR was to gain the stronghold on this corner of Midlothian. The Esk Valley Railway Company became the Polton Branch, which was opened in 1867. The NBR took it over in July 1871, having worked it since its inception.

Carstairs & Larbert Junction Railway: 1872

In November 1872 the Caledonian Railway gave notice of their intention to construct a completely new line of railway from a point near Cobbinshaw to their Scottish Central line near Larbert. It was intended that this new line would remove the Caledonian Railway's dependence on running rights over the short, very short, portion of the NBR line from Gartsherrie Junction to Garnqueen North Junction on the former Monklands & Kirkintilloch Railway. This proposed line was to run due north, crossing the counties of Lanarkshire, Edinburghshire (Midlothian), Linlithgowshire (West Lothian) and Stirlingshire, and would be formed by nine separate railways on the line of route. It would strike into the heart of what was NBR Territory. As previously mentioned in Chapter 3, under the Agreement reached to construct the Wester Dalry Branch between the NBR lines and Edinburgh Princes Street in 1876, a condition of this Agreement required the Caledonian Railway to withdraw the proposals for seven of these railways, and the remainder of the scheme was thus abandoned.

The precise dates for the following aspirations are not known.

Slateford to the E&G Main Line

With the passing of Caledonian Railway freight traffic over the Wester Dalry Branch prohibited, this later project sought to construct a new connecting line from Slateford to connect with the E&G main line at a point north and west of the suburb of Sighthill. It was intended to permit freight traffic from Stirling and the north, direct access to Lothian Road Goods station. It was never built.

Leith North to Albert Dock (Leith East)

The Caledonian sought to improve their presence in the Leith Docks complex by constructing a new line of railway from North Leith to the new Albert Dock which had been built, lying to the east of the Leith Docks complex. In truth, through access already existed but required the Caledonian to run over the NBR dock tramway lines, the latter being but a single line connection, crossing over the swing bridge at the mouth of the Old Port of Leith (Water of Leith).

PRINCES STREET UNDERGROUND RAILWAY TO LEITH

See Chapter 3 (Newhaven & Leith Link Line) for full discussion.

MID CALDER TO SOUTH QUEENSFERRY AND PORT EDGAR

A branch line from Mid Calder, running via Clifton to connect with the E&GR branch line from Queensferry Junction to Dalmeny, South Queensferry and Port Edgar was proposed. This may have been a joint venture between the E&GR and the Caledonian, but it did provide another indication of the close working relationship which existed between the two companies and which was to disappear when, in 1865, the NBR absorbed the E&GR.

MID CALDER BRANCH: CIRCA 1887

Given complaints received from the public regarding the distance between Midcalder station (formerly Kirknewton) and Mid Calder village, the company sought Parliamentary Approval under the 1887 Act to address this matter and to construct a branch line, some two miles and 83 yards in length, commencing at a junction with the main line of the company, some 440 yards eastwards from the level crossing by that railway of the public road on the westwards side of Midcalder station, and running on the north side of that road, to by-pass East Calder and terminate on the eastern side of the village of Mid Calder, at a point about 400 yards north-westwards from the mansion house of Mid Calder Hall. This line was never to be built, but in 1975, Lothian Regional Council demanded that BR rename Midcalder station as Kirknewton in order to avoid public confusion. Thus, the wheel turned full circle!

BARNTON BRANCH TO CORSTORPHINE: 1895/96

A scheme was mooted to connect Corstorphine into the Barnton Branch by a curving extension but it was never approved. Corstorphine was to be most adequately served by a short branch constructed by the NBR from Haymarket West Junction and serving intermediate stations at Balgreen Halt and Pinkhill. The Caledonian proposal would have required intending passengers from Corstorphine to make a very long and convoluted journey into the city, via the Barnton Branch.

BALERNO BRANCH, MALLENY LIGHT RAILWAY: 1899

In this year, the Caledonian Railway considered a request from an Army Officer, General Chapman, to construct, under Light Railway Regulations, a new branch line of railway, diverging from the Balerno Branch at a point between Balerno station and Currie station. This Light Railway was to run southwards, striking up into the Pentland Hills proper, to serve a rifle range which had been built there in the 1880s for use of the 4th/5th Royal Scots Queen's Edinburgh Rifles. A further 440-yard-long spur was to be provided from this light railway to provide access to Balerno Bank Paper Mill (Hill, Craig & Co.) lying at Harlaw, immediately south of Balerno village. This Malleny Branch was proposed to be 2¼ miles in overall length, but with quite prohibitive gradients required to gain the necessary height, ranging from 1 in 24, 1 in 25 to 1 in 33 in that short distance. It was envisaged that such a line could become popular with weekend walkers and visitors venturing into the Pentland Hills, but the idea was quietly shelved.

Ex-L&NER Class 'D49' No. 62712 *Morayshire*, now relieved of stationary boiler duties at Slateford (see page 107), stands at Dalry Road shed pending withdrawal and preservation. Bought by the National Museum of Scotland, this engine can now be seen in L&NER green livery, working on the SRPS railway at Bo'ness. *Stuart Sellar*

17 The Former Caledonian Railway Lines in the Twenty-First Century

Although Dalry Road MPD and Edinburgh Princes Street station are now, in 2018, long gone and nothing more than fond memories, thankfully valuable historical photographic material remains and much of the former Caledonian Railway routes are, happily, still with us.

The West Coast Main Line route from Edinburgh to Carstairs is now electrified with the 25KV overhead line system. In the bold new world of the privatised railway, the route continues to see some colourful operators and colourful trains: Virgin West Coast Pendolino high speed, tilting, fixed-unit electric trains; Virgin East Coast (at the time of going to press) Inter City 225 electric trains (running from Glasgow Central to London King's Cross via Edinburgh Waverley and the East Coast Main Line) Trans Pennine Class 350 EMUs and 185 DMUs; Abellio ScotRail Class 380 EMUs which run between North Berwick and Glasgow Central via Carstairs, as a means of getting the EMUs to Shields Depot for routine maintenance, although there is also a daily North Berwick/Glasgow Central passenger service and a North Berwick/Ayr through service; Arriva Cross Country Class 220 Voyager High Speed DMU and EMU trains (built by Bombardier) use the route to serve a variety of destinations, including a morning Birmingham New Street to Glasgow Central service which runs via Leeds and the East Coast Main Line to Edinburgh Waverley, thence West Coast Main Line via Carstairs, to Glasgow.

The overnight sleeping car services operated by Caledonian Sleepers as part of First ScotRail up to 2015, but now by Serco, consist of two trains overnight between Edinburgh and London Euston over the West Coast Main Line. The earlier evening

Two views of Dalry Road station in 2017.

Above: What is left of the island platform looking towards to former Dalry Junction. *John Furneval*

Left: The island platform looking westwards. The Western Approach Road can be seen on the left-hand side of the image. *John Furneval*

departure from Edinburgh combines at Carstairs (shades of the old Caledonian Railway) with a portion from Glasgow Central, whilst the later train runs with portions starting their journeys from as far afield as Aberdeen, Inverness and Fort William. These portions combine at Edinburgh Waverley to run as one train southwards. On the northbound journey, the early departure from London Euston splits at Carstairs, whilst the later train, with four destinations, splits at Edinburgh Waverley, running forward as through coaches to Fort William, Inverness and Aberdeen.

The 1869 Mid Calder to Cleland Railway still carries an Abellio ScotRail passenger service between Edinburgh Waverley and Glasgow Central, formed by DMUs, and the route is, as this book is prepared for press, being electrified under the wider Edinburgh/Glasgow Route Improvement Project (EGIP). This route gained a further enhanced, limited stop, express passenger service a few years ago (shades of the old Caledonian Railway and its Grampian coaching sets). Breich station, on this line, with a usage amounting to no more than three passenger journeys per week, has also been the subject of a failed closure attempt.

The Slateford/Haymarket Branch, after a 100-year wait, is finally a main running route for Anglo-Scottish services to and from Edinburgh Waverley and a number of English destinations such as Manchester Airport, Liverpool, London Euston and the south and west, and electric services to and from Glasgow.

From a freight traffic point of view, there is no longer much use of either route on a regular basis. A regular Scunthorpe to Dalzell Steel Mill service runs via Shotts on the outward leg, and the empties returns via Cobbinshaw. There is a fortnightly (approximately) DRS nuclear flask from Sellafield to Torness over the Cobbinshaw line and the Slateford curve to Millerhill. The Freight Operating Company, COLAS, runs cement trains from Oxwellmains to Brunthill (Carlisle) on an as required basis. The only other freight paths are for Network Rail Engineering ballast trains between Carlisle and Millerhill, and also Mossend to Millerhill, but use of these is wholly dependent upon planned engineering works.

The many main freight branches suffered a significant reduction as goods and mineral traffic levels decreased, before finally disappearing, and nothing now remains between Edinburgh and Carstairs, or Benhar Junction, other than the visual evidence on the ground to indicate that railways once ran there.

The entire Edinburgh Area signalling is controlled from Edinburgh Signalling Control Centre, the fringe interface with Glasgow Signalling Control Centre being milepost 183 at Woolfords on the WCML, and Benhar Junction on the Shotts line.

Breich station, West Lothian. This former Caledonian Railway station was scheduled for complete closure in 2017/18 by Network Rail, being the least used passenger station in Scotland, but was given a reprieve by the Scottish Government in November 2017. Seen here looking east towards Edinburgh with a 4-coach train consisting of two Gloucester 'Twin' DMUs, leaving on a Glasgow Central bound passenger service in the 1960s. *Roy Crombie/SRPS*

BIBLIOGRAPHY

E&GR Directors Minutes (various): National Archives of Scotland
Edinburgh District Control Log Report on ECML Flooding: 12th August 1946

Cornwell, H.J. Campbell, *Forty Years of Caledonian Locomotives 1882-1922*, David & Charles, 1974
Fleet, Chris and Daniel MacCannell, *Edinburgh: Mapping the City*, Birlinn, 2014
Hobbs, Col. M.H., *The Railways of Great Britain: A Historical Atlas*, 2nd Edition, 2006
Howell, David, *Respectable Radicals*, Ashgate, 1999
Knox, Harry, *Steam Days at Haymarket*, Irwell Press, 2007
Knox, Harry, *Haymarket MPD: A History*, Lightmoor Press, 2011
Knox, Harry, *The Scottish Shale Oil Industry*, Lightmoor Press, 2013
Knox, Harry, *St. Margarets MPD 1844-1967*, Lightmoor Press, 2015
Knox, Harry, *Vanished Railways of West Lothian*, Lightmoor Press, 2017
LM&SR, *Centenary of the Caledonian Railway*, 1947
Marshall, Peter, *The Scottish Central Railway*, Oakwood Press, 1968
McKillop, Norman, *The Lighted Flame*, Nelson, 1950
Neele, George P., *Railway Reminiscences*, EP Publishing Ltd, 1974
Nock, O.S., *Scottish Railways*, Nelson, 1961
Nock, O.S., *The Caledonian Railway*, Ian Allan, 1963
Nock, O.S., *The Caledonian Dunalastairs*, David & Charles, 1968
Reed, Brian, *Crewe Locomotive Works*, David & Charles, 1985
Shaw, Donald, *The Balerno Branch*, Oakwood Press, 1989
The Water of Leith Project Group, *The Water of Leith*, McDonald Printers, 1984

Caledonian Railway Association, *The True Line* Journals (various)

Class 'J37' No. 64569 shunts at Leith East Depot. *Stuart Sellar*

INDEX

An unusual visitor at Dalry Road on 20th March 1955. Ex-L&NER Class 'K2' 2-6-0 No. 61781 *Loch Morar* of Keith shed stands alongside ex-CR McIntosh 0-6-0T '3F' No. 56283 outside Dalry Road shed. *Stuart Sellar*

Ex-CR McIntosh Class '439' 0-4-4T No. 55210 acts as station pilot in Princes Street and is seen shunting coaching stock.
J.L. Stevenson/ Hamish Stevenson

A slightly overgrown Colinton station on the Balerno branch, with an Officers' Inspection train in the platform in July 1961. Colinton Tunnel can be seen to rear. *Stuart Sellar*

About the Author

Born in West Calder, Midlothian (Scotland) and educated at West Calder High School.
Joined British Railways as Junior Clerk, at Shotts (Lanarkshire), on the 15th October 1956, transferring to Haymarket MPD as an Engine Cleaner in February 1957. Acted as Cleaner/Fireman until late summer 1959. Re-entered the clerical grades at Haymarket Depot in 1959. In 1961, appointed Relief Station Master in Glasgow South District and thereafter served, amongst other roles, as a Divisional Freight Inspector, Civil Engineering Fleet Manager, Assistant Area Manager and then Area Manager at Bathgate and finally Operational Signalling & Safety Officer for the Scottish Region of BR.
Avoiding Railtrack plc at rail privatisation in 1994, joined Halcrow Transmark as an Operations & Safety Consultant. Worked in the UK and India, and relocated to Australia as Operations Projects and Safety Manager with GHD/Transmark in Sydney, working with all of the Australian Rail Authorities and also with the New Zealand Government and TranzRail.
Returned to the UK in 1999 and, as part of Halcrow Business Solutions, worked with Iarnród Éireann in Dublin as a Principal Rail Operations & Safety Consultant, but with a brief return to New Zealand in 2000. Retired from the railway industry on 31st December 2006.